C000180694

ADRIADNE'S THREAD

Margaret Mac Curtain, c. 1978

Margaret Mac Curtain

ARIADNE'S THREAD
Writing Women into Irish History

ARLEN
HOUSE

Published in 2008 by
ARLEN HOUSE
an imprint of Arlen Publications Ltd
PO Box 222
Galway
Ireland
Phone/Fax: 00 353 86 8207617
Email: arlenhouse@gmail.com

Distributed in North America by
SYRACUSE UNIVERSITY PRESS
621 Skytop Road, Suite 110
Syracuse, NY 13244–5290, USA
Phone: 315–443–5534/Fax: 315–443–5545
Email: supress@syr.edu

ISBN 978–1–903631–42–3, *paperback*
978–1–903631–62–1, *hardback*

Typesetting ¦ Arlen House
Printing ¦ Betaprint
Cover Art ¦ Leo Whelan
'The Kitchen Window'
Reproduced with the permission of the Crawford Art Gallery, Cork

CONTENTS

ACKNOWLEDGEMENTS

First and foremost I wish to thank Alan Hayes of Arlen House for his determination to give shape and definition to this collection, and for inviting Professor Maureen Murphy to write such a generous foreword. Thanks also to Sister Jo Dorran, O.P., Sion Hill, for her work in preparing the manuscript. Over the years during which these essays were written I owe debts of gratitude and helpfulness to many people: the notes to the texts give some indication of my indebtedness to the scholarly community in Ireland and abroad. Colleagues, graduate and undergraduate students in the History Department, University College Dublin supported my efforts to integrate women's history into the curriculum. The exchange of ideas with women's networks country-wide that accompanied the growth of Women's Studies challenged my assumptions. Yet a further stimulus was provided in the conferences organized by the Women's History Association of Ireland. Eilish Pearce, my sister, has always been an unblinking observer of Irish society and I have benefitted greatly from her insights.

The publisher has endeavoured to credit all known persons holding copyright or reproductive rights for articles republished, passages quoted and for illustrations reproduced in this book, especially:

Mike Collins, Cork University Press.
Fred van der Zee at Rodopi, Amsterdam.
Professor Nancy Netzer, Boston College.
Brian Burns, Boston College.
Colleen O'Sullivan, Registrar, Crawford Art Gallery, Cork.
The National Gallery of Ireland, Dublin.

The publisher would like to sincerely thank Professor Maureen Murphy for her invaluable contributions to this book; Mary Paula Walsh and Kay Conroy for their encouragement to commission the collection; and embattled colleagues at NUI Galway for their practical and moral support.

To Catherine Rose
and Róisín Conroy (1947–2007)
pioneers of feminist publishing

Maureen Murphy

Foreword
THE MANY VOICES OF MARGARET MAC CURTAIN

The first four essays in Margaret Mac Curtain's *Ariadne's Thread: Writing Women into Irish History* establish the major themes of her studies of Irish women's history. 'St. Mary's University College' (1963) announces her interest in women's education, particularly at third level. 'Women, the Vote and Revolution' (1978) discusses the diminished status of women after the Irish Free State was established – it is a call to write women's experience into Irish history. 'Towards an Appraisal of the Religious Image of Women' (1980) explores new ways of looking at Irish women's religious and spiritual experiences, including an historical survey of women in religious life in twentieth-century Ireland and an analysis of the distinct features of Celtic women's spirituality. 'The Historical Image' (1985) integrates women's history with gender analysis, reflecting the intellectual energy that informed the first decade of women's historical studies.

These essays representing four aspects of women's history must be considered in the context of Mac Curtain's other voices – those of teacher, religious sister, editor, human rights activist, educational reformer and media commentator. Like other Irish academic historians such as Mary Hayden and Eoin MacNeill of University College Dublin (UCD) and Mac Curtain's mentor James Hogan of University College Cork (UCC), she has *made* as well as studied and written about Irish history. Unlike the others, however, Mac Curtain, born in 1929, the last year of Ireland's most troubled decade, was a member of the first post-independence generation. As a school girl and as a student leader at UCC, she was aware of her family's part in that process. To be a Mac Curtain in Cork in the 1940s was to be identified with the history of the city. Her father Seán, a member of the Cork 1st Brigade of the Irish Republican Army (IRA) during the War of Independence, was clerk of a Republican court in Cork city; his cousin, Tomás Mac Curtain, Lord Mayor of Cork, was murdered, it is believed, by the Royal Irish Constabulary in March 1920.

Margaret Mac Curtain took an overall first class honours degree in History and English, the Peel Memorial Award and the Gold Medal for the most outstanding student in her 1949 year. Her external examiner J. R. R. Tolkein invited Mac Curtain to study medieval literature with him at Oxford, but she opted instead for the Higher Diploma in Education at Cork to prepare to enter the Dominican novitiate at Kerdiffstown House, Co. Kildare in 1950. Assigned to Sion Hill, Blackrock and given responsibility for senior history in 1956, she asked permission to study for a graduate degree in Early Modern Irish History at UCD. When Professor R. Dudley Edwards saw Mac Curtain in her Dominican habit, he said, 'Of course, you must do a bishop for your thesis'. He suggested Dominic O'Daly, the Dominican diplomat who founded the Monastery of Corpo Santo and the Convent of Bom Sucesso in Lisbon. Mac Curtain attended lectures after her own classes and wrote her MA thesis, *Dominic O'Daly 1595–1662: A Study of Irish-European Relationships in the Seventeenth Century* (1958), by candlelight – there was no electricity in the sisters' rooms until later in the sixties.

Encouraged to continue for her doctorate, Mac Curtain studied O'Daly in the wider context of the diplomatic relations between Ireland and Europe in the seventeenth century. Her research took her, a cloistered Dominican, to the Vatican archives and to libraries and archives in Spain, Portugal and France. Not only did she find research fascinating, she found Rome exciting in the years leading up to the opening of the Second Vatican Council and exhilarating with its promise of church reform that would include addressing the role of religious women. She earned a certificate of Theological and Biblical Studies from Regina Mundi Institute.

Mac Curtain's thesis, *An Agent of the Irish Counter-Reformation: Dominic O'Daly*, earned her a doctorate in history from the National University of Ireland (NUI) in 1963. She appeared in a front page photograph in *The Irish Times* on 29 October 1963 at her conferring wearing an academic hood over her habit, a first for religious in those times. Another first was her article in *Archivium Hibernicum* that examined the Irish manuscripts in Fondo Santa Sede, the foreign affairs archives in Madrid where she discovered religious women's voices in the Irish records.

While she continued to publish on church diplomatic history, Mac Curtain began her thirty-year career as Lecturer in History at UCD in 1964, the year after she took up Lorna Reynolds' invitation to contribute a study of St. Mary's University College to *University Review*. She would revisit the theme of women and education many times. Signed Sister M. Benvenuta, O.P., as she was known in those years, 'St. Mary's University College' introduced readers to a unique voice – the voice of a professional historian, a woman and a religious who was as widely read in literature and biography as she was in Irish historiography and who had found, in the life and letters of an unusual Dominican, an untold chapter of the history of Irish women.

She traced Archbishop of Dublin William Walsh's role in the matter of education for young women in St. Mary's University College, but she did not make any judgments about that role. That reticence and the phrase, not meant ironically, 'It would be an impertinence here to examine Msgr. P. J. Walsh's study [of Archbishop Walsh] critically' give the reader a snapshot of Mac Curtain in the early 1960s, an enclosed religious woman beginning her career out of cloister as a secular academic. Reticence did not equal timidity. When, in 1964, Archbishop John Charles McQuaid asked to review Mac Curtain's lecture notes for her classes on the counter-reformation, she refused on the ground of academic freedom and her superior supported her.

In retrieving Mother Patrick Shiels, O.P. from the Dominican Archives, and in telling the story of her efforts to improve educational opportunities for Irish catholic girls, Mac Curtain was taking the first step of what would be her programme to write women into history. 'St. Mary's University College' anticipated Mac Curtain's own role as an educational innovator and reformer, a role that came naturally to one with teachers on both sides of her family. Trained as a national school teacher, her father was recruited for the first generation of Free State School Inspectors; her aunt Sister M. Bonaventure McKenna was a legendary principal of St. Aloysius School in Cork. Her uncle Eoghan Mac Cionnaith, Professor of Mathematical Physics at University College Galway (UCG), was the father of Mac Curtain's beloved cousin Siobhán McKenna. Early in her teaching career she worked with Senator Owen Sheehy Skeffington to abolish corporal punishment, published 'From Renaissance to Bourbaki' (1968), an article about teaching the new maths and co-authored *The Birth of Modern Ireland* (1969) with Mark Tierney O.S.B. for schools, but her most significant educational contribution happened when she took a career break from UCD from 1980–1983 to be the founding Principal of the Senior College Ballyfermot with a vision for a post-secondary education that would offer innovative programmes for students in a community that had not had the advantage of higher education.

Toward the end of her teaching career at University College, Dublin, Mac Curtain published another article on the education of Irish women, 'Women, Education and Learning in Early Modern Ireland'. Written for *Women in Early Modern Ireland* (1991), a collection of essays she edited with Mary O'Dowd, Mac Curtain's authoritative wide-ranging essay considers how class, religion, language and literacy affected the education of young women in sixteenth- and seventeenth-century Ireland compared with education of women among christian humanists in England and on the continent. After the dissolution of Irish monasteries by Henry VIII, Irish girls in Tudor Ireland were educated with their brothers at home. Girls also appeared on the rosters of European boarding schools – experiences that encouraged young Irish women to consider religious life in those continental convents as an alternative to marriage and child-bearing.

The Post-Reformation emphasis on bible reading supported the growth of literacy for upper-class women as well as men, and women used that literacy to keep diaries and household records. While there was increased attention to literacy in the seventeenth century, Mac Curtain argues that the increased authority of husbands and fathers in Old English catholic as well as in puritan families of the new landed ascendancy in Ireland ignored the intellectual development of young women. Papal decrees also limited the development of religious women in the seventeenth and eighteenth centuries by issuing directives maintaining cloister. Mac Curtain's Lisbon research documents the literacy of nuns in English, Irish and Portuguese as well as reading knowledge of Latin among the community of Dominicans in the convent of Bom Sucesso.

The twenty-one essays in *Women in Early Modern Ireland* demonstrated that women's history had moved into the mainstream of Irish historical scholarship. The mark of Mac Curtain's pioneering scholarship appears in many of the essays in the collection which was published in the final years of her teaching career at UCD. By then she was offering courses in women's history regularly, directing graduate research and mentoring scholars in Ireland and abroad. Before she retired from teaching, she set forth, with Mary O'Dowd, 'An Agenda for Women's History in Ireland, 1500–1900: Part 1', which was published in *Irish Historical Studies* in 1992. Mac Curtain's section 'Education in Ireland before 1880' in *The Field Day Anthology of Irish Writing: Irish Women's Writing and Traditions, IV–V* (2002) revisits 'Women, Education and Learning in Early Modern Ireland' and adds texts like Máire MacNeill's discussion of the fosterage of Máire Rua, a vivid figure in the folklore of seventeenth-century Clare, with a branch of the MacFhlannchadha at Urlan Mór near Carrigoran.

In 1971, Mac Curtain had proposed a women's history course to her colleagues in the History Department at UCD. It was rejected. Four years later, in October 1975, UCD offered the first women's studies extramural course in Earlsfort Terrace. After writing extensively on early modern Irish history, including her monograph *Tudor and Stuart Ireland* (1972) and editing, with James Lydon, the eleven-volume 'Gill History of Ireland' (1970–1973), she returned to women's history. Mac Curtain organized the series of Thomas Davis

Lectures in 1975 for RTÉ Radio to commemorate International Women's Year. She edited the series with Donncha Ó Corráin into a book of essays titled *Women in Irish Society: The Historical Dimension,* but the collection was refused by major Irish publishers as not having sufficient commercial interest. Catherine Rose of pioneering feminist press, Arlen House, accepted the book and it appeared in 1978. An expensive book for its time, it sold more than 10,000 copies, going into three Irish printings and a major North American edition.

Asked by Thomas O'Loughlin in a 1994 interview in *History Ireland* to name her most significant book, Mac Curtain said *Women in Irish Society* because it demonstrated the 'intellectual and creative energy of the 1970s'. For Mac Curtain, it was a decade that began with the student revolution of 1969–70 and ended with Wood Quay. A student leader herself at UCC where she was Lady Vice-President of the Students' Council and Cathaoirleach of An Comhchaidreamh, Mac Curtain was sympathetic to student rights at UCD and she argued that students had a voice in college governance. A newspaper photograph of Mac Curtain in her Dominican habit standing on a table addressing students earned her a certain notoriety that was not lost on the College Commission of Inquiry who summoned her with other faculty they considered radicals. They were exonerated and Mac Curtain topped the poll of graduates at the next election for the senate of the UCD governing body. She joined the faculty of the School of Irish Studies established for American students in Ireland by Michael Scott and Mary Lavin in 1972 and taught there until 1989; she participated in the UCD history exchange with the University of Kansas in 1978 and made three lecture tours to America in the 1970s. The decade ended with the occupation of Wood Quay which began 1 June 1979. She represented the Group for the Study of Irish Historic Settlement which she chaired, and, with F. X. Martin, O.S.A. and the archaeologist Leo Swan, confronted the night security officer with his guard dog and accompanied academics, writers and prominent citizens into the contested site.

Mac Curtain's own contribution to *Women in Irish Society*, 'Women, the Vote and Revolution' is one of her most cited works. In the essay, Mac Curtain departed from her attention to women in the early modern period to raise questions about the relationships between nationalism, suffrage and trade unionism before and after the Easter Rising. She concludes that nationalism dominated the other movements after 1916 – the potential for divisiveness over votes for women put the matter on hold. An effective mediator and negotiator herself, Mac Curtain observed that the fierce mourning women who argued against the Treaty could have held the balance in the debate had they been more 'constitutionally agile'. As the vote for women was sidelined in deference to nationalism, women's issues were subverted in the 1970s by the focus in the revisionist debate about 1916 that emerged after the Troubles began in Northern Ireland.

'Women, the Vote and Revolution' marked a new methodology as well as a new subject for Mac Curtain. Her interviews with Sighle Ní Dhonnchadha and Eithne Coyle about the history of Cumann na mBan illustrate the value of women's oral histories to the researcher. Readers who remember the fiftieth anniversary commemorations of the 1916 Rising produced by RTÉ recall that the ambitious re-creation of the events of Easter Week as eyewitness news reports were quickly forgotten, but Nora Connolly's plain-spoken recollection of being driven with her mother across the smouldering city to see her father for the last time was riveting and unforgettable. Familiar with the written records of women's voices, Mac Curtain recognized the immediacy of living memory.

'Women, the Vote and Revolution' opened the field for other scholars. Beth McKillen responded to it in her 'Irish Feminism and Nationalist Separatism', a thoughtful two-part essay in *Éire-Ireland* (1982), arguing that the post-1916 relationship between nationalism, feminism and trade unionism was reciprocal rather than limiting. Clíona Murphy's *The Women's Suffrage Movement and Irish Society in Early Twentieth Century* (1989), women's histories like Sarah Anne Lawrenson and Lucy Olive Kingston's *Emerging from the Shadow* (1994), and the biographies of the women of 1916 and the Troubles are all indebted to Mac Curtain.

Mac Curtain's 'The "Ordinary" Heroine: Women into History', introduced Medb Ruane's *Ten Dublin Women* (1991), the catalogue for the Dublin Civic Museum exhibition organized by the Women's Commemoration and Celebration Committee. The only *ordinary* thing about these extraordinary women was, for some, their modest circumstances – street trader, midwife, news vendor, domestic servant. What they shared was a commitment to improve the lives of others. The heroines organized biscuit workers, fought for better conditions for workers, campaigned for votes for women, founded a children's hospital, and sat on the bench of a Sinn Féin court.

Mac Curtain might have titled her essay 'Women into History for the Ordinary Reader' because she not only introduced the ten women featured in the exhibition, but she also used the occasion to introduce Irish women's history to the general reader. She outlines the steps necessary to write women into history, placing their history into the context of classic historiography –

recovering and archiving sources that document women's history, creating a chronology that includes those sources and the dates that are significant to women's experiences, and interrogating and interpreting those primary sources, perhaps developing new methodologies in doing so. Mac Curtain argues that to write women's history is to challenge the accepted narrative as much as to recover and reclaim women's voices. The purpose of her essay was, in part, to enlist her reader in that process. Never republished until now, 'The "Ordinary" Heroine: Woman into History' contextualizes the lives of the ten Dublin women, while it creates the model for a legitimate women's history.

In 'Marriage in Tudor Ireland' (1985), Mac Curtain returned to the period of her *Tudor and Stuart Ireland* where she had examined the rivalry between the Butler and Fitzgerald men over the Ormond earldom. In this article she focuses on the women of the period clarifying their positions with regard to property, dowry rights and marriages to broker alliances, to secure land or to end feuds. Using her wide knowledge of civil and canon law and their archival sources, Mac Curtain discovered that when Brehon and Gaelic law codes sanctioned closer degrees of affinity and consanguinity and allowed clandestine marriages and divorce to be subordinated to English common law, marriage became a formal ecclesiastical institution. As a result, women of the Pale lost their autonomy as land-holders. Plantation certificates established land ownership in the seventeenth century, a change that reflected the constitutional changes in the relationship between Henry and Ireland. Writing a complex and technical essay using legal evidence about the status of women was not without irony in 1985, for the previous autumn Mac Curtain successfully sought an interlocutory injunction from the High Court against UCD when the

Professor of Modern Irish History arbitrarily reassigned her teaching duties to others after she was elected Prioress of her Sion Hill community in 1984. Arguing that the office of Prioress was 'totally unremunerated and wholly spiritual', Mac Curtain won her case, but was never promoted beyond College Lecturer.

A decade after 'Marriage in Tudor Ireland', Mac Curtain used her 'Reflections on Walter Osborne's *Study from Nature*' (1996) to look at another aspect of Irish women and land – the woman domestic gardener from bawn to suburb whose history reflects the changes in Irish economic and social life over more than three centuries. The topic interested her as much as gardener as historian. She enumerates the plants in the seventeenth-century garden in Tully Castle, a garden restored by the Northern Ireland Department of Interior; she reconstructs Máire Rua O'Brien's pleasure garden on the edge of the Burren in County Clare. The gardens, pond and summer house like the broad, open façade of Leamaneh house were a departure from the fortified tower house and represented the O'Briens' hope for the future, a hope soon dashed by the collapse of the Catholic Confederacy and the beginning of the Cromwellian wars. The eighteenth century demesne was not the fortified compound that Mac Curtain had described in 'A Lost Landscape: the Geraldine Castles and Tower Houses on the Shannon Estuary', her essay in the *festschrift* for F. X. Martin, O.S.A.; she described the demesne as a secured property that used a system of walls, ditches and fences to protect the residents. Even the family's pleasure garden was enclosed. Diaries and letters like those of Mrs. Delany offer an appreciation of the woman gardener as amateur botanist and landscape designer. Her flower collages establish her as a botanical artist. Mac Curtain's attention to the records of women as domestic gardeners anticipated the range of women's roles that would be written into women's history in *The Field Day Anthology of Irish Writing, IV–V*.

By the 1990s, Mac Curtain's own writing agenda in women's history became clear – church, state and women in twentieth-century Ireland. Specifically, she would identify and examine the religious experiences of Irish women – both laywomen and religious women and the expression of their spirituality in historical documents and in the oral and written tradition of Ireland's two languages. 'Towards an Appraisal of the Religious Image of Women' (1980) established Mac Curtain's interest in the subject. Long before John O'Donohue's popular *Anam Cara: Spiritual Wisdom from the Celtic World* (1997) used Irish poems and prayers to limn the sensibility of the Celts, Mac Curtain had been thinking and writing about the nature of Irish women's spirituality. Often invited to speak on the subject, interviewers have always been curious about the development of her own spirituality – one which embraces intellectual independence and social activism on the one hand, with a commitment to a traditional religious community life on the other. 'Towards an Appraisal of the Religious Image of Women' opened the discussion. Mac Curtain gave the essay as a plenary address to the American Conference for Irish Studies' 1980 meeting and it was published the same year in *The Crane Bag* special issue, 'Images of the Irish Woman'. The Crane Bag was an appropriate symbol of the issue and, indeed, for Mac Curtain's accomplishments in founding Irish women's history. At the end of the Editorial to 'Images of the Irish Woman', the editor told the story of Aoife and the Crane Bag:

> The title of this journal is derived from the Celtic legend of Mananann the god of the sea who, wishing to punish his wife Aoife, transformed her into a crane. She

retaliated by ensuring that his secret alphabet of wisdom, which he treasured, would be shared with the populace. Consequently, whenever cranes are in flight they form images in the sky of the secret alphabet for all to read. Aoife, symbol of any repressed woman, overcame barriers of communications through her forceful use of images.

Aoife, like Ariadne, overcame the silence imposed on women to find new ways to broadcast their messages and share their stories.

Mac Curtain argues in 'Towards an Appraisal' that the shift in the mythological model from Maeve to Mary brought a change in attitude toward Irish women. She demonstrates the similarities in strength and psychological freedom of the early christian saints Brigid and Íte and Maeve. However, the preoccupation with male chastity compromised the status of women, and the very thing that guaranteed her autonomy in pre-christian Ireland limited her autonomy in the Irish church after the seventh century. Mac Curtain speculates that post-Reformation Ireland embraced the cult of Mary because it was a cult appropriate to the sacred and secular hardships in seventeenth-century Ireland. It was a change in a model from a figure who was active to a figure who was passive, from one who chose to one who was chosen.

A second consideration of the matter of Irish women's spirituality was prompted by the sighting of moving statues at Marian shrines in the south and southwest of Ireland in the summer and autumn of 1985 that attracted crowds of the faithful to witness the phenomenon. Was the episode a projection of the anxiety of the community? Was it a contemporary manifestation of the co-existence of a folk religious tradition with Roman Catholic ritual? Did it become, as Mac Curtain argues in her introductory note, 'the vehicle for interpreting the moral anxiety that engulfed catholic believers in the aftermath of the angry exchanges during the debate over the 1983 8th Amendment to the Constitution'? Mac Curtain's 'Moving Statues and Irish Women' ranges beyond an interrogation of the moving statues phenomenon to a prescription for Irish women's spirituality to face what Nell McCafferty called 'the desolate situation of Irish women'. Mac Curtain bases her strategy on elements in the life of the Irish storyteller Peig Sayers – an intense sense of the presence of God, the contemplation of God in nature, charity, stoicism and steadfastness in time of grief and a sense of one's core identity.

Mac Curtain returned to Peig Sayers for 'Fullness of Life: Defining Female Spirituality in Twentieth-Century Ireland', an essay for Maria Luddy and Clíona Murphy's *Women Surviving. Studies in Irish Women's History in the 19th and 20th Centuries* (1989). The work of the Feminist History Forum encouraged research focusing on women who received little attention from Irish historians. Mac Curtain contrasted the faith-world of the rural Blasket storyteller with that of the Dublin middle-class lay missionary Edel Quinn. This ambitious essay concentrates more on Quinn whom she locates in the spiritual context of catholic Ireland in the decade after the foundation of the Irish Free State. She charts the course of Quinn's spirituality as an example of Irish middle-class women's spirituality – from the French influence in secondary schools to their sodalities that shaped catholic values and encouraged vocations, to their work for the catholic action group, the Legion of Mary. Mac Curtain herself was a member of the Legion as an undergraduate. She credits the experience for developing her social consciousness and supporting her vocation. Tuberculosis ended Quinn's plans to enter the Poor Clare contemplative community of Franciscan nuns, but despite the fatal disease she accepted the challenge to go as a lay missionary, an envoy of the Legion of Mary, to Africa in 1936 where she travelled widely and strenuously until her death in May 1944.

Constrained by the length of the essay perhaps, Mac Curtain gets Quinn to Africa and ends her story there saying simply 'Her historical presence is assured'. The abrupt ending is particularly tantalizing given Mac Curtain's own African credentials. Her long interest in South Africa and her record as an early, energetic patron of the Irish Anti-Apartheid Society barred her from obtaining a visa so that she missed the experience of her Dominican generation teaching young women of the townships. Her summer in Kenya in 1982 to investigate Quinn's work in the Diocese of Nairobi seemed in some way a compensatory project, so one wonders why she put aside her plan to write Quinn's biography? The reader who knows that Mac Curtain lived in Tralee some twenty years after Edel and that her sisters attended the same Presentation school as Quinn wonders what she, a devout schoolgirl, would have heard about Edel Quinn in the 1940s and what such stories would have contributed to her own spiritual formation? Five years after Mac Curtain's essay, Quinn was venerated by Pope John Paul II and there is an update of Cardinal Suenens's 1954 biography by Dr Desmond Forristal. Quinn's centenary in 2007 has been observed with religious celebrations and historical markers in Kanturk and Dublin.

Mac Curtain wrote 'Late in the Field: Catholic Sisters in Twentieth-Century Ireland and the New Religious History' for the Conference of Irish Historians held at Queen's University, Belfast in 1993. It subsequently appeared in *Chattel, Servant or Citizen: Women's Status in Church, State and Society* edited by Mary O'Dowd and

Sabine Wichert (1995) and in *Irish Women's Voices: Past and Present* (1995). An ambitious and magisterial survey of the writing about twentieth-century Irish nuns, Mac Curtain also outlines requirements for a new religious feminist history – an interdisciplinary approach that draws on the rich archival sources including annals, letters and other documents which religious communities are taking more responsibility for conserving and for making available to scholars.

She might have added to her discussion the disciplines of literature, art and architecture that she is using in her current work – literature of nuns in short stories like Mary Lavin's 'A Nun's Mother', Seán Ó Faoláin's 'The Man who Invented Sin', in novels like Kate O'Brien's *The Land of Spices*, in poems by women religious like Bríd Dáibhis and Joan Sweetman or about women religious like Eiléan Ní Chuilleanáin's 'J'ai mal â nos dents' and convent architecture, a subject she is pursuing in her study of medieval nunneries. While she does not include the literature and documentaries of the Mercy Sisters' treatment of women in their Magdalen laundries, her parting shot in 'Late in the Field' reminds readers that the matter of class in religious life, the division between lay and choir sisters, still needs to be addressed.

Mac Curtain's long introductory note to 'Late in the Field' brings developments in the historiography of Irish women religious up to the beginning of the twenty-first century. The ground rules established, the reader looks forward to Mac Curtain and other scholars' studies of religious life and to the broader theme of women's spirituality in twenty-first-century Ireland with a diminished presence of Sisters. She believes that there will be religious women at a future time with the same idealism, who will reinvent themselves in new models of service and spirituality.

Four years later, Mac Curtain wrote a further study of Irish religious women in the twentieth century 'Godly Burden. Catholic Sisterhood in Twentieth-Century Ireland', for the American Conference for Irish Studies volume *Gender and Sexuality in Modern Ireland* (1997) edited by Anthony Bradley and Maryann Gialanella Valiulis. After providing the demographic data about convents and congregations in nineteenth- and twentieth-century Ireland, the essay traces the evolution of the alliance between convents and the State that was institutionalized in 1924 when catholic schools were recognized as state schools. W. B. Yeats illustrated that alliance in his poem 'Among School Children' that begins during his senatorial visit, in 1926, to inspect the new curriculum at a Montessori school run by an order of nuns in County Waterford.

She includes the demographics and the somewhat different history of Irish nuns and nuns in Irish orders in the United States, information from Suellen Hoy's 'The Journey Out: The Recruitment and Emigration of Irish Religious Women to the United States, 1812–1914'. Their counterparts in Irish religious orders in America had a very different experience. Education is under the jurisdiction of each state and, historically, there is a separation of church and state. The state or public schools, particularly in urban centres of the northeast, were regarded by Irish catholics as promulgating a protestant ethos even down to the reciting of the *Book of Common Prayer* version of the 'Our Father' in morning exercises in the 1940s. Those of us who attended public schools would sit pursed lips in silence while our fellow students recited the end of the prayer. Nuns in the United States lived in community – however, they moved more easily out of cloister in the 1950s and early 1960s, and the Vatican II reforms were implemented earlier.

Mac Curtain cites the idealism after 1916 and World War I and the disappointment of the Irish Civil War as contributing to the rise of vocations. Her example of religious women who were members of Cumann na mBan (Catherine Dixon) or who served as volunteer nurses (Mary Martin) is a departure point for a longer study of the experiences that prompted women to choose religious life. In addition to the vocation of choir nuns, Mac Curtain describes the attractions of the life of the lay sister and explains that the lay/choir division reflected the social stratification in Irish society of the time. Nevertheless, the matter of lay sisters rests uncomfortably with Mac Curtain's egalitarian sensibility. Were there other factors that contributed to the rise in vocations in the twentieth century? Did the Eucharistic Congress in Dublin in June 1932, the high watermark of Irish catholic triumphalism, with its address by the Archbishop of Edinburgh to 200,000 women in the Phoenix Park contribute to vocations in that decade? Mac Curtain ends 'Godly Burden' with the exodus from convents that began in the 1970s and continued through the end of the twentieth century, but by then Mac Curtain had founded a new community – historians who were writing women into history, and she continues to provide new themes and models for those narratives.

Mac Curtain's 'The Historical Image' (1985) introduced the broad theme of 'image and reality' in the construction of the position of women in Irish history. Written for an American lecture tour in 1979 and published in a pioneering collection celebrating women's achievement, *Irish Women: Image and*

Achievement, is a *tour de force* that uses her knowledge of Irish law to describe the reality of women's lives as their power and status waxed and waned over four hundred years and to pose the question why a '… society whose literature attributes such independence to women would deny it or rigidly curtail it in real life'. She starts in the great years of the sixteenth century where Gaelic law protected women's rights and property. She describes Irish women's impoverishment and powerlessness in the seventeenth century when the subordination of women was a mark of Ireland's colonialism in the wake of the Cromwellian wars and the subsequent plantations. She points out that it was not surprising, under the circumstance, that Ireland was cast as a woman – the *spéirbhean* of the eighteenth century *aisling* and Cathleen Ni Houlihan, the poor old woman.

Mac Curtain considers the ways that women imaginatively addressed their historical conditions. Their responses represented the shapes of women's sorrow – the *caoine*, the lament, the love song of the abandoned girl. There were also their more active efforts to change their circumstances by emigration, by entering religious life or by becoming aware of and working for their rights.

Women in religious life, particularly those who entered the native Irish religious orders – the Presentation Sisters, the Irish Sisters of Loreto and the Sisters of Mercy – played pioneering roles in educating Irish children and relieving human suffering. In the nineteenth century the Irish continental religious orders opened convent boarding schools. We know from contemporary reports like those of Asenath Nicholson in *Annals of the Famine in Ireland* (1998 [1851]) that the Presentation Sisters kept their schools open and fed the children of the poor. The Presentation Convent in Tuam,

Co. Galway was the one place in Ireland in 1848 that Nicholson observed children with normal affect. The Intermediate Act (1878) brought the opportunity to prepare Irish women for third level education, the story Mac Curtain told in 'St Mary's University College'. Despite a strong record of at least a basic education for girls at every level, the falling status of women in post-Famine Ireland can be read in the demographics. Mac Curtain provides census and employment data that explain another figure – the some 310,000 Irish girls who arrived at the Port of New York between 1883 and 1908.

Mac Curtain returns to 'Women, the Vote and Revolution' to describe the counter-revolutionary pressures that witnessed women relegated to a subordinate position in the Irish Free State when social legislation was designed to keep woman in her place in the home. Were Mac Curtain to have published 'The Historical Image' in 2008 instead of 1985, the conclusion would have charted a history of improved conditions for women. Perhaps the most radical social legislation was the Right to Remarry Campaign of 1995 that carried the Judicial Separation Act to its logical conclusion by allowing for separated partners to remarry. Mac Curtain agreed to be a Patron to the Campaign and took responsibility for media relations with local radio. A full-page ad in *The Irish Times* carried her signature right above Bono's. Reuter's carried the story with the headline 'Maverick Nun backs Divorce in Ireland'. However, their quote from Mac Curtain underscores her argument that catholic teaching was not at odds with the State's concern to resolve the matter of civic divorce:

> I would hope my stand would be seen as a plea for the liberty of conscience which catholics have been exhorted to exercise and as a plea for reconciliation and generosity which has been absent in Ireland.

Her reason and compassion aside, it was a controversial, high profile campaign with a potential for abuse. Mac Curtain received threatening calls and letters and during the campaign her car, parked in front of the Sisters' residence, was stolen and trashed. In the end, the campaign succeeded – just, but it is clear that Mac Curtain's courageous stand on the principle of the separation of Church and State on this matter made a difference.

'The Real Molly Macree' (1993) reveals most dramatically the disparity between the romantic image of the Irish colleen in art, music and literature and the reality of her life in post-Famine Ireland. The occasion for the essay was the exhibition at Boston College of paintings on loan from the National Gallery of Ireland during Mac Curtain's tenure as Burns Visiting Scholar at Boston College in 1992–93. The late Adele Dalsimer, Co-Director of the Irish Studies Program, invited Mac Curtain to contribute to a collection of reflections on particular paintings in the exhibition. Mac Curtain chose Thomas Alfred Jones's watercolour 'Molly Macree' (ca. 1869). In her essay, Mac Curtain reads the Jones painting and then, using evidence from post-Famine economic and social history, makes the case for the reality of the life for young women in rural Ireland. Her treatment is a case study of how the reading of a painting in the context of social, economic and political history can inform the study of culture in a particular period. The essay anticipated those ideas in Brian P. Kennedy and Raymond Gillespie's collection *Ireland: Art into History* (1994) that examine visual images in a cultural context.

Heeding her own caution to resist taking art too literally, she concludes that the silence behind the colleen's calm, steady gaze masks the reality of rural women's lives in post-Famine Ireland – her worn apron is the metaphor for that condition. The power of the image Mac Curtain creates reminds the reader of another iconic colonial image, one from Joseph Conrad's 'Heart of Darkness'. It is the magnificent, fierce African woman who stands silently at the edge of the Congo River watching the boat carrying Marlow and Kurtz downstream. 'She looked at us all as if her life had depended upon the unswerving steadiness of her glance'. The silence of those women would be broken by post-colonial interrogation.

Mac Curtain's most recent essay in this collection is 'Writing Grief into Memory: Women, Language and Narrative' that started as a plenary address to the International Association for the Study of Irish Literatures conference at the University of Limerick in 1998 and was later published in the conference proceedings edited by Patricia Lynch, Joachim Fischer and Brian Coates titled *Back to the Present: Forward to the Past: Irish Writing and History since 1798* (2006). Taking up the conference theme of 'Memory', Mac Curtain's paper is a survey of texts that recover expressions of women's grief from oral and written tradition, in Irish and in English. Taking as her starting point the study of memory Mac Curtain proposes to demonstrate 'how women's voices use memory to create a narrative around mourning and grief'. The substance of the paper draws on the wide range of texts of spiritual writings that Mac Curtain collected for her contributions to *The Field Day Anthology of Irish Writing, IV–V*. Her return to the study of literature, a subject she studied with the formidable B. G. MacCarthy at UCC, enriches her readers' appreciation of the insights that literature offers the historian.

Mac Curtain begins with a feminist reading of the traditional women's genre, the *caoine* and analyses Eilís

Dillon's translation of 'Caoineadh Airt Uí Laoghaire' ('The Lament for Art O'Leary') returning to the *caointe* of contemporary Irish language poets Máire Mhac an tSaoi, Caitlín Maude and Nuala Ní Dhomhnaill. She includes Lady Gregory's 'Alas, a woman may not love', a poem of her love affair with Wilfrid Scawen Blunt, but not Gregory's best known love lament, her translation from the Irish of 'Domhnall Óg or The Grief of a Girl's Heart', the cry of a girl who has been seduced and abandoned. Arguing that the storyteller's *oeuvre* demands attention after years of being marginalized as a school text, Mac Curtain examines the theme of loss in Peig Sayers' three volumes of autobiography, memoir and memorate. To read Mac Curtain on Sayers is to wish she had added a full-length study of the storyteller including the manuscript materials in the Archives of UCD's Delargy Centre to her *oeuvre*. Her command of Irish, her wide knowledge of social history and her empathy for the subject would have produced the definitive biography of Peig.

If 'Writing Grief into Memory', is Mac Curtain's closing essay in this collection, *The Field Day Anthology of Irish Writing, IV–V* is her harvest knot, the symbol for the *meitheal* (working party), the metaphor for the *modus operandi* of the volumes' senior editors. The genesis of *Field Day IV–V* is a well-known story. When *Field Day I–III* was published, the editors were confronted with the charges that women's texts were under represented, that there was a lack of attention to feminist scholarship and that there was not a single woman on the editorial board. Seamus Deane, Editor of *Field Day I–III*, offered the opportunity for an additional volume by women writers and scholars. When it appeared eleven years later, it was a two-volume, 3200 page work. By then Ireland had changed and *Field Day IV–V* reflected that change. Seamus Deane said that *Field Day I–III* took its authority from the present moment: Northern Ireland since 1969. *Field Day IV–V* took as its moment the European Court of Human Rights rulings affirming the status of women and the successful Right to Remarry Campaign. For *I–III*, the moment was England and Ireland: colonizer and colony; for *IV–V* the moment was globalization with the Celtic Tiger rampant. For *I–III*, the moment was governed by Margaret Thatcher; for *IV–V*, the moment was the presidency of Mary Robinson. For *I–III*, the moment was the end of the twentieth century; for *IV–V*, the moment was the beginning of the twenty-first century.

Mac Curtain played a key role in the *Field Day IV–V* project. She served as a senior editor; she was one of the authors of the Foreword to the two volumes; she headed the 'Religion, Science, Theology and Ethics 1500–2000' section recruiting contributing editors, making her own selection of texts, providing introductions, notes and bibliography and even translating texts from the Irish. Her introduction to the section surveying five hundred years of women's writings on religion, science, theology and ethics provides the *coda* to her earlier essays and, as always, reminds the reader that there is still work to be done. She raised the matter of working on similar projects in different places or within different communities. One might ask what was the experience of Irish women in the same religious community working in America or in rural Ireland? What was it about Barbara Heck's life as a Methodist in Ireland that gave her the courage to recruit Philip Embury to preach to fellow Methodists in New York '… lest we shall all go to hell together'? Was there any influence at all of the Lowell mill girls who produced the *Lowell Offering* (1840–45) and then the *New England Offering* (1847–1850) on the mill girls of the Ulster Revival of 1859?

Speaking of the parallel but separate women's philanthropies in the late eighteenth century, Mac Curtain observes that such isolation may have contributed to the sectarian rivalries of the next century. She might have included the most bitter example of those rivalries, 'souperism', the use of food as an instrument of proselytism during the Great Irish Famine. Irene Whelan's fine study, *The Bible War in Ireland* takes the reader up to 1840 but not through the harrowing years 1845–52. More work needs to be done on religious women: nuns, clergy wives, Quaker women during the period. The experience of editing the 'Religion in Early Modern Irish' section of *Field Day* prompted Mac Curtain to investigate Kilculliheen and Grace Dieu further for her study of convents of the Pale, and it gave her the answer to a question she came back to frequently in her earlier writings – why had women remained subordinate in the Irish State that they had helped to create? She found an answer in the recollections of catholic girlhoods in Ireland in the first half of the twentieth century.

Retirement from UCD in 1994 brought new challenges. She was the Baldwin Scholar in the College of Notre Dame of Maryland (Baltimore) in spring 1995. When she returned to Ireland she was a member of the Coimisiún ar Eagraíochtaí Deonacha na Gaeilge, a ministerial commission to advise on the Irish language. She chaired the National Library of Ireland Society for four years after her return from Baltimore. In 1997, she was named to a five-year term as Chair of the National Archives Advisory Council, the same year she was named in a list of the sixty most influential women in Ireland by *The Sunday Tribune.* The same paper put her on the short list of candidates to succeed Mary Robinson as President of Ireland. In 1999, at the request of the New York State Department of Education, she chaired the

International Advisory Committee for the New York State Great Irish Famine Curriculum that won the National Council for Social Studies Project Excellence Award in 2002. During the 1990s she continued to serve her Dominican community chairing the Board of Governors of St. Catherine's College of Home Economics, but especially as a member of the community that supported the education of children with special needs. RTÉ TV and Radio, Raidió na Gaeltachta and TG4, the Irish language medium TV station, frequently invite her to appear as a commentator, panellist and presenter as in the recent feature that took her and her friend and UCD colleague Maribel Foley to Spain in search of St. Teresa of Avila. While she protests that she is retired, producers argue that her telegenic persona and her wise, well-informed and witty repartee have made her a *sui generis* presence in the Irish media.

The 1990s brought Mac Curtain recognition for her life's work as scholar and activist for human rights. She was awarded honorary degrees from three American colleges: Merrimack College (1994), the College of Notre Dame (1995) and The College of the Elms (1999) In 2007, the NUI recognized her lifetime achievement with a Doctor of Literature degree presented by the Chancellor and her old friend and colleague Garret Fitzgerald. She was the recipient of the Gold Medal of the Éire Society, Boston 1993, the Women's International Center's Living Legacy Award in 1997 (San Diego) when she was cited as a champion of justice especially for women and children, and the UCC Alumnus Achievement Award in 2000. She was a founding member of the Women's Education, Research and Resource Centre (WERRC) and the Women's History Association of Ireland (WHAI), which, on its tenth anniversary in 1999, created the

Cullen-Mac Curtain Prize in Women's History for an undergraduate essay on women's history.

Mac Curtain chose *Ariadne's Thread: Writing Women into Irish History* as the title for this collection of essays. While it is an apt metaphor for her book and for her work in Irish history, I think of Mac Curtain also as a faithful Penelope – patiently weaving her tapestry of Irish women's experience. However she does not wait for a man to return to set things right. Instead, she weaves and invites Irish women to join her and pick up the threads of their own history.

– Hofstra University, New York,
February 2008

Maureen Murphy is a former president of both the American Conference of Irish Studies and the International Association for the Study of Irish Literatures. She is Interim Dean of the School of Education and Allied Human services and Professor of Secondary Education and English at Hofstra University, Long Island. Among her academic work, she has edited (for The Lilliput Press, Dublin), Asenath Nicholson's *Annals of the Famine in Ireland* (1998) and *Ireland's Welcome to the Stranger* (2003).

Sometimes an artist captures a mood in a painting – an arrangement of objects, a figure posed against a background of light and shade which expresses eloquently what a creative writer portrays in a work of fiction, or more laboriously what a historian tries to convey in a complex study of a period. Leo Whelan's *The Kitchen Window* painted about 1926 is a social document as well as a fine example of a Dutch interior translated into a modern Irish domestic scene.

A woman is standing beside a table. Pausing in her work of polishing a silver teapot, she glances abstractedly away from the viewer, back into the kitchen behind her. Her hair is bobbed and her wide-set eyes have an expression of resigned forbearance mingled with a flash of reserve, perhaps of independence, the latter declaring itself in the set of her head and shoulders. The large window to the right produces strong effects of light and shade on the wooden texture of the table and cupboard. The red and white check-patterned curtain behind the woman's upper body contrasts agreeably with the yellowish cupboard doors and the woman's dark-blue spotted blouse. The peeling paint-work, the large re-polished silver trophy on the table provoke the viewer's curiosity. Even more interesting to the eye is the manner in which the artist conveys, by a skilful use of lines and rectangular spaces, the boxed-in atmosphere of the woman's environment. In a painting of exquisite sensibility, Whelan conveys the solitary existence of the woman in the kitchen in the years when the new Free State and a partitioned Ireland faced an uncertain future.[1]

Leo Whelan's woman in the kitchen belonged to the generation which inherited the legacy of the Irish revolution, 1916–23. Born during or after the last decade of the nineteenth century they influenced the cultural, political and moral climate of the post-civil-war decades subliminally, despite their absence from the public life of the country. What happened to a generation who had won the rights to university education, to women's suffrage and to political office is connected with their participation in, or distancing themselves from the consequences of a revolution which partitioned their country after a bloody civil war. Exclusion from public office took place almost immediately with the passing of the Civil Service (Amendment) Act, 1925 which restricted women to junior positions in the Civil Service. The Juries Bill 1927 exempted women as a class from serving on juries. They were debarred from joining the police force and the national army of the Free State.

Maryann Valiulis, in her study of this period, *Power, Gender and Identity in the Irish Free State* analysed the Dáil debates of the founding years and considered:

> that the government's position was based upon a rigid and hierarchical gender dichotomy. The government and its supporters authoritatively asserted that the primary role of women was marriage and motherhood, that women's place was in the home, tending to the needs of their husbands, raising their children.[2]

A decade later a small lobby protested about the status of women expressed in Article 41.2.1 of the Constitution of the Irish Free State, *Bunreacht na hÉireann,* 1937 which allocated them a role supporting the State by a 'life within the home'. Their views were dismissed as representing a radical minority of feminist politics. However, the lobby of feminists comprised the National University Women Graduates' Association, the Irish

Women Workers' Union, the Joint Committee of Women's Societies and the Standing Committee on Legislation Affecting Women. Indeed the early feminism of the most vocal activists of the generation which had campaigned on the 'votes for women' issue was unpopular and unfashionable in the middle decades of the twentieth century.

The social and economic forces which shaped women's lives, north and south, in the decades after the civil war and partition of the country were the sub-text for a gendered division of labour. In the Free State the middle-classness which dominated politics and church-institutions in the first half of the twentieth century was rooted in prosperous family-owned farms which benefited from the land acts around the turn of the century. With the 1921 Treaty the land-owning aristocracy, no longer the ruling class, handed over central and local government to their former tenants and their presence in the new Ireland became a token of their former power. Implicit in the governing structures of Ireland, north and south, was the assumption that leadership positions belonged to men, and the task of consolidating family power and finances fell to women less as partners than as subordinates. With few, though notable exceptions, women accepted their role in the new order. Joanna Bourke in her study *Husbandry to Housewifery* suggests that 'the changes in rural Irish society between 1890–1914 created a non-market household sector which demanded skilled labour which was met by women'. Girls' education at school level she argues persuasively prepared them for a life of useful domesticity and the new household economy was part of a larger state economy.[3] In the inter-war years the Irish Free State's thinking around women's place in the order of society projected an ideal of family, motherhood and home. Diarmaid Ferriter suggests in his study of the

Irish Countrywomen's Association, *Mothers, Maidens and Myths: A History of the ICA* 'that the 1930s was the time for a real independent rural Ireland, and that was an Ireland true to the home'. Deeply committed to raising levels of skills and economics of domestic living in rural Ireland, the Irish Countrywomen's Association was not part of the women's coalition which opposed the role of women defined in *Bunreacht na hÉireann*.[4]

Many unresearched questions invite exploration about the situation of women in the formative decades after the Irish civil war. Did rural values dominate the thinking of church leaders and politicians, idealising the simplicity of country living? How boxed in, how content were women to live in the confined space of farm kitchen, or family room in towns and cities as Leo Whelan's painting suggests? Were they silent and unquestioning when their adventurous sisters left the countryside and, either emigrated, took religious vows in convents or remained unmarried to pursue a career? The 2000-strong membership of the Irish Countrywomen's Association urged their president in 1939 to resist the cliché 'a woman's place is in the home' and replace it with, 'a woman's place is where she can best help her home'.[5] Facing into the decade of the second world war rural women struggled with the hardships occasioned by Ireland's neutral position in the war and the priorities of a gendered state in bringing electricity and piped water to the farm, but not necessarily to the farm kitchen.[6]

Were women relegated to a 'woman's sphere' when *Bunreacht na hÉireann* set constitutional boundaries to their position? Girls' education, and the complex hierarchy of which cohorts of girl children received secondary education in the decades between 1937 and 1967, the year when the Irish state introduced free education in the Republic, raises troubling questions about gender, class and equal opportunity. All-female secondary schools conducted and managed by female religious orders reached their zenith in the 1940s and 1950s and will, in time, provide a rich quarry for investigation. There were gains and losses but women in those decades did not recognize that they had a history and, though they saw themselves reflected in fiction and drama, they were alienated from any critique of their own experience.

The decades between 1920 and 1960 are regarded as a valley period between two 'waves' of the women's movement in Ireland, in North America and in Europe. Understanding the experiences of Irish women in that period gives meaning to the whole century. Comparing the life-situations of Irish women with those of women in countries on the periphery of World War II, Norway, Finland, Portugal and Greece (rather than Britain, France, Germany and Italy) brings a sense of proportion to the accusations of isolationism and backwardness levelled against Ireland in those decades. Irish women had campaigned for suffragism and for civil liberties in the early part of the century and when the second wave of the women's movement erupted in the 1960s they knew what they wanted. It was a global movement in the 1960s concerned with issues of equality in the workplace, with child-care and with birth-control. It was the decade when a contraceptive pill became available on prescription in 1961. For Roman Catholics worldwide the summoning of the Second Vatican Council, 1962–65 was epoch-making in its agenda and decrees. When Pope Paul VI issued *Humanae Vitae* in 1968, side-stepping the report of a papal commission which had the previous year recommended that the decision to regulate the size of the family be left to the individual couple, there were murmurs of dissent with the ban against artificial methods of birth control in Ireland whose largely catholic and church-going population was, in general, docile to Rome's precepts.

The detailed memorandum which the women's organizations in Ireland, such as the Irish Countrywomen's Association, the Irish branch of the Soroptimists and the Irish Housewives' Association presented to the Irish government in 1968 recommended the establishment of a Commission on the Status of Women as a pre-condition for entry into the European Economic Community which the Irish government was then seeking. In 1970 a commission, chaired by Dr Thekla Beere (1902–91) secretary of the Department of Transport and Power (and the sole female representative of her sex in the upper levels of public service) was set up. The *Beere Report* appeared in two volumes: an interim report on Equal Pay in 1971, and the following year a full report containing forty-nine recommendations for improving the status of women. Together they constitute one of the most important documents for charting the position of women in the Irish state. Before the Republic of Ireland joined the European Economic Community (EEC) in 1973, its government set up the Council for the Status of Women entrusting it with the task of monitoring the implementation of the recommendations of the *Beere Report*. It was also empowered to act as an umbrella body for women's organizations within the State and to represent them officially.[7] The government appointed Hilda Tweedy (1911–2005) to chair the Council for the Status of Women, a position she held from 1972–78.

The *Report* expressed the aspiration that women would retrieve their own history. Hilda Tweedy was committed to that goal. Among other activities she had co-founded with Andrée Sheehy Skeffington the Irish

Housewives' Association in 1942, an important pressure group which brought its influence to bear on government policy towards rationing and price controls when a state of emergency was decreed in the 1940s. During her term as chair of the Council she organized seminars and workshops where women discussed the new legislation on women and work coming from European directives to the Irish government. One of her most enduring achievements was her history of the Irish Housewives' Association, *A Link in the Chain*, an exemplary account of relations between women and the Irish State in the mid-twentieth century.[8]

Writing women into Irish history became a subversive activity for women historians in the 1970s. The universities were not ready for an innovation which, in the opinion of the historical establishment, possessed neither a sound methodology nor reliable sources.[9]

Outside Ireland there was an emerging scholarship on the subject of women as a distinct group for historical research. International workshops and models of the 'new women's history' in the United States, in France and in England mentored its advance and quality. Women's history in Ireland as elsewhere developed in a climate of forced activity which made heavy demands on the resources of those professional historians willing to give papers, to guide theses and to publish. Accompanying this intellectual ferment, and partly the reason for it, was a real hunger for discovering the roots of the women's movement in the opening years of the twentieth century. As women learned more about their own participation in the beginnings of democracy in Ireland they internalised and to some extent identified with the struggle for women to win the right to vote, to acquire property in their own name, and to aspire to political office. Attendance at conferences and evening classes led to a demand for women's studies as part of a university curriculum, and by the mid-1980s Irish universities had acceded to that demand.

The acceptance of women's history as course material for a university history syllabus fared less successfully than the introduction of women's studies. Centres for Women's Studies were founded as degree-conferring institutions within the academic community, whereas the goal of women's history was its integration within mainstream history departments. Women historians taught history, and directed research within the Centres for Women's Studies, but in the 1970s and early 1980s, the case for teaching women as a course in an undergraduate history syllabus was weak in a male-dominated profession. The irony was that thirty years earlier women's roles and contribution had figured on history syllabuses in Ireland. Professor James Hogan who held the chair of History, including Irish history, in UCC lectured on sixteenth-century political women as a topic for examination. At the oral examination for my doctoral dissertation in 1963 my defence of convent archives as valid, historical deposits gave rise to a vigorous and enthusiastic discussion among my examiners. Less than a decade later 'revisionism' began to influence the teaching of Irish history and unwittingly stifled discussion around alternative ways of constructing the historical past of the island.

Were it not for the establishment of the Irish Association for Research in Women's History in 1987, it is possible that women historians would bow to the inevitable and limit women's history to becoming a component of women's studies. By founding the Irish Association for Research in Women's History, Irish practitioners of women's history formed international links with similar bodies worldwide and participated in conferences and exchanges on a global network. The first president of the Irish Association for Research in Women's History, Mary Cullen, established links with the International Committee for Historical Sciences (which regulates the teaching of history at university level) through Ida Bloom, professor of women's history at the University of Bergen in Norway and at that time president of the International Federation for Research in Women's History. By the beginning of the 1990s women's history was being taught and researched in mainstream history departments in Irish universities and in other third-level colleges in Ireland.[10]

For the first time in the history of the Irish State there was a woman president, Mary Robinson, whose strong advocacy of women's issues in the law courts had given her a wide constituency over the previous two decades. During her seven years as president she actively encouraged women's studies and the history of Irish women. Much had been accomplished in a short time. Historians had given back their place in the life of the country to women of past centuries. Irish publishers had taken risks in publishing theses and biographies creating a reading public and raising the level of awareness by ensuring that women's books were reviewed.[11] The temptation to remain with the task of rendering women visible is attractive. Restoring the women 'missing from history' is the initial step accordIng to American historian, Gerda Lerner, author of *The Majority Finds its Past: Placing Women in History.* She wrote in 1979:

> Women are made to fit into the empty spaces of traditional history. Once engaged in this enterprise and confronting the vast untapped riches of primary sources, the historian becomes aware of the inadequacy of the concepts with which she must deal, of the limitations or inapplicability of the traditional questions she is asking. The search for a better conceptual framework for the

history of women begins at this stage. One is led, step by step, to new definitions, to the search for more appropriate concepts, to dissatisfaction with periodization in traditional history.[12]

The work of restoration and making visible will continue but for trained Irish historians at the beginning of the twenty-first century the task of reconstructing mainsteam history is of major concern to the future of the discipline. While the 'revisionist' debate took centre stage in the 1980s and early 1990s other studies of history not perceived to be relevant to revisionism grew apace supported by groups committed to expanding their new fields. Thus studies of settlement history have enriched the approach to heritage and town planning. Labour history has advanced greatly an understanding of working conditions and trades unions since its beginnings in 1973. The publication of *Women Surviving: Studies in Irish Women's History in the 19th and 20th Centuries*, a collection edited by Maria Luddy and Cliona Murphy in 1989, was hailed as the coming of age of women's history as a professional discipline.[13]

Revisionism was never a 'school of history'. It was an interrogation of the accepted past in controversial topics such as the interpretation of the Great Famine (1846–52), the 1916 Easter Rising and the development of twentieth-century Ireland, north and south. It was the main intellectual discourse that accompanied the progress of the northern conflict, hovering uneasily between the legitimate goal of historical research to re-interpret the myths and long-established 'facts' of history and the more journalistic endeavour to dislodge nationalist history from its popular appeal with a large reading public. D. G. Boyce, editor with Alan O'Day of *The Making of Modern History: Revisionism and the*

Revisionist Controversy suggests that the most unsatisfactory aspect of the revisionist controversy was:

> that it did not move historical scholarship forward at all ... it did not encourage a debate about the historian's method, but rather sought to prevent historians talking to each other about their method, inviting them to take refuge in their 'own' primordial loyalties.[14]

Irish identity has tormented writers of every creed and class throughout the twentieth century. Philosophers, creative writers, artists and communicators on radio, screen and stage, all have endeavoured to convey the specificity, the individuality of being Irish and the 'personality' of Ireland. National identity raises even more questions and when examined reveals a shared sense of belonging and loyalties to political creeds, sometimes at the expense of the outsider. Irish identity evokes powerful, even passionate responses which, when scrutinised, lay bare complicated attitudes to language and religion. Misunderstandings and self-contradictions abound in the assumptions of what constitutes Irish identity, all the more painful in the context of north-south relationships.

Any discussion of identity in the 1990s led to the issue of gender as one of its components. Gender is sometimes confused with sex. Sex is that by which an animal or plant is male or female on the basis of their reproductive functions. In making the further distinction between sex and gender in human beings, sex is the biological difference between men and women. Gender is the manner in which culture and power construct definitions of sexuality and assign roles and activities deemed proper for each designated sex. Joan Scott, a leading theorist in the field of women's history threw down a challenge with the publication in 1988 of *Gender and the Politics of History*, a treatise which examined the construction of masculine and feminine identities in the field of history. Scott defines gender as 'the social organization of sexual difference ... the knowledge that establishes meanings for bodily differences'. She argues that gender is a primary way of signifying relationships of power and should have its place in the study of history.[15] Georges Duby and Michelle Perrot, co-editors of a five-volume *History of Women* reject 'the idea that women in themselves are an object of history'. They insist that their *History of Women* is 'fundamentally relational; because we look at society as a whole and our history is necessarily also a history of men'. The introduction of gender as a legitimate study in the historical sciences was recognized in the programme of the 1995 International Congress of Historical Sciences, the most authoritative body in the realm of professional history. Its main theme was 'Women, Men and Historical Change: Case Studies on the Impact of Gender History'. The proceedings indicated that the new emphasis on difference and diversity posed a threat to the concept of women's history in a wider context whereas the conventional 'women and work' model favoured by social and economic historians retained its position.

Does a gendered approach place an obstacle in the way of studying women as a group and not as a set of relationships? It certainly has inserted a note of defensiveness and even of apology into the reasons for studying women in isolation from men.[16] Has the history of women lost its appeal for a new generation of students in the twenty-first century? Pirjo Markola, a Finnish historian explores the tension in her essay 'Constructing and Deconstructing the "Strong Finnish Woman": Women's History and Gender History'. Her analysis offers a useful comparison with Irish women in several instances. Finnish women were the first in

Europe to gain the right to vote in 1906 and to be eligible to stand as candidates in national elections. In Finland 'votes for women' was not a woman's issue: women's political citizenship, achieved without struggle, became a 'bipartite citizenship'. This meant in practice a gendered approach to social policy, involving problems of social security, health and home economics which parliamentary women were expected to pursue. Finnish research has concentrated on female activity in the labour force and the reasons why it was at such a high level of involvement. Markola concludes that women's history, while under threat from those who advocate gender history is all the more challenging and necessary as Finnish women move into a new phase.[17]

The themes 'women and work', the pursuit of the goal of women's franchise, the motives and activities of revolutionary women in Irish freedom movements, are subjects that present a serviceable comparisons with the researched history of Finnish women, but the contribution of women to the main contours and shape of twentieth-century Ireland have eluded historians and remain firmly in the domain of creative writers.[18] The powerful impressions with which the artist and writer have suffused the Irish imagination challenge the historian to hold a mirror up to the recent past in an unemotional and objective context. The Irish memory remains a prisoner to the shaping influences of childhood in an age when men and women live longer lives and pass on ancient sorrows and deprivations to a more fortunate generation. The enormous popularity that the memoir and autobiography *genre* enjoyed at the end of the twentieth century testifies to the coldness and harshness of childhood experiences before the mid-century. '1 once said to John Synge "Do you write out of love or hate for Ireland?" and he replied "I have often asked myself that question"'. The interrogator was W. B.

Yeats. The historian is handicapped who cannot interpret the ways subjectivity filters the Irish memory in its selectivity of past events.

Irish women's history at the beginning of the twenty-first century is not harassed by the epistemological problems prevalent in historical debate in countries where there have been strong schools of social history – France and the United States in particular. Revisionism has preoccupied Irish historians and unintentionally has permitted women's history to develop. The support of influential historians, men and women, and a proven record in writing about women is evidence of a receptivity which is reflected in audiences at summer schools such as the annual Merriman School and the Parnell School. The second president of the Women's History Association of Ireland, Professor Mary O'Dowd, Queen's University, Belfast, actively encouraged the awareness of women's history in Northern Ireland as well as in the Republic through shared conferences and projects. The major achievement of her years as president was her support for the compilation of *A Directory of Sources for Women's History in Ireland*, undertaken by Maria Luddy with a team of specialists for the Women's History Project funded generously by the Department of Arts, Heritage, Gaeltacht and the Islands to catalogue women's issues within the state and official archives of the country.[19] The Women's History Project marks a further stage of development following on from the two-part historiographical essay undertaken for *Irish Historical Studies* at the behest of the editors in 1992.[20]

My main reason for assembling this collection of essays is to encourage women and men to study and write women's history. Prompted by many students who questioned me after class, or at the end of a discussion with one of the women's networks that mushroomed in the last twenty years of the twentieth century, I have made a selection of essays from my own work which demonstrates different approaches to researching and writing the history of women. My objective was to create a workshop atmosphere in which an essay is examined in its context, that is in the circumstances which gave rise to it: how I set about writing the piece, what problems I had to overcome when method was unclear, and the provenance of documents either unknown or uncatalogued. I also suggest to the reader what to expect from a piece of historical writing about women and in what ways the study of women's history has advanced since I published my first researched essay in the early 1960s.

The title, *Ariadne's Thread,* is a metaphor for the project of women's history as it attempts to find recognition within the academic study of Irish history. Metaphors are significant so far as they direct the gaze to that which they resemble. In the Greek legend, Ariadne, a captive of the Minotaur, gave Theseus a ball of yarn which he unravelled behind him in the labyrinth as he searched for the Minotaur. After slaying the Minotaur, Theseus retraced his steps, following Ariadne's thread and escaped with her to Naxos. Ariadne's labyrinth, the Minotaur, the thread of escape, in the ways they resemble the enveloping culture of twentieth-century Ireland for so many women and men has more to do with how an ancient myth embodies a rich, intricate set of meanings which illuminates a historical background, than with matching symbol to reality. Nuala Ní Dhomhnaill, poet and essayist, in an address to women writers in 1999, reminded them that:

> the threads that bind us to life, to family, to community are not to be cut but are to be spun out of ourselves.

Ariadne and her thread which leads in and out of the labyrinth of the self is the myth that is at work here, not that of the conquering hero.[21]

The artist supplies the clues for the historian and, like Leo Whelan's woman in the kitchen, invites the historian to look at a hidden thread.

NOTES

1   Leo Whelan (1892–1956), *The Kitchen Window,* painted about 1926, is housed in the Crawford Art Gallery, Cork. cf. Brian P Kennedy, *Irish Painting* (Dublin, Townhouse, 1993), p. 118.

2   Maryann Gialanella Valiulis, 'Power, Gender and Identity in the Irish Free State', in Joan Hoff and Maureen Coulter (eds), *Irish Women's Voices: Past and Present,* a special issue of the *Journal of Women's History,* Vol. VI. No. 4/Vol. VII. No. 1 (Bloomington, IN, Indiana University Press, Winter/Spring 1995), p. 122.

3   Joanna Bourke, *Husbandry to Housewifery* (Oxford, Clarendon Press, 1993) p. 275. Part three of Bourke's study, 'Houseworkers' pp 201–83 supply the context for her assertion.

4   Diarmaid Ferriter, *Mothers, Maidens and Myths* (FÁS/ICA History Project, 1994), p. 10.

5   *Loc. cit.* p. 17. See also Aileen Heverin, *The Irish Countrywomen's Association: A History 1910–2000* (Dublin, Wolfhound Press, 2000); Caitríona Clear, *Women of the House* (Dublin, Irish Academic Press, 2000).

6   Mary E Daly, '"Turn on the tap": The State, Irish Women and Running Water', in Maryann G. Valiulis and Mary O'Dowd (eds), *Women in Irish History* (Dublin, Wolfhound Press, 1997), pp 206–19.

7   Ailbhe Smyth, 'The Contemporary Women's Movement in the Republic of Ireland', in Ailbhe Smyth (ed.), 'Feminism in Ireland', special issue of *Women's Studies International Forum* (New York, Pergamon Press, 1988), Vol. XI, No. 4, pp 331–41.

8   Hilda Tweedy, *A Link in the Chain: The Story of the Irish Housewives' Association 1942–1992* (Dublin, Attic Press, 1992), p. 116.

9   The founders of *Irish Historical Studies* (1932–) Professors Theo Moody and R. D. Edwards expressed privately to the author their scepticism concerning women's history as a subject meriting validation at university level in the early 1970s.

10 Mary Cullen, 'Women's history in Ireland', in Karen Offen, Ruth Roach Pierson and Jane Rendall (eds), *Writing Women's History* (Bloomington IN, Indiana University Press, 1991), pp 492–441.

11 Alan Hayes, *The Irish Feminist Publishing Archive at NUI, Galway* (Galway, Women's Studies Centre, 1998), a pamphlet outlining the activities of feminist publishing initiatives 1970s–1990s on the occasion of placing the archives of Arlen House and Women's Community Press at NUI, Galway, 4 December 1998.

12 Gerda Lerner, *The Majority Finds its Past: Placing Women in History* (New York, Oxford University Press, 1979), p. xiv in paperback edition, 1981.

13 Seán Hutton and Paul Stewart; 'Introduction: Perspectives on Irish History and Social Studies', in Hutton and Stewart (eds), *Ireland's Histories: Aspects of State, Society and Ideology* (London, Routledge, 1991), p. 3.

14 D. George Boyce and Alan O'Daly (eds), *The Making of Modern Irish History: Revisionism and the Revisionist Controversy* (London, Routledge, 1996), p. 12.

15 Joan W. Scott, *Gender and the Politics of History* (New York, Columbia University Press, 1988).

16 Francoise Thebaud, 'Explorations of Gender', in Georges Duby and Michelle Perrot with Francoise Thebaud (eds), *A History of Women: Toward a Cultural Identity in the Twentieth Century* (Cambridge MA, Harvard University Press, 1994), pp 1–11.

17 Pirjo Markola, 'Constructing and Deconstructing the "Strong-Finnish Woman": Women's History and Gender History', *Historiallinen Aikakauskirja Historical Journal*, No. 2, pp 153–160 (University of Tampere, 1997), translated by Brian Fleming.

18 Anne Fogarty, 'Uncanny Families: neo-Gothic Motifs and the Theme of Social Change in Contemporary Irish Women's Fiction', *Irish University Review,* Vol. XXX, No. 1, (Spring/Summer 2000), pp 59–81; Pat O'Connor, *Emerging Voices: Women in Contemporary Irish Society* (Dublin, Institute of Public Administration, 1998); Gerry Smyth, *The Novel and the Nation: Studies in the New Irish Fiction* (London, Pluto Press, 1997).

19 The Women's History Project sponsored by the Women's History Association of Ireland, was inaugurated in 1997 with funding from the Department of Arts, Heritage, Gaeltacht and the Islands. The aim of the project was to survey, list and publish historical documents relating to a history of women in the Republic of Ireland and Northern Ireland. The information gathered is entered on a

database, A *Directory of Sources for the History of Women in Ireland.* See www.nationalarchives.ie.

20 Maria Luddy, Margaret Mac Curtain, Mary O'Dowd, 'An Agenda for Women's History in Ireland 1500–1900', *Irish Historical Studies,* Vol. XXVIII, No. 109 (May 1992), pp 1–317.

21 Nuala Ní Dhomhnaill, 'A Spectacular Flowering', *The Irish Times,* 29 May 1999, Section 4: The Arts (unpaginated).

My first introduction to women's history was a study of Irish women's struggle to win the right to university degrees at the end of the nineteenth century. Trained as a traditional historian of high politics and international diplomacy in the early modern period I was without map or compass in unknown territory and had to rely on methods I used in European archives when researching my seventeenth-century subject for my dissertation. I have always maintained that sources should not dictate the formulation of the historical problem, so instead of pursuing the insistent question: why were women so tardy in demanding access to university degrees, I considered how Irish women succeeded in reaching their goal. Subsequently Eibhlín Breathnach completed a major thesis for her MA in 1981 on 'Women and Higher Education in Ireland 1860–1912' and published two valuable articles from the body of the thesis, see Crane Bag, *Vol. IV, No. 1, (1980) and Cullen,* Girls Don't Do Honours, *cited below.*

Why women were deprived of educational opportunities has proved a more elusive problem to investigate, but the collection of essays edited by Mary Cullen, Girls Don't Do Honours: Irish Women in Education in the 19th and 20th centuries *(Dublin, Women's Education Bureau [Arlen House], 1987) was a vigorous contribution to a neglected topic. The study of St. Mary's University College appeared in* University Review, *Vol. III, No. 4 (1963) and was suggested to me by the editor, Professor Lorna Reynolds.*

> Now that everything is over, I am sure there need not be
> any ill-will on either side. We both, I am sure, fought for
> what we held to be the best for the students. I shall, of
> course, be very happy to leave things as they are about
> the vice-presidentship, since you wish it.[1]

This extract could, without much literary effort, be incorporated into a contemporary college novel; Randall Jarrell's *Pictures from an Institution*, or even C. P. Snow's *The Masters* suggesting themselves irrepressibly to one reader. It is, then, refreshing to find that the quotation is from a letter dated 21 April 1910, and bears the address, 7 Stainer Street, Dublin. Moreover, its writer was a person whose name is a household word for two generations of Irish students – Mary Hayden.

Old letters, when they are the personal ones of the great, are a source of temptation to the historian. Like faith, they are the evidence of things not seen, and provide proof of intangible qualities of personality. They reflect passing moods, sudden enthusiasms, depressions, irritations, whimsies, anxieties and fancies. If they were written by a great man over a number of years to the one person, then the researcher is indeed fortunate because such a series of letters succeeds in establishing more concrete facts than transitory emotions. It is possible to trace, or discern, a politician's line of action, and change of policy; or a church man's attitude towards ecclesiastical and national issues. Writing to his sister, Newman expressed this trenchantly:

> It has ever been a hobby of mine, though perhaps it is a
> truism, not a hobby, that the true life of a man is in his
> letters. Not only for the interest of a biography, but for
> arriving at the inside of things, the publication of letters
> is the true method. Biographers varnish, they assign
> motives, they conjecture feelings, they interpret Lord
> Burleigh's nods, but contemporary letters are facts.[2]

Such was the method used in the biography of Archbishop Walsh of Dublin which appeared in 1928, and helped to make it the definitive biography of a great man. It would be an impertinence here to examine Monsignor P. J. Walsh's study critically but, thirty-four years later, it is possible to re-assess certain aspects of the man who led the catholic church in Dublin during the troubled years that lay between Parnell's downfall and the establishment of Dáil Éireann. In this essay I have endeavoured to take one section, to the documents of which I have access, and trace the Archbishop's handling of an educational problem which was a recurring pre-occupation in his busy career: namely, women's colleges in the university scheme for Ireland.[3]

From 1825 onwards the idea of a collegiate education for women was developing rapidly in certain countries. In the States, always a few decades earlier than Europe, the Wesleyan college at Macon in Georgia was chartered in 1830 and conferred its first degrees in 1840. About the same time the state of Ohio allowed the first college-level institute of a co-educational nature to hold a charter. The state universities quickly followed suit, and the civil war period brought even more opportunities in higher education for women with the establishment of co-ordinate colleges of the Radcliffe variety, where the teaching is done by members of the Harvard annex. Yet a fourth type of college evolved at the turn of the century, and has proved to be the most popular in the contemporary American scene, the liberal arts college.[4]

In England and Scotland, the nineteenth century was marked by numerous and far-reaching changes. A series of statutes revised the system of examinations and degrees; religious tests were abolished at English universities in 1871, at Scottish in 1892. London University, founded in 1825, and chartered as an examining and degree-conferring institution in 1838, was re-organized on a broader basis in 1889. Women were admitted to examinations and degrees at London in 1878, Cambridge in 1881, Oxford in 1884. In Scotland women were admitted as students in 1892.

In Ireland the situation was a little more complicated. The project of a Catholic University was launched at the Synod of Thurles in 1850. The story of Newman's University is well known. What is not generally appreciated is the fact that after the departure of Newman in 1859, the university survived another twenty years in its original constitution, and then took new life in different forms. The Liberal plan of a supplemental charter incorporating the Catholic University as a college, not as a university, and enabling the students educated in its halls to obtain degrees from the enlarged Queen's University, failed in 1866. Two years later the Conservative scheme for a purely Catholic University with charter and endowment was announced by Lord Mayo, considered, and abruptly withdrawn because of an imminent general election.

The next suggestion came from Gladstone in 1873. He proposed one university comprising catholic and other colleges without public endowment, Belfast and Cork Queen's Colleges with their endowments continued, Magee Presbyterian Theological College, Derry, and such others as would fulfil certain conditions. It met with strong opposition and was defeated by a majority of three votes. Feeling was growing in parliamentary circles however that some solution must be acceptable and in 1879 on the second reading of a University bill introduced by the O'Connor Don, the Beaconsfield administration announced that they would themselves introduce a University bill for Ireland. Accordingly on 25 June a bill was introduced setting up in place of the

Queen's University, the Royal University of Ireland. This was, in fact, an examining body, which was provided with 26 so-called Fellowships, evenly divided between catholics and protestants, the holders of which were to be examiners in the university and professors in teaching institutions approved by the Senate, at salaries of £400 a year.[5]

The Royal University was then merely an examining body but it had the effect of getting the catholic colleges of higher education to associate and stand together in competition against the endowed Queen's Colleges. Thus the framework of the Catholic University was considerably modified in 1882. In that year, University House in St. Stephen's Green became University College, and the Catholic University, of which Maynooth since 1876 had been constituted a member, was made to embrace an association of colleges, each of which retained its own independent collegiate organization.

Every movement has its pioneers, and in the last quarter of the nineteenth century it was not an ardent feminist that sparked off the controversy concerning women's rights to university education, but a Dublin-born nun. Mary Jane Shiel came of an old Dublin family and was born at Anne Street on 24 February 1844, being the daughter of William Shiel and the sister of John Shiel who later became a well-known judge of the High Court in South Africa. Subsequently the family moved to Lower Dorset Street and an old roll-book in Sion Hill bears the record of the little girl's entrance to the boarding school at the early age of seven years. It was the time of uncluttered curricula before the claims of public examinations had impinged on parents' consciences, and education for the well-to-do middle classes in Ireland was directed on broad lines of general culture. The study of languages, ancient and modern, formed the basis of a wide appreciation and study of literature. History, the fine arts, and the graces of feminine living all found their places on the timetable. Mary Jane Shiel had a brilliant mind and was an ambitious student. To an astonishing degree, she manifested in later middle-life an all-round culture which was evidenced in such diverse ways as lecturing at college-level in French language and literature; producing Shakespeare with distinction; and directing an orchestral society good enough to give public recitals to a critical Dublin audience.

While still in her teens she entered the novitiate in Sion Hill on a day made splendid by the visit of Cardinal Wiseman to the convent. In due course she was professed and as Sister M. Patrick she began to teach and eventually direct the studies in her old alma mater. An indefatigable worker, all her energies were channelled into improving educational facilities for Irish catholic girls.[6]

Meanwhile the Intermediate Education Bill had been introduced in 1878. It proposed to endow denominational schools indirectly by means of result fees, and was passed the same year. Under the new system of the Royal University, any and every school might prepare students for university examinations. The avenue to catholic women's higher education was opening up, and Sister Patrick was one of the first to explore its possibilities. For some years it had troubled her that no provision was made for catholic women students, although Alexandra College, founded in 1866, had provided a course of undenominational education for Irishwomen which was attracting the intelligentsia of all creeds.[7] It was a situation that could be found in many continental countries. If catholic schools, Sister Patrick argued, did not provide a course of higher education for young Irish women, they would seek university courses in colleges that were non-catholic.

On the establishment of Dominican Convent, Eccles Street, in 1882, Sister Patrick was appointed sub-prioress in the new foundation. Almost at once university classes were started in a room still known to many as University Room 2, where as yet no plaque marks the wall to commemorate the hours that the young Mr. de Valera spent lecturing in mathematics. Perhaps one of Mother Patrick's greatest gifts as a woman was her disinterestedness in the service of education. Possessed of a wide culture and undoubted teaching ability, she realized that this venture was not to be an off-shoot of convent-school status but a fully-fledged university centre. Accordingly she never hesitated to use money and persuasion in enlisting the services of lecturers intellectually equipped to establish a tradition of catholic scholarship which would prevail over counter-attractions for academically-minded young girls. In 1887 the first university honours were won and a growing list of successes and exhibitions were regarded with appreciation by the *Freeman's Journal*. The editorial for 29 October 1892 ran as follows:

> It is with special gratification that we today chronicle the proud triumph achieved by Catholic education in the person of Miss K. Murphy, M.A., who was yesterday awarded the Studentship in Modern Languages at the Royal University. We warmly congratulate Miss Murphy on her brilliant success, and we feel confident that we but share her own feelings when we speak of her victory as the triumph of a larger interest than a mere personal one. The interest is that of Catholic education.[8]

It was inevitable that Mother Patrick, working in such a milieu, should encounter the two greatest influences in Catholic higher education just then: Archbishop Walsh of Dublin and Fr. W. Delany, S.J., President of University College from 1883 to 1888, and again from 1897–1909. Fr. Delany was perhaps the single most authoritative voice in the various decisions leading up to the settlement of 1909, and was deeply interested in every aspect of university education. It was not surprising, therefore, that he became intimately associated with the groups working in Dublin for the betterment of women's academic training. On the whole he remained a hidden influence in St. Mary's, and though it is obvious from council books and minutes of the Literary Academy in Eccles Street that he was closely connected with the work going on, only one letter from him is extant in this connection. He was a careful man and rarely committed to pen what he had to say.[9]

Far different was Archbishop Walsh. Thirty-four letters from him to Mother Patrick and her later Superiors bear testimony to his genial and forthright personality. William Walsh had been President of Maynooth, and was a former student of the Catholic University. He was elected Archbishop of Dublin in 1885 after a lengthy and hotly-contested struggle at Rome between the Irish bishops and the interfering government who considered him dangerously national. He had been a member of the Senate of the Royal University, but resigned in 1884 owing to a dispute about the distribution of the University Fellowships. Nevertheless, on assuming office as archbishop, he immediately made the question of university education for catholics a live issue. It is not necessary here to follow the intricacies of the problem for the next few years, bound up as they were with the Home Rule issue and the Land Question. In a statement made at the opening of the academic year of the Medical School of the Catholic University (7 November 1889), Dr Walsh made clear his position and that of his fellow-bishops in a celebrated speech. He reviewed the whole field of Irish university education, and exposed the unjust and intolerant attitude of the Ascendancy. He made it clear that there was no secret understanding between the Tory government and the Irish bishops. In the same speech he attacked mixed education, and put forward his own solution which he was to maintain until forced to submit to the compromise of 1909, of which he was to become the first Chancellor.[10]

He now concerned himself actively with the problem of women's education at university level. The first letter to Mother Patrick on this subject is dated 24 March 1893, and beyond a promise to call at Dominican Convent, Eccles Street, in the next few days, it gives no hint of the business he had in mind. The second, over a fortnight later, sees his project well ahead. Without further preamble he begins:

> I am making a few further slight changes in the MS before sending it to the printers. These regard, the *first* sentence, the sentence about *the college curriculum,* that about *application* for *Boarders,* and the *last* sentence, about application for the present. I am also making a few small changes in my letter – especially one to bring out that the students are to be free to abstain from 'taking any part in the *competitive* examination' etc., etc.[11]

He then went on to discuss with surprising frankness the line of action he wished the *Freeman* leader writer to take in his comments. It would be tempting to trace the policy of the Archbishop in the leader-articles of the *Freeman* but it is outside the scope of the present study. In due course the *Freeman* printed His Grace's letter. 'We have to recognize', he wrote:

> that a gap still remains to be filled and that it can be filled only by the establishment of a well-equipped college, set apart as this new college of yours will be,

exclusively for the work of higher education. In every such work, the absence of concentration is fatal to all chances of success. As Cardinal Newman used to say, in speaking of the steps that should be taken for the organization of an Irish Catholic University 'we cannot have the best of everything' ... As for any help that it will be in my power to give to your work, you may always count upon it. As an earnest of my good wishes, I shall at once place at the disposal of the college council £500 to be applied in scholarships and exhibitions to the amount of £100 a year for the first years of the work of the college, or in any other way that the council may consider better calculated to encourage that work and promote its development.[12]

It became one of his pet projects. It was he who chose the name St. Mary's, because, as he quaintly stated:

it takes us out of the difficulty about 'ladies' or 'girls'. To my mind 'young ladies' is an abomination. 'Women' is the only generic word I know of. But it is objectionable on many grounds.[13]

It was he who advised the renting of a house in Merrion Square, and not the Kildare Place mansion which he described as a wreck. As a gift, he paid the first year's rent (£200). 'I find I can, by a little management, afford to do so'. Of more concern to him was the selection of the House Council, the members of which he solicited personally. Shrewdly he warned Mother Patrick:

It is better not to *publish* any of the names of the Council until we are fairly filled up; but the names of those who have accepted may be *freely* mentioned. It would be well also to take every opportunity of making it known that, as regards laymen, I have asked only those who are members of one of the three public bodies that have to do with University and Intermediate education.[14]

No. 28 Merrion Square was a fine old Georgian mansion, formerly the town residence of Lord Howth. It provided a chapel, study, classrooms, as well as accommodation for the community. The students' residence was opened at No. 17 Upper Mount Street under Mrs. Gray, who acted as Lady Superintendent. The College Council was composed of the following members: His Grace the Most Rev. Dr Walsh, Archbishop of Dublin, who acted as president; members of the Senate of the Royal University of Ireland; Commissioners of Education in Ireland; Heads of Colleges and Schools. Among those who served on the Council were Dr Healy, bishop of Clonfert; The Rt. Hon. Christopher Palles, The O'Conor Don; Sir Patrick Keenan; Mgr. Molloy; Fr. Delany; Francis Cruise; Christopher Nixon and Edmund Dease. The prospectus drawn up by Mother Patrick and approved by the archbishop was as follows:

St. Mary's University and High School has been founded for the purpose of affording Catholic ladies complete facilities for Higher Education in all its branches. In the College, Students will be prepared in all subjects included in the Intermediate and University Programmes. No public examination, however, will be compulsory. Students can make their own choice among the various subjects included in the College Course, and there will be provided a well-organized system of College examinations, by which their success in study can be efficiently tested. The College Curriculum will include the ordinary subjects of the Intermediate and University Courses; and, in addition, Music – Instrumental and Vocal – and the other subjects indicated in detail. Students who have made a two years' Course at the College, and have satisfied the examiners as to their proficiency will be awarded a College certificate. The Teaching Staff will consist of distinguished Graduates of the Royal University, and of eminent Professors; also of members of the Dominican Community, whose success as teachers has been so amply demonstrated by the results of the Intermediate and Royal University Examinations for the last eight years. The assistant staff will include a number of the former students of the College who have distinguished themselves most highly during their College Course, and have been specially successful at the Intermediate and University Examinations. There will be no students resident in the College itself. Students who so desire can be accommodated in a Residence House in the vicinity, under the responsible supervision of the Nuns, and in the charge of ladies appointed by them. The general course of studies in the College will be directed by the College Council, composed of University Graduates and gentlemen of distinguished position in the educational world, under the presidency of His Grace the Archbishop of Dublin. There will be a tutorial committee consisting of the principal members of the Teaching Staff, who will form a deliberative Council to advise regarding all details of the teaching work of the College. An advanced course of Religious Instruction will form a very important part of the programme.[15]

The list of professors and lecturers is impressive. Fr. Delany proved generous of time and gifts, and helped Mother Patrick to select those best suited for the posts. In the early years the Archbishop usually came to the annual distribution of prizes, and expressed his satisfaction at the progress of the students. 'Three successes such as these', he remarked on the occasion of Mary Hayden's and K. Murphy's Fellowships, and Mary Barniville's Scholarship in 1895:

> to say nothing of the array of University Honours and of Intermediate Exhibitions and Prizes to the credit of St. Mary's are surely sufficient in themselves to prove that we are no longer open to reproach for having failed to provide for Catholic girls a college in which they can pursue with the most eminent success, and up to the

very highest grades, the study of the various branches of learning.[16]

By October 1899 in the summary of results which the new self-conscious catholic Ireland was publishing and watching, St. Mary's was third in the list, which was headed by Queen's College, Belfast, and seconded by University College, Dublin. 'Its triumphs', trumpeted the *Freeman*, 'have been too numerous to regard it from any other point of view than that of the most successful and indispensable of the educational institutions of the nation'.[16] A little later, St. Mary's was moved to Muckross Park in Donnybrook, then a fine mansion standing in quiet and secluded grounds, some distance from the city. In September 1900, work was commenced in the new surroundings, and a contemporary account gives us a glimpse of university life in a women's college sixty years ago. Eleanor Butler, the well-known geographer, wrote as follows:

> Ard Eoin (the house of residence) smelt strongly of new timber and mortar. The bedrooms, with their bare, white-washed walls, bare floors and curtainless windows were the perfect setting for the earnest young student determined 'to scorn delights and live laborious days'. After tea, candles were divided round; Latin dictionaries, books of trigonometry, of logic, and I know not what, were exchanged. Next day, lectures were at 9.30 a.m. I found my way through the fields at the back of Muckross Park. Very fresh and pleasant the grounds appeared a veritable platonic academy!

At that time Mother Patrick Shiel took First Year French, and another remarkable nun, Mother Albertus Hochburgher, a native of Munich, took German. On the staff were, among others, Mary Hayden, Mr. Semple, Arthur Clery, P. J. Merriman, later president of University College, Cork, and Mary Ryan, who was to become professor of French in UCC:

Tea was at seven, after which some good public meeting at the University College might draw us to town again. We were able to let ourselves in, for we had the honour of locking up Ard Eoin for the night. 'Strange', remarked a friend [to Eleanor Butler], 'that the nuns do not keep a watch on these young ladies but leave them free to come and go as they please'.[17]

It was typical of Mother Patrick, who expected the best in others. Though the quality of work was not impaired by the move, the distance from the city was a serious disadvantage to the 'Royal' lecturers, and in 1903, St. Mary's was transferred to Eccles Street, where it ran its last short brilliant course for eight years.

The letters from the Archbishop concerning the college continued to flow, though he had written in vexation as far back as 1893:

I am afraid I shall have to ask you to get Dr Molloy or someone else that takes an interest in the good work, to look after details for you. It is simply hopeless here at times to get even a moment to spare from urgent work.[18]

So far from abandoning the work, his Christmas letter of the same year was full of plans for beginning a scheme of secondary teaching training for women on the lines of Girton College in Cambridge. Quite early on Mother Patrick had seen the need for training university graduates for the teaching profession and had suggested the idea of establishing a training college in connection with St. Mary's. How much she was influenced in this by Mother Eucharia of the Loreto College, Stephen's Green, another gifted educationist, and by Mother Peter McGrath, O.P., Dominican College, Eccles Street, is a matter for mild surmise, but evidently as early as 1893, she and the Archbishop had discussed the project and were in agreement as to its necessity. In fact the scheme was not implemented until 1908, when Archbishop

Walsh supervised personally the drawing up of the prospectus and acted as one of the guarantors of the loan fund which was set up.[19] This new venture set out to supply a course of studies and training for graduates to qualify for the Secondary Teachers' Diploma granted by Cambridge University. When the Higher Diploma courses were established in the National University, the majority of the students in the training college at Eccles Street adopted them.

One of the most distinctive features of old St. Mary's, and one which flourishes today in Dominican Hall is St. Mary's Literary Academy. It was founded in Eccles Street in 1889. Miss Katharine Tynan was the first vice-president and Rosa Mulholland came frequently to the meetings in her capacity as reporter. In its early days one of the chief functions of the Literary Academy was to sponsor a series of lectures for the public in English and French. These were well attended and of a sufficiently high standard to qualify for the claim of being a course of extra-mural studies. Thus for the Michaelmas term 1893 Mlle. Decoudin gave a magnificent set of lectures of the following themes: Bossuet; La Fontaine; Mme. de Maintenon et Mme. de Sevigne; Boileau; Chateau-briand; and Corneille. Like all lively debating societies it, too, had its moments of being 'anti-establishment'. An explosive letter from the Archbishop on 28 October 1894 must have seared the soul of the dismayed Mother Patrick. 'I look upon the whole occurrence as practically the deathblow to St. Mary's', he prophesied gloomily, and debates stopped. Years afterwards he reminisced humorously to his secretary 'about the featherbrained young lady who was put up by someone known to you and me, to make an attack on the Catholic Schools'.[20] Turning over the pages of the first minute book, one finds the signatures of chairmen like Fr. Delany, S.J.; Fr. Finlay, S.J.; Professor Mary Macken; Miss Louise Gavan

Duffy; Dr Finbar Ryan, O.P.; Professor Robert Donovan and a host of other well-known scholars.

Irish nationalism, too, found a voice in the Literary Academy and the choice spirits of a new age participated in debates that were becoming bilingual. Thus in 1900 Agnes O'Farrelly read a hard-hitting paper, *The Reign of Humbug*, later published as a pamphlet by the Gaelic League, in which she underlined the dangers of 'cosmopolitanism'. In less than two years, the Gaelic revival was in full spate, and Máire Ní Chinnéide, Studentship holder, read a paper in Irish called 'An Craobh Rua'. The chairman was Professor Douglas Hyde and among the speakers to the paper was a man called Pearse. On 4 April 1906, the first 'Irish' night was held. Josephine O'Sullivan was the auditor and spoke on the 'Schools of Ancient Ireland'. A significant feature of the social gathering was the number of St. Mary's students who answered to it, speaking in Irish, only less fluent, as the *Freeman* puts it graciously, than the Rev. Chairman, Fr. P. S. Dinneen, M.A. Finally in December 1908 a branch of the Gaelic League was founded in St. Mary's. Known to many as Cumann Fódla, it ran classes for beginners and advanced students of Irish at No. 21 Eccles Street.

But the climate of opinion which had been so favourable to the college in the 1890s changed with the new century. In July 1901 the Royal Commission on Irish Education was set up 'to inquire into the present condition of the higher, general, and technical education available in Ireland outside Trinity College'. It has since become famous as the Robertson Commission, and its findings were the subject of controversies and counter-proposals, that were finally solved by the Irish Universities Act of 1908. The Archbishop declined to give evidence before the Commission, but Fr. Delany in his testimony, emphasised the need for a separate university for Irish catholics. Here he was in opposition to Dr Walsh who favoured a completely catholic college within an enlarged University of Dublin.

Mother Patrick also found herself unwittingly in opposition to the Archbishop. The first hint of a difference in policy between them is contained in a note from His Grace's secretary. Dated 4 July 1900, it runs:

> I mentioned the project to His Grace, and he looked upon it as utterly impossible. I believe that, especially in your present circumstances, it would be sheer folly to attempt it, and that if it was attempted, it would bring disaster to your present work. I return Mother Pius's letter.[21]

Unfortunately the accompanying letter is missing, but unexpectedly Mary Hayden sheds light on the matter. Ten years later she reminds Mother Patrick of the incident. 'You will remember', she wrote:

> that when I gave evidence in your name before the University Commission, my evidence, prepared under your directions and submitted to you (I mean the then Superior and yourself) was in this sense and asked that the existing women's colleges should be made into hostels and endowed with bursaries for poorer students. I admired at the time your unselfish and public-spirited action ...[22]

On reading Mary Hayden's magnificent defence of women's rights to higher education before the Robertson Commission, it is well to know that Mother Patrick Shiel endorsed every word of it.[23] To her in that year it was apparently of far greater moment than the recognition of a separate women's college, and her triumph, for which she was to pay bitterly later on, was in the opinion expressed by the Robertson Commission in its *Report:* full equality of men and women within the university being set forth, both should attend and obtain degrees on the same conditions.

A year after the Robertson Commission had published its *Report*, Lord Dunraven proposed a scheme not unfavourable to the Archbishop. It did not materialise, however, during the two years left to the Unionists in government. It led to the setting up of the Fry Commission by the Liberal Government in 1906. This commission inquired into the state of Trinity College with a view to increasing its usefulness to the country. Early in the new year James Bryce, Liberal Chief Secretary, proposed the inclusion of all the Irish University Colleges, including Trinity College, in a single National University. He was supported by Archbishop Walsh and opposed by Fr. Delany, and by Trinity College. Fr. Delany was not alone in his rejection of this scheme: an unanimous resolution against it was passed in 1906 by the Senate of the Royal University. It was left to Augustine Birrell, who succeeded Bryce as Chief Secretary, to offer a compromise and effect the settlement of Ireland's University Question: the setting up of two new universities in Ireland; one to meet the needs of the catholics, the other for the presbyterians. The Bill was finally passed in 1908, to come into force on an appointed day within two years after the passing of the Bill. By November 1909, University College, Dublin, assumed its teaching role and the Statutory Commission brought its work to a finish on 31 July 1911.

What of the relatively minor question of women's colleges? St. Mary's had expanded under the organizing genius of Mother Patrick, and there were other colleges developing along similar lines. Since 1895 Loreto College, St. Stephen's Green, had been catering for Loreto students from different parts of Ireland. The solution offered by the University Bill made co-education, which had seemed so remote a possibility at the Robertson Commission, an actuality. At that Commission, Loreto College had declared through their representative that their first preference was for recognition of a separate women's college which, adequately equipped and staffed, would be endowed by the university. Alexandra College, too, made a stand at the Fry Commission, when Miss White, the Lady Principal, made a statement which was tantamount to seeking recognition for a women's college on the lines of the English women's colleges. Subsequently Miss White clarified her line of action in a letter to Mother Patrick. She had hoped, she said, to strengthen the women's position with both universities if Alexandra College kept its demands quite separate, thus showing that there were two distinct movements in favour of women's colleges.

What finally caused Mother Patrick to send in the application for recognition of St. Mary's as a constituent college of the new National University was probably the example of Loreto College and Alexandra College. She urged, in her application, the undesirability of co-education; the precedent of London University; the record of St. Mary's successes. Her application was considered and refused. Dr Clancy, bishop of Sligo and a friend of Mother Patrick's, put the case against separate women's colleges with a fine and humorous objectivity:

> I am entirely in favour of a separate Residential House for girls being provided by Parliament, or by the Senate of the National University out of Dublin funds, and of the supervision of this House being handed over to some religious body. I am also a strong advocate of subsidizing out of public funds a tutorial system of preparation for lectures in such a House of Residence. But when I come to consider what is involved in the petition of your 'sweet girl graduates' – how it would

demand a second staff of Examiners, and the setting up of a different standard of knowledge for men and women – I regret I cannot see my way to sign it.[24]

He then pertinently asked if such colleges as Mother Patrick envisaged would be set up in Cork and Galway, and why not Sligo?

As for the Archbishop: man-like he saw no difficulty. As early as 20 January 1896, he had written: 'I must keep myself free in all matters of detail concerning the University Question'. Though he was disappointed at the turn taken by the case for women at the Robertson Commission, he still had hopes of establishing a women's college within the projected university. In a letter of 16 August 1908, his tone was one of cordiality and he was full of the scheme for setting up a Students' Aid Fund to which he contributed £200. A year later, caught between the responsibility of being Chancellor of the National University of Ireland and his own private wishes, he declared stiffly to St. Mary's that, as Chancellor, he was unable to interfere in the matter of the application. In two subsequent letters he urged his own solution: let there be one women's college. That it would have to be undenominational or, possibly, multi-religious did not occur to him.[25]

Their dilemma caused no lasting resentment between the two religious orders concerned and characteristically they both set about implementing the alternatives which allowed the setting up of hostels. '49' and '77' have sprung from noble traditions of scholarship. Looking back from the vantage point of fifty years one is allowed to speculate on what might have happened to Irish education if a liberal arts college or a secondary training college had been recognized in 1909. The problem then ceases to be an historical one and becomes an educational one.

from Lorna Reynolds (ed.), *University Review*, Vol. III, No. 4 (1963), pp 33–47.

NOTES

1   Mary Hayden to Mother Patrick, 21 April 1910. The letter is among MSS in the convent archives, St. Mary's, Cabra.

2   Newman to Mrs. Mozley, 18 May 1863, in Anne Mozley, (ed), *Letters and Correspondence of John Henry Newman During his Life in the English Church, with a Brief Autobiography* (London and New York, Longmans, Green and Co, 1890), cf. Introduction.

3   My thanks are due to the authorities, St. Mary's, Cabra, for permission to use documents from the archives there, and to the Prioresses of Eccles Street, Muckross Park and Sion Hill for access to papers and documents in the archives of those convents.

4   Carter Victor Good, *Dictionary of Education* (New York, McGraw Hill, 1945), p. 83. 'The liberal arts college is an institution of higher learning usually offering a curriculum in the liberal arts and sciences and empowered to confer degrees; a major division of a university (usually that of arts and sciences) especially one that requires for admission no study beyond that of completion of secondary education'.

5   Fergal McGrath, *Newman's University, Idea and Reality* (London and New York, Longmans, Green), p. 490; Alfred O'Rahilly, 'The Irish University Question', *Studies,* Vol. V, No. 199, pp 225–70; Vol. VI, No. 201, pp 147–70.

6   Register of Professions and other registers kept in convent archives, Sion Hill, Blackrock, Co. Dublin.

7   I am indebted to Miss Morgan, Lady Principal, Alexandra College, for putting at my disposal certain facts concerning the foundation of Alexandra College. The word 'undenominational' according to the *Oxford English Dictionary*, was apparently first introduced in 1871; that is five years after the foundation of Alexandra College, and cannot properly be .used to describe the College in 1866. When the College and School were incorporated in 1887 under the Education Endowments (Ireland) Act, 1885, it was laid down that 'every member of the Council shall be a member of the Church formerly established by law in Ireland, and in the "Irish Church Act, 1869" referred to as the Church of Ireland. The Visitor shall be the Archbishop of Dublin of the said Church for the time being'.

8   Editorial, *Freeman's Journal,* Vol. 126, p. 5.

9   A. Gwynn, 'The Jesuit Fathers and University College', in Michael Tierney (ed.), *Struggle with Fortune: A Miscellany for the Centenary of the Catholic University of Ireland, 1854–1954* (Dublin, Browne and Nolan, 1954), pp 19–50.

10 Patrick J. Walsh, *William J. Walsh, Archbishop of Dublin* (Dublin and Cork, The Talbot Press, 1928), pp 543–45.

11 Archbishop Walsh to Mother Patrick, 7 April 1893 (*Loc. cit.*).

12 Editorial, *Freeman's Journal*, Vol. 127, p. 5.

13 Archbishop Walsh to Mother Patrick, 5 August 1893 (*Loc. cit.*).

14 *Ibid*, 6 August 1893.

15 For full text cf. 'St. Mary's University College', *The Lanthorn, Yearbook of Dominican College, Eccles Street,* Vol. VII, No. 2, 1932, pp 187–8.

16 Editorial, *Freeman's Journal*, Vol. 134, p. 5.

I7 Among documents in convent archives, Muckross Park, Donnybrook.

18 Archbishop Walsh to Mother Patrick, 6 November 1893 (*Loc. cit.*).

19 *Ibid*, 16 August 1908.

20 Dr Petit for Archbishop Walsh to Mother Patrick, 4 July 1900 (*Loc. cit.*).

21 *Ibid*.

22 Mary Hayden to Mother Patrick, 14 March 1910 (*Loc. cit.*).

23 *Royal Commission of University Education in Ireland,* Vol. III. 357–9.

24 Bishop of Sligo to Mother Patrick, 4 April 1910 (*Loc. cit.*).

25 Archbishop Walsh to M. Prioress, Eccles Street, 4 July 1910; 21 May 1911 (*Loc. cit.*).

In 1966 the Irish state commemorated the fiftieth anniversary of the 1916 rebellion in Dublin. The occasion was marked by numerous public lectures and by the publication of scholarly studies about the 'making' of the Easter Rising. Irish television, RTÉ, presented a memorable series of programmes based on archival material, both photographic and documentary, as well as interviews with survivors of the Easter Rising. It was living history. For the first time women were perceived to have taken an active role in the Irish revolution.

Euphoria quickly gave way to dismay as the conflict in Northern Ireland plunged Irish people, south and north, into a re-assessment of the origins of the conflict. Historians 'revised' interpretations of the 1916 Easter rebellion and engaged in what became the Revisionist Debate. A questioning of the impact of Irish nationalism on the canon of Irish history, in particular on the founding of the Free State and the position of Northern Ireland after partition was formally recognized. Revisionism became the major intellectual discourse of the 1970s in Irish academic circles.

It was not the sole discourse in that decade. Women had re-grouped in what became known as the 'second wave' of the women's movement and their concerns were published in the two-volume Report of the Commission on the Status of Women *(the Beere Report). This was an important prelude to the Republic of Ireland's entry into the European Economic Community in 1973. Women wanted to know their own past and proposed its inclusion in school and university curricular – a demand that began to be met in the mid-1980s. In the interim women acquired the skills and methods of writing their own history, assisted by professional historians, both groups learning together from models and research techniques developed in the international field of women's history.*

The essay, 'Women, the Vote and Revolution' originated as one of a series of Thomas Davis lectures delivered over Radio Éireann, towards the end of 1975 to mark the beginning of the International Decade of Women. Women in Irish Society: The Historical Dimension *when published in 1978 established itself as a valuable reference book. While researching 'Women the Vote and Revolution' in 1975 I had the opportunity of interviewing survivors of the Easter Rising; Sighle Ní Dhonnchadha, Eithne Coyle and Máire Comerford which gave me an enduring interest in oral history. Not surprisingly the revolutionary period around the 1916 Rising has attracted historians and biographers of distinction and the volume of studies on women in that period increases yearly. The need to evaluate that generation of women born towards the end of the nineteenth century in terms of a larger historical context remains. That analysis will take into account the many paradoxes of their upbringing and situation, their utopian vision of a better Ireland and their declining power in the public realm once the revolution was over.*

Throughout the nineteenth century there was a growing consciousness about women's rights which found expression in a demand for participation in government by means of the vote and, less noticeably, in organizing trade unions for women. The passing of the 1867 Reform Act in the British Parliament with its use of the word 'man' in defining electoral qualifications marked a definite stage in the demands of women for civic status, and the following decades witnessed an organized effort on the part of women to get the vote. This culminated in the founding of the Women's Social and Political Union led by the three Pankhursts in the exciting years before World War One.[1] In Ireland women had been active in the education of girls and in schemes of social welfare since the middle of the eighteenth century. After the Famine religious orders of nuns set up hospitals, schools and orphanages on a hitherto unprecedented scale. Moreover they managed their own institutions and handled their large financial commitments with farsightedness and, at times, with expertise. Irish women showed the same ability to handle practical affairs of shop-keeping and farming in the changed economic conditions after the Famine. In rural areas many women became strong supporters of the Land League. Parnell's two sisters, Fanny and Anna, with the encouragement of Michael Davitt, founded the Ladies Land League as an auxiliary to the main organization. For a year and a half the Ladies Land League took over the direction of the land war when Charles Stewart Parnell was imprisoned in 1881. Parnell found it a serious embarrassment and had it dissolved the following year, estranging Anna from himself and indeed from the Home Rule Party in the process. According to Anna, it was this episode which turned her eventually towards Sinn Féin.[2]

Annie Besant deserves mention as one who influenced a generation of Irish women. Of Irish descent, she took a prominent part in social and political protest with the Bright brothers in England. She was a member of the Theosophite Movement and later still an advocate of Home Rule for India when she went to live there.[3]

In 1876 Anna Haslam, a native of Youghal, founded the Irish Suffrage Society. A married woman she had been a signatory of the first Women's Suffrage Petition presented to the British House of Commons by John Stuart Mills. She and her husband, Thomas, were later to be described as the 'pioneers of Feminism in Ireland' by

Francis Sheehy Skeffington.[4] Membership spread beyond the confines of the Society of Friends and the scope of the association expanded to include the extension to women of the Poor Law Guardianship and the Local Government vote. Twenty years later the Women's Poor Law Guardian Bill was passed and in 1898 the Local Government vote was granted to women. The next year eighty-five women were elected as Poor Law Guardians, thirty-one of those becoming Rural District Councillors. The Haslams had brought an influential group of Irish women and their male sympathisers into their association and the following years were to reap the benefits of their persistent, non-militant penetration of Irish public opinion.[5]

The opening decades of the twentieth century were full of movement and creativity in Ireland. Women made their contribution to the Irish renaissance. Lady Gregory and Máire Nic Shiubhlaigh founded traditions in the Irish theatre. Sinéad Ní Fhlanagáin, later to become Mrs Eamon de Valera, assumed a position of personal influence by her teaching in the Gaelic League. Alice Stopford Green was one of the first to write the new national history and had a reading public in Ireland and Britain for her book, *The Making of Ireland and its Undoing*. Estella Solomons' paintings of the 1916 leaders hang in the Municipal Gallery in Dublin. It seemed as if Irish women of all creeds and backgrounds were making significant statements on aspects of Irish life, except politics from which they were excluded.

The Intermediate Act in 1878 had opened higher education to girls and throughout the nineties women were taking degrees for the first time and carrying off university honours. Mary Hayden won the Junior Fellowship in the Royal University in Dublin. This, had she been male, would have entitled her to lecture in

History, and her unpublished diaries are wry about the position of being an unhired woman scholar.[6] Hanna Sheehy took her Master's degree in French and won the coveted Gold Medal. She married Francis Skeffington who subsequently resigned the registrarship of the Royal University over the non-recognition of women graduates. Agnes O'Farrelly took a degree in Celtic Studies, gave lectures in the Gaelic League, became a professor of Irish poetry and later still was a founder-member of Cumann na mBan. Possibly at the beginning the women graduates were untouched by what Queen Victoria described as 'the strange infection of feminism'. 'The Queen' she wrote:

> is most anxious to enlist everyone who can speak or write to join in checking this mad, wicked folly of 'Women's Rights', with all its attendant horrors, on which my poor feeble sex is bent, forgetting every sense of womanly feeling and propriety.

In Ireland women's higher education was swept into the great debate whether women should be educated separately from men at university level which led to the establishment of the National University of Ireland with its constituent colleges in Cork, Galway and Dublin in 1909. Mary Hayden's magnificent defence of women's rights to higher education before the Robertson Commission led to the decision: full equality of opportunity between men and women at university. She herself was later to hold the professorship of Irish History at University College, Dublin.[7]

In the atmosphere of intellectual ferment little attention was paid to the suffrage movement for some years: it had all the appearance of being another force in a decade which had produced the Theosophite movement, the founding of Sinn Féin, the start of the Abbey Theatre and Sir Horace Plunkett's ideas of a new rural society. There was a growing interest in pacifism but there was also a new militancy about trade-unionism. The first stirrings of militant trade-unionism had already occurred for women in Belfast in the series of strikes which preceded the setting up of the Irish Transport and General Workers' Union in 1908 in Belfast. Mary Galway, secretary of the Textiles Operatives' Society, played a leading role in mobilising the women workers in the city and organized the mill-girls strike of 1911 with its '3,000 cheering, singing and enthusiastic females and not a hat among them'.[8]

It was then understandable that women became concerned with acquiring the vote and right through the first decade of the century there was a rapid growth in societies concerned with organized suffragism. The largest, and apparently only militant, society was the Irish Women's Franchise League founded by Hanna Sheehy Skeffington and Margaret Cousins in 1908 which from its inception harried the Irish Parliamentary Party on the injustice of excluding women from the Home Rule Bill. There were at least three Belfast societies with branches in the province: the Conservative and Unionist Women's Franchise League being the most influential. The Munster Women's Franchise League had branches throughout the province and was ably organized by the remarkable pair of novelists, Sommerville and Ross. In 1911 the Dublin woman, Louie Bennett, who was to act as a catalyst between the Labour and Woman Movements later on, founded the Irish Women's Suffrage Federation to bring together the various societies. The decision towards the middle of 1912 to print a weekly suffragist paper, *The Irish Citizen*, under the joint editorship of Francis Skeffington and James Cousins was of major significance to the Franchise movement. In that paper were to be reflected over the next few years the issues which affected not only the position of women in Ireland but the growing awareness of war, strikes and eventually revolution.[9]

When Christabel Pankhurst spoke at the Rotunda in Dublin in 1910 huge crowds flocked to see her. This meeting occasioned the first brush with the law. Mrs Garvey Kelly was brought before the courts for chalking advance notices of it on the pavements. Tim Healy, MP, defended her and the case was dismissed. In November she and four other members of the Irish Women's Franchise League were up in court again, charged with breaking the windows of Mr Birrell's house. On that occasion they all spent a month in jail.[10]

Members of the Irish Parliamentary Party declared they were personally sympathetic to the cause but John Redmond, its leader, told a deputation of women in April, 1911, that he was against votes for women as it would increase the power of the clergy. Privately he told Hanna Sheehy Skeffington that what he really feared was a massive conservative vote from the women.[11] Sinn Féin too were hesitant and their spokeswoman, Mrs Wyse Power, expressed the opinion that women would have the vote from an Irish parliament, but should not go seeking it from a British one.

The campaign was kept up by the suffragettes, and began to pay off. The Lord Mayor of Dublin, Alderman Farrell, crossed over to Westminster to petition at the Bar of the House that the franchise be given to women for the offices of county and borough councillors. He was successful. An Act was passed and as a result Dublin and Waterford Corporations had their first women councillors in the persons of Miss Harrison and Dr Strangman respectively. These early years were characterised by a good-humoured, bantering note exemplified in the sermon of the parish priest of Ventry, County Kerry, who remarked 'that it was a sure sign of the break up of the planet when women took to leaving their homes and talking in public'. However with the prospect of Home Rule becoming brighter a growing hostility to the feminists began to show itself and the movement was accused of being anti-nationalist in its preoccupation with votes for women. They held a Poster Parade to draw attention to the Votes for Women Issue and it was attacked by a mob allegedly mustered by the Ancient Order of Hibernians. The suffragists retaliated. Sunday, 31 March 1912, was Home Rule day and great was the chagrin when the platform was found to be daubed with the slogan, 'Votes for Women'. John Redmond reiterated in public his sentiments about giving votes to women, and so the rift between the Suffrage movement and the Irish parliamentary party widened.[12]

In June there was a mass meeting in Dublin to protest against the exclusion of women from the proposed Home Rule Bill. From all parts of the country representatives of the women's societies poured into the Rotunda, not merely the suffrage groups but also women from the trade unions, Sinn Féin and Inghinidhe na hÉireann. Mary Hayden took the chair and the resolutions were forwarded to the members of the Irish Parliamentary Party. They were ignored and the Irish Women's Franchise League turned to militant action.

In general the militancy was confined to breaking of government windows, though on one occasion the bust of John Redmond in the Royal Irish Academy was found painted with arrows! The visit of Mr Asquith, the English Prime Minister, in July 1912 was the occasion of a major demonstration during which Francis Sheehy Skeffington, who had been banned from entry to the Theatre Royal, succeeded in heckling Asquith on the votes for women issue, using as disguise the sober garb of a cleric, until he was caught and ejected. More seriously two unauthorised English suffragettes flung a small blunt hatchet at the prime minister grazing his ear slightly. Irish newspapers echoed the growing annoyance of sections of Irish public opinion, one reporter even suggesting the return of the birch.

It was a grim summer for the Irish suffragettes. There were increasing convictions: Margaret Cousins spent a month in Mountjoy, Hanna Sheehy Skeffington went on hunger strike with three others, the first Irish group to attempt that searing experience. Another Irish woman, Dr Kathleen Lynn, attended the hunger-strikers as medical officer. In all there were thirty six convictions between 1912 and the outbreak of war, though the only example of forcible feeding in Ireland was in the case of the two English suffragettes in jail over the Asquith insult.[13] It meant a great deal when James Connolly came to Dublin to speak on the IWFL platform in the Phoenix Park: it marked the beginning of co-operation between the Suffrage movement and the cause of Labour, the gradual realization, as Hanna Sheehy Skeffington remarks in her *Reminiscences* that it was votes for women and not for ladies they were pursuing.[14]

In November 1912 seventy one members of the Irish Parliamentary Party by their vote defeated the Women's Suffrage Bill, as well as Women's Suffrage Amendments to the Home Rule Bill. When they again voted, later on, for the ignominious 'Cat and Mouse Act' whereby temporary discharge of suffragettes enduring forcible feeding was permitted until they were fit enough to be re-committed, widespread protest arose on all sides. Sympathy in Ireland began to flow back towards the suffragettes. At a mass meeting in the Mansion House in June 1913, Padraic Colum, Tom Kettle, Countess Markievicz and others spoke against the 'Cat and Mouse

Act'. P. H. Pearse sent a message which read: 'the heart of every man and of every woman in Ireland, whatever his or her politics, must be against the government that proposes to torture our women'.

Meanwhile the great lockout strike in the second half of 1913 had brought the women into the orbit of the Labour movement. There had been a growing awareness among women workers that theirs was the right to organize. In 1911 Jim Larkin, his sister Delia, and Helena Molony with support from the Irish Trade Union Congress formed the Irish Women Workers Union. Its object was 'to improve the wages and conditions of the women workers of Ireland and to help the men workers to raise the whole status of labour and industry'. It was a period of great hardship for workers and the class struggle sharpened considerably before erupting in the great lock-out strike. Delia Larkin, commenting on the term 'women workers' in her column in *The Irish Worker* wrote:

> to the idle class it conveys very little because 'never do they think of these workers as human beings'; to the employing class women workers has a sweet sound. They know that in these workers they have an extraordinary cheap means of producing wealth.

James Connolly stated it more tersely: 'in Ireland the female worker has hitherto exhibited in her martyrdom an almost damnable patience'.[15]

The women at Jacobs' Biscuit Factory were among the most militant of the strikers in 1913, and the entire membership of the Irish Women Workers Union came out and shared the six months' distress of their class. Louie Bennett, from being a casual observer of the strike was drawn to Liberty Hall and testifies to the links that were being forged between the feminists and the workers in her essay written later from notes and memory, *Our Heritage from Dublin 1913 Strike*:

> At that time I belonged to the respectable middle-class and I did not dare to admit to my home circle that I had run with the crowd to hear Jim Larkin, and crept like a culprit into Liberty Hall to see Madam Markievicz in a big overall, with sleeves rolled up, presiding over a cauldron of stew, surrounded by a crowd of gaunt women and children carrying bowls and cans.

Soup kitchens were organized by the suffragettes and the sight of their green and orange colours as they ladled out soup was not forgotten by the strikers that winter.[16]

In November 1913 the Citizen Army was founded to protect the workers and 'to bring discipline into the distracted ranks of labour'. A week later Larry Kettle announced 'there will also be work for women to do, and there are signs that the women of Ireland, true to their record, are especially enthusiastic for the success of the Irish volunteers ...' The occasion was the inauguration of the Irish Volunteers. Six months later, April 1914, at a meeting convened in Wynn's Hotel, Dublin, Cumann na mBan was formally constituted, Agnes O'Farrelly taking the chair for the occasion.[17]

It is true as Countess Markievicz asserted in a piece she wrote for *The Irish Citizen* that three great movements were going on in Ireland those years, the national movement, the women's movement and the industrial one, yet as each converged on 1916 they moved at their own pace. When war broke out in August, 1914, *The Irish Citizen* and particularly its editor, Francis Sheehy Skeffington, came out against it and alienated many suffragists in the process. His pamphlet, *War and Feminism,* was answered by his friend, Thomas Mac Donagh who addressed a suffragist meeting on the theme, 'Ireland, women and the war'. While his speech supported the anti-war stand it carried overtones of ambiguity about the aims of the volunteers. He was questioned sharply about his views and Hanna Sheehy Skeffington, who presided, closed the meeting with sentiments of doubt about the words 'liberty' and 'people' used at the Irish Volunteers' Convention, They should be defined, she said, so as to make certain they included women.[18]

Throughout 1915 Cumann na mBan was wresting initiative away from the feminist organizations, divided now over participation in the war effort. It was a split which also reflected the growing estrangement between north and south, all the more painful because of the sincerity of the women involved. Cumann na mBan gained the stature of a national movement. In October, 1915, it adopted a uniform. Enthusiasm among its rapidly increasing membership was high. Louise Gavan Duffy in her recollections, written in Irish, states:

> there were women on the Cumann na mBan committee who were suffragists; others of different opinions, but so urgent, so important was the work of the Volunteers, that we could not afford to divide. Everything was put aside and we were ready to do what we were told: carry messages, give first aid, make meals, in short any work … we knew that there would be a Rising, what time, where, how? We would know when the time was ripe and we left it to the leaders. When the time came it was, however, without my foreknowledge.[19]

On 7 March 1916 Countess Markievicz was in Cork under the auspices of Cumann na mBan. The subject of her speech was 'The Sacrifice of Robert Emmet'. There were then forty three branches of the Cumann affiliated with headquarters in Dublin. Elsewhere in her essay Louise Gavan Duffy comments on Markievicz: 'perhaps there were young women who took a more militaristic part in the national cause – it is not my purpose to discuss the Citizen Army – I do not really know about the women who were with Countess Markievicz. I think they had another outlook'.

Constance Markievicz appears at all stages of the story. The links between the Gore-Booth sisters and Mrs Haslam's Suffrage Society went back to 1896 when they founded a branch in Sligo; but it was through artistic Dublin that Constance became involved with Irish nationalism. At AE's home she met Arthur Griffith and Bulmer Hobson. In 1908 Helena Molony and Maud Gonne persuaded her to join Inghinidhe na hÉireann which for some years had articulated the cultural nationalism of the period by its patronage of drama. Maud Gonne's stage interpretation of Cathleen Ni Houlihan written by Yeats epitomised to many nationalists the sacredness of the cause they were engaged upon. Popularly known as the Daughters of Erin they merged with Cumann na mBan in 1913 but never quite lost their identity as a group who were feminist as well as nationalist.[20]

'Fix your minds on the ideal of Ireland free, with her women enjoying the full rights of citizenship in their own nation', Markievicz advised the Students' National Literary Society in a widely-circulated lecture in 1909. That same year she founded the Fianna, or as Lady Gregory called them 'the boy scouts she trained against the English troops'. P. H. Pearse remarked that had the Fianna not been founded, there would have been no volunteers and by implication no 1916. Though Markievicz became increasingly separatist in her political ideology, she continued to appear on suffragist platforms and she also identified closely with the Labour movement through meeting Larkin and Connolly. Lady Gregory's rather cool judgment on Markievicz is worth noting:

I knew her in her Castle days when she was a rather jealous meddler in the Abbey and Hugh Lane's gallery. But her energy found a better scope when she took up the Labour Movement, and then a more violent one in 1916 ...[21]

Under Connolly's leadership the Citizen Army prepared for revolution. As a lieutenant in that army Markievicz poured her immense energies into drilling and training programmes. On Easter Monday 1916 she and Commandant Michael Mallin occupied Stephen's Green and the College of Surgeons. Her courage was magnificent and after the Rising she unflinchingly accepted the death penalty imposed upon her while in prison. Great was the joy when she was freed under the general amnesty. The best tribute to her came in a joint ceremony of the Irish Transport Workers Union and the Irish Citizen Army after the Great Lockout strike when they presented her with an illuminated address:

Inspired and enthused by your example, we were proud to have you amongst us, and now that the fight is over, we desire that you remain one of us, and to that end we unanimously elect you Countess as an Honorary member of our fighting Irish union.

The events of Easter Week changed the sentiments of Irish women utterly. James Connolly who had understood the importance of the votes for women issue had been executed. As he had warned the women two years earlier the national question took precedence over both it and the industrial question; indeed nationalism sublimated all lesser concerns for the next few years. Many of the suffragettes took fire from the revolution and parted from the constitutional movement. Hanna Sheehy Skeffington was confronted with the senseless murder of her husband, and pacifism, learnt from him, deserted her. She published in 1917 a pamphlet on

British militarism. Louie Bennett admitted that 1916 convinced her of the force of nationalism: she did not welcome its intrusion on the Labour Movement, but, she argued in one of her essays, she had clarified through the events of 1916 what her order of priorities must be.[22]

As for Cumann na mBan it effectively radicalised the women towards revolution. Essentially conservative in its aims, in the aftermath of the Rebellion it proved tireless in organizing political prisoners. Its opposition to Conscription was, from a tactical aspect, vigorously effective in the pledge it demanded of women and young boys: 'not to do, or even learn to do, work being done by men in Ireland'. Their contribution to the Sinn Féin election victory, and that of Markievicz, has been under-estimated. In Dublin, for instance, they were tireless in rallying voters to go to the polls.[23] Cumann na mBan capitalised on the spent forces of the Franchise groups by acquiring speakers like Hanna Sheehy Skeffington to speak on their platforms, thus identifying the national cause finally with that of women, the very point upon which Hanna Sheehy Skeffington had queried Thomas Mac Donagh some years previously. It injected new vitality into the women workers and, despite Markievicz's original misgivings about the subsidiary role of Cumann na mBan to the volunteers, it captured and held her charismatic leadership as its president for over seven years. The annual convention of Cumann na mBan in 1921 reported that there were nearly eight hundred branches in the country as well as in England and in Scotland. Throughout the Anglo-Irish War its members undertook scouting, despatch-carrying, intelligence work and first aid, often in high-risk zones. Several had been wounded and a number of women served jail sentences as active members. Michael Collins in March 1922 at a huge meeting in Cork organized by Cumann na mBan thanked them for their contribution to the war but, like Thomas Mac Donagh at an earlier meeting, left them deeply divided about their ultimate role in the nation's destiny.[24]

The unanimity and powerful rhetoric of the women's speeches in the Treaty Debate where they one and all took the republican side has not yet received an explanation fully satisfying. The complexity of anger indicated by the women speakers who it must be pointed out, had obtained a political education over the previous twenty years not often afforded to a generation of women, is puzzling. Even if Erskine Childers was the mentor of these first women parliamentarians, they were a group who had been exposed to all the pitfalls of the kind of situation in which they found themselves. What is clear from their speeches was their inflexible and doctrinaire republicanism. Their political ideology had not kept pace with the change in atmosphere after World War One.[25] Had they been more constitutionally agile in the Treaty Debate they might well have held the balance of power between the two sides. Five of the six women in the First Dáil were relatives of men executed in 1916, or killed in the Anglo-Irish War. Mrs Pearse, Mrs Clarke, Mary Mac Swiney, Mrs O'Callaghan, Dr Ada English, all had suffered loss of their menfolk, and Markievicz had been through the Rebellion. This electoral mannerism rapidly became a criterion for selection of women to the Dáil and to this day has been carried into the party system of the southern State. Irish women in post-revolutionary Ireland did not make the political traditions: they inherited them from fathers, husbands and brothers.

James Connolly as early as 1914 in Belfast, warned the suffragettes there not to believe that the possession of the vote would solve all ills and he entreated them to familiarise themselves with the conditions of women's work, housing and with the difficulties facing working mothers. 'Ideals', he said, 'could not as society was today constituted dominate humanity unless they had a sound economic basis'. Connolly's death and the departure of the Larkins from Dublin created a vacuum of leadership in the new small Labour Party, and even more seriously in trade union circles. Yet the Irish Women Workers Union survived. In 1917 Helena Molony, Markievicz, Mrs Ginnell, Dr Kathleen Lynn and the Dublin newspaper vendor, Rosie Hackett – all of them coming from a common involvement with the Easter Rising – joined forces with Louie Bennett and Helen Chenevix to push forward the organization of women workers. Two important strikes, the Women Laundry Workers and the Women's Dispute in the Printing Trade were settled by the Irish Women Workers Union in the following months. It was the Treaty issue and the resulting civil war which divided the industrial classes of the country and fragmented solidarity.

After the Civil War, as after the Famine, once again a generation of sorrowful and purposeful women turned their faces forward to reconstruction of their shattered country. North and south, Irish women possessed the freedom to vote, the right to hold office – even to become cabinet ministers as Markievicz demonstrated – the expertise to set up and manage their own trade unions, and to a limited extent they availed of the developing technology of domestic and farm work to control their environment. In many respects it was a spectacular victory but the paradox remains to be explained: Irish women were free in the areas they had struggled for, why then were they content to remain subordinate in a society they had helped to create?

from Margaret Mac Curtain and Donncha Ó Corráin (eds), *Women in Irish Society: The Historical Dimension* (Dublin, Arlen House, 1978, 1979, 1984; Westport, CT, Greenwood Press, 1979), pp 46–57.

NOTES

1   E. Sylvia Pankhurst, *The Suffragette Movement* (London and New York, Longmans, Green and Co, 1931); N. Blewett, 'The Franchise in the United Kingdom', *Past and Present,* No. 32, December 1965, p. 54. For more general accounts cf. Sheila Rowbotham, *Hidden from History* (London, Pluto Press, 1974), pp 75–89; Andrew Rosen, *Rise Up, Women* (London and Boston, Routledge and Kegan Paul, 1974).

2   T. W. Moody, 'Anna Parnell and the Land League', *Hermathena,* No. CVVII, 1974, pp 5–17.

3   Arthur H. Nethercot, *The First Five Lives of Annie Besant* (Chicago, IL, University of Chicago Press, 1960).

4   Margaret and James Cousins, We *Two Together* (Madras, Ganesh, 1950) contains an excellent first-hand account of the Irish Suffrage Movement. See Francis Sheehy Skeffington, 'The Haslams', *The Irish Citizen,* No. 43, 21 March 1914, p. 347.

5   Rosemary Owens, 'How we Won the Vote', *Votes for Women, Irish Women's Struggle for the Vote,* pamphlet edited and published by A.D. Sheehy Skeffington and R. Owens, Dublin 1975.

6   Mary Hayden's Diaries, 59 Vols., 1878–1903, deal mainly with her life in Dublin from the age of twelve to her meeting with P. H. Pearse in 1903. MS 16,627–16,683 in National Library, Dublin.

7   Testimony of Mary Hayden, *Royal Commission of University Education in Ireland,* Vol. III, 357–9 (The Robertson Commission, 1901).

8   Unpublished paper, 'The Role of Women in the Early Irish Labour Movement' delivered by Miss Una Claffey, B.A., at a symposium, 'Woman in Irish History' in Liberty Hall, 21 April 1975.

9   *The Irish Citizen* was a weekly until January 1916 when it became a monthly paper. It was closed down in 1920 by the Auxiliary Forces.

10 Unpublished reminiscences of Maurice Wilkins whose wife Eva Stevenson was an active member of the Irish Women's Franchise League and took part in the window-breaking episode, cf. vol. 1, *The Irish Citizen,* 1912.

11 Hanna Sheehy Skeffington, 'Reminiscences of an Irish Suffragette', in A.D. Sheehy Skeffington and R. Owens (eds), *Votes for Women, Irish Women's Struggle for the Vote* (Dublin, 1975).

12 The best account of these events is found in *The Irish Citizen* Vol. 1, Nos. 1–33 (1912).

13 Militant feminists were described as suffragettes to distinguish them from suffragists of both sexes who sought the vote by legal means.

14 Hanna Sheehy Skeffington, *loc. cit.,* p. 22.

15 James Connolly was the darling of the IWFL and his chapter on 'Women' in *The Re-Conquest of Ireland* (1915) was undoubtedly influenced by the Irish suffragist agitation.

16 R. M. Fox, *Louie Bennett, Her Life and Times,* (Dublin, Talbot Press, 1957).

17 Interviews by author with Sighle Ní Dhonnchadha and Eithne Coyle in Dublin 1975; cf. E. Coyle, 'The History of Cumann na mBan', *An Phoblacht,* No. 8 (April 1933); Lil Conlon, *Cumann na mBan and the Women of Ireland* (Kilkenny, Kilkenny People, 1969).

18 'Irish Suffrage Activities', *The Irish Citizen,* Vol. III, No. 30, 12 December 1914, p. 239.

19 Louise Gavan Duffy, 'Insan G.P.O: Cumann na mBan', in F.X. Martin, OSA (ed.), *1916 and University College, Dublin* (Dublin, Browne and Nolan 1966), p. 90.

20 Jacqueline Van Voris, *Constance de Markievicz in the Cause of Ireland,* (Amherst, MA, The University of Massachussetts Press, 1967).

21 Lennox Robinson (ed.), *Lady Gregory's Journals* (Dublin, Putnam and Co., 1946), p. 238.

22 Louie Bennett, *loc. cit.,* p. 62.

23 Interview between author and Sighle Ní Dhonnchadha, Dublin 1975.

24 Lil Conlon, *Cumann na mBan and the Women of Ireland,* p. 263.

25 Dáil Éireann, *Official Report. Debate on the Treaty Between Great Britain and Ireland,* signed in London on 6 December 1921 (Dublin, Talbot Press, 1922).

TOWARDS AN APPRAISAL OF THE
RELIGIOUS IMAGE OF WOMEN

The early writing of history of women appeared in journals whose editors were supportive of feminism and of feminist aspirations to write women back into history. The Crane Bag, *a cultural and political journal edited by Mark Patrick Hederman and Richard Kearney was regarded, during its short career of ten numbers in five volumes, 1977–81, as a forum for different approaches to literature, myth, religion, nationalism and philosophy. It drew on modern European thought as well as on indigenous sources of intellectual traditions, creating what the editors described as an 'actualised space' for different ideas and attitudes. The seventh issue of* The Crane Bag, *Vol. IV, No. 1 (1980), was given over to 'Images of the Irish Woman' and its guest editor, Christina Nulty, took an inter-disciplinary approach in line with European trends, to provide 'a reflection of the many faces of women in Ireland'. The collection of essays opened up new areas in cultural studies and in the history of social and cultural representations.*

What strikes the observer of how the Irish church has influenced the image of women in the long history of the island is the absence of scholarly studies on this important subject which occupies a central position in our literature and mythology. Taking the long view, the power of myth in image-making was an element of the early Celtic churches and bore significantly on the church's shaping role of Irish womanhood in the first centuries of christianity, yet when one examines the image of women as mediated by religious influences after the Famine in mid-nineteenth-century Ireland what becomes apparent is the centrality of model in the evolving expectations of what modern Irish society demanded of its womenfolk. It is under both aspects, myth and model, that the following pages will investigate the image of women in Ireland, testing the hypothesis at two periods, early Celtic christianity from Patrick onwards, and post-Famine Ireland of recent times.

Austin Farrer in *The Glass of Vision* (London, Dacre Press, 1948) argues that God has always manifested himself through 'inspired images' rather than creeds or doctrines, and he assigns to the religious community an active part in developing and interpreting those religious images which have influenced them. Religious images become embedded in the complex stories of a society's understanding of the cosmic order which historians, anthropologists and those who study ancient civilisations call myths. In general it may be remarked that historians of Celtic christianity have been occupied with the internal content of the myths that cluster around the Irish saints of that first period. Readers are indebted to the studies of Kuno Meyer, Ludwig Bieler, and, especially in investigating the nature of early Celtic christianity, the contributions of Nora Chadwick and Kathleen Hughes are particularly helpful. What I propose to examine in this essay (following Ian Barbour)[1] is the model of woman as she emerges in the myths concerning the early Celtic saints, and examine in the light of that model, later models after the great Famine that project certain images of women into our twentieth century literature. 'A model', proposes Barbour 'represents the enduring structural components which myths dramatize in narrative form'. Moreover, one model may run consistently through many myths:

> Models result from reflection on the living myths which communities transmit ... they summarize the structural elements of a set of myths ... they are neither literal pictures of reality nor useful fictions. They lead to conceptually formulated, systematic, coherent religious beliefs which can be critically analysed and evaluated.[2]

As I shall hope to demonstrate in the post-Famine period models may also fulfil non-cognitive functions of myths, particularly in the expression of attitudes. Under this aspect, a model evokes commitment to ethical standards and policies of action. But first let us look briefly at the cognitive function of the hagiographical myths of Celtic christianity in their projection of female image and model.

Not a great deal is known about early Irish paganism but two survivals in rural Ireland are linked with the transition from paganism to christianity. Fertility cults appear to have been widespread and were associated with sacred wells, and the pagan year hinged around four festivals, Imbolc (February 1), Bealtaine (May 1), Lughnasa (August 1) and Samhain (November 1). The first, Imbolc, in the Celtic christian takeover was assigned to Saint Brigid, the mythical powerful founder-abbess of Kildare monastery. She occupies a central position in Irish hagiography. Of dubious origin, Brigid of Kildare has been transmitted to us as the daughter of a nobleman whose mother was a slave-girl. Moreover, Brigid as founder of the great monastery of Kildare which, under its abbess, laid claim to a wide *paruchia* of over thirty churches in its heyday, 630 AD, appointed the bishop and wielded immense power as a churchwoman.

The similarity between the strength and psychological freedom of Saint Brigid and Medb in the great myth of the *Táin Bó Cuailgne* has never been drawn out but they were indeed the same 'model' in the sense that Barbour speaks of. Brigid remains static in the various hagiographical accounts which eulogise the central facts of her miraculous power, generosity, wisdom, fertility in a spiritual sense, her practical charity and her virginity (the last-named not overly highlighted). Medb comes across from the *Táin* as a woman of the Celtic world, Brigid's secular sister with all her human passions and vulnerability, but possessing the same strength and fertility as her saintly counterpart. More real than Brigid, though not as well known, is Saint Íte of Kileedy who emerges from Charles Plummer's *Vitae Sanctorum Hiberniae* as an awesomely powerful woman, the foster mother of Jesus the Divine Infant who was reputed to nurse him nightly. In connection with Íte the word *caille* and *cailleach* take their first airing in a double-meaning. *Caille* meaning a veil[3] made its way into primitive Irish no later than the fifth century and became incorporated into the word *Cailleach* meaning a nun and almost simultaneously becomes in secular mythology the word for 'an old hag'. In the Íte hagiographical incident she is addressed as *cailleach* conveying the reverence and ruefulness which runs through the holy literature of Celtic christianity concerning women. W. B. Yeats with his infallible ear picks up the same echoes in his great poem of the old nun: 'Among School Children': 'self-born mockers of man's enterprise'.

One other aspect of Celtic christianity deserves an airing in the context of female images. It is that form of spirituality and asceticism which links it to the hidden stream: of Gnosticism and to the Johannine traditions of primitive christianity in Ireland, rather than to the Pauline and Latin shape it gradually assumed after Patrick. Celtic pre-patrician institutions of christianity were not Roman; Latin itself was probably not adopted until after Saint Patrick's journeys. Hermits, *Gielts* and wandering bearers of the christian message seem to resemble more the ideas of eastern monasticism in that first age of christianity in the sixth century. Celtic women who converted to christianity needed the protection of the small christian community. Frequently they were rejected by their families as we know from Patrick's *Confession:* 'not that their fathers agree with them (the Virgins); no – they often even suffer persecution and undeserved reproaches from their parents'. In return for protection they helped with catechizing and 'in the performance of ministries around the sacred altars'. They were lauded for their virginity but we know from Patrick that a great number of them were married and he adds 'how many of them have been reborn there so as to be of our kind? I do not know – not to mention widows and those who practise continence'. What is perplexing to the average student of Celtic christianity is the scant reference to the practice of syneisactism.[4] In the East the practice of syneisactism was found in the orthodox hermit culture of the Nitrian desert. There men and women lived chastely together, which is the basic description of syneisactism, a realized eschatology of men and women cohabiting in chaste asceticism. Now in one of the earliest Celtic sources, the *Tripartite Life of St. Patrick* mention is made of its practice *viz.* St. Mel: 'Bishop Mel of Kildare was assisted in prayer by his kinswoman' and this delightful saint whose name signifies 'sweetness' or 'honey' was accused 'of sinning with his kinswoman', a charge investigated by Saint Patrick and proved to be false. Syneisactism in the west was regarded as both a trial and a temptation. Perhaps the most famous account of the practice in Ireland is found in the Martyrology of Oengus the Culdee. Oengus recounts the nightly victory of Saint Scothine in the realm of chastity. In this narrative the role of *virgines subintroductae* as seductive temptresses who register the saint's powers to resist or to capitulate is undoubtedly a downgrading of the role of female ministry in the Celtic church and puts women in the category of Eve and the apple. With the writing of *De Virginitate* by the Pseudo-Clement, and its widespread use as a manual of monastic formation for young men, misogyny and fear of women drove the sexes apart in their following of christian celibacy and the freedom of the first order of Celtic women saints gradually disappeared. In a number of the saints' lives in *Vitae Sanctorum Hiberniae* there is present a distrust of women: thus Saint Enda used only to talk to his sister through a veil though she had travelled many miles to visit him; Saint Ciarán would not look into the eyes of a woman. Saint Coemgen (Kevin), the most famous Irish celibate of all, is credited with fleeing to Glendalough away from the sound of sheep or cow because 'ubi ovis, ibi mulier, ubi mulier, ibi peccatum, ubi peccatum, ibi diabolus, et ubi diabolus ibi infernus'. There is present in the tenth-century poem, *Éirigh, a ingen an righ*,[5] a familiar gleeful ring of male chauvinism in its recounting of female temptations overcome. Seán Ó Faoláin's translation has Finbar, Ciarán, Scuitin, Columcille and even Patrick himself 'rejecting the blazing brightness of the maiden daughter'.

> I have pondered on victorious Fionnbarr,
> whose mind was lofty,
> who denied the raging princess,
> the daughter of Dangail d'uib Ennaig.

> I have thought on Ciarán of Cluan,
> much have I heard of his piety,
> who denied Aillind the Daughter of Bran,
> and slept beneath a woman's breasts.

> I thought also of the great piety
> of Scuitin of Sliabh Mairce Moir

who used to lie, God willed it in his love,
between the white breasts of women.

And I thought then of Columcille
who for the love of the King of Truth
denied – for all her great fame –
(the pleasure) of Aidan's fair daughter.

I recalled Patrick and his austerities,
the chief apostle of Erin
who rejected the blazing brightness
of the maiden daughter of the valiant Milchu.[6]

Increasingly as we enter Ireland's Golden Age of Sanctity there is a preoccupation with male chastity which in Irish hagiography becomes the crown of perseverance, the white martyrdom. Gradually, Irish women were regarded as seductresses, temptresses and the cause of man's downfall. In *Saltair na Rann* and in Kuno Meyer's edition of 'Eve's Lament' Eve is a self-confessed engineer of Adam's woes:

'Tis I that brought the apple down from
above and which went across my gullet: so
long as they endure in the light of day,
so long women will not cease from folly.[7]

What is missing from the mythology of early Celtic christianity is the figure of Mary. The images of women that flit across the pages of these old manuscripts are recognizably Irish whether they are those of Íte who fondled the Christ-child nightly but who also had a mettlesome temper, or Gobnait, patron of agrarian prosperity in west Cork, or Saint Ciarán's glorious princess, Aillind, the daughter of Bran, or Aedhan's fair daughter rejected by Columcille. Mary comes just before the Normans but it is not far-fetched or improbable to speculate that the cult of Mary, Mother of God, developed 'from hardship and adversity when the Irish people chose catholic christianity after the Reformation in the centuries of plantation and colonisation. There is extant in the devotional bardic literature of the late middle ages many poems to Mary bridging the divide between sacred and secular in the sense of Mary being sinless and above all women, in the courtly poetry tradition of Hiberno-Norman Ireland.

O master stroke of women;
O chart of the sea-path home;
O fair-tressed sinless lady,
O branch over wood, O bright sun.
O spring unfailing, peace-bond of the six hosts,
before whom war recoils;
O subduer of God's wrath.
O help of the living world, let me not
cause thy poverty to have been in vain,
O ivy bearing fresh wine,
O guardian of God's child.
O banquet of apostles and virgins, O love
never too dearly purchased; O unsullied
heart; O sister; O clear guide to heaven.
O Mary, queen of all men, and of women
too; to thy help must we flee; thou art
refuge of all, even of thy foes.[8]

In seventeenth-century Ireland there was a rise in the cult of the Rosary authorised by the papacy to meet the needs of a people debarred from liturgical practices of a more sophisticated type by the secular laws of the time.

It was however in the nineteenth and twentieth centuries that the cult of Mary, Mother of God became that of model in the sense discussed by Barbour at the beginning of this essay:

Broadly speaking, a model is a symbolic representation of selected aspects of the behaviour of a complex system for particular purposes. It is an imaginative tool for ordering experience, rather than a description of the world.[9]

He continues:

> one of the main functions of religious models is the interpretation of distinctive types of experience: awe and reverence, moral obligations, reorientation and reconciliation, interpersonal relationships, key historical events, and order and creativity in the world.

The Famine in the 1840s was an event of psychological horror and disaster to the society of Ireland who experienced its biblical dimensions. Men, women and children were confronted with an act of God so terrible in its manifestation that a society which had been increasingly involved in the liberating processes of self-improvement, searched providence for an answer. It was given at Knock, Co. Mayo in 1879 with an apparition of Mary, the Blessed Mother. What happened at Knock to a rural population which was undergoing yet another famine has yet to be interpreted in the history of religious sentiment. In an essay exploring the devotional revolution which occurred in the second half of the nineteenth century, Professor Emmet Larkin demonstrates how institutional religion was affected by the piety of a people shocked into church-going and other religious observances by the post-Famine anxiety to rationalise the changed *Weltanschauung* of a people whose cosmology had hitherto been free of a punishing God. Attendance at Sunday Mass which before the Famine had been around forty per cent rose to ninety per cent by the 1890s, and the values of a sombre church-going society were reinforced by the system of a late-marrying rural society.[10]

In Britain those decades coincided with the reign of the widowed Queen Victoria, a gloomy black-clad figure who set the mood of unsmiling seriousness for her court and government. In Ireland, Mary, Mother of Sorrows was the most appropriate model for a generation of women, the death of whose elderly husbands left them widows at a relatively young age. But it was specifically in the family setting of mothers and sons that the Marian model is most clearly visible. Patrick Pearse's poem, 'The Mother' written shortly before his execution associates the mother of an Irish nationalist with the Mother of Jesus at the foot of the Cross. Even before Pearse's theme of a mother offering up her sons to heroic death, Maurya in Synge's *Riders to the* Sea reinforced the lonely strength and spiritual resources of the Irish widow left without her menfolk. After the Civil War the image is further extended in O'Casey's women. Mrs. Tancred in *Juno and the Paycock* is the suffering face of republican motherhood in twentieth-century Ireland north and south when she identifies her sorrow with that of the Mother of God and turns to her for solace as she sets out to her son's funeral:

> Mother o' God, Mother o' God, have pity on the pair of us! ... O Blessed Virgin, where were you when me darlin' son was riddled with bullets, when me darlin' son was riddled with bullets! ... Sacred Heart of the Crucified Jesus, take away our hearts o' stone ... an' give us hearts o' flesh! ... Take away this murdherin' hate ... an' give us Thine own eternal love![11]

Later in the same play, Juno re-echoes her words when she too is told that her son has been murdered by his former associates.[12]

> Tragedy is only possible to a mind which is for the moment agnostic or Manichean. The least touch of any theology which has a compensating Heaven to offer the tragic hero (heroine) is fatal,

remarks I.A. Richards.[13] What saves Juno, Mrs. Tancred and their real-life prototypes from despair is their faith in an understanding God and their sense of identification with the Mother of Jesus. They are alone and they learn to live with solitude of spirit even before the blow falls but their lives are essentially in harmony with a future eschatology which in some as yet unknown way, contains for them fulfilment, meaning and peace.

It is Mary Lavin in her short stories who breaks the ritualistic spell that freezes Irish women in the sorrowful role of bereft widowhood created by Synge, O'Casey, Pearse and even to some extent by Yeats. Space and a sense of the magnitude of my task preclude a full examination of the Lavin women that come alive in the countryside of Meath or inhabit Baggot Street and the streets around 'the Library'. Mary Lavin restores vitality and a richly variegated emotional and imaginative life to the women of her stories.[14] They move with a vigour of their own making. Their reassurance is that of the earth-mother, life-enhancing, fertile, essentially alone, possibly celibate through widowhood but catching the note of celebration which flows through the manuscript accounts of Brigid of Kildare and Íte of Kileedy. Her short story, *Happiness,* is a magnificent lyrical complex unfolding of what female survival in twentieth-century Ireland is about:

> By magic then, staring down the years, we'd see blazingly clear a small girl with black hair and buttoned boots who, though plain and pouting, burned bright like a star.

Mary Lavin's women, to the historian always looking for the clues to interpret the secret voicings of a society, represent the non-cognitive model of which Barbour speaks, the subconscious monitoring, the studied behaviour and 'the formative repressions of a strict religious and moral code operating within the narrow boundaries of a predominantly rural society that

influenced every second of one's waking life'.[15]
Elsewhere in *Happiness* the daughters discuss Mother:

> What was it, we used to ask ourselves – that quality that
> she, we felt sure, misnamed? Was it courage? Was it
> strength, health, or high spirits? Something you could
> not give or take – a conundrum? A game of catch-as-
> catch-can?

The past is always influencing the present: the hidden
stream flows on. It is the mingling of the subconscious
gnostic elements of Celtic christianity with the orthodox
strands of post-Famine Roman Catholicism in the lives
of Mary Lavin's women which compels this essayist to
find in the short stories of Mary Lavin the image of
woman most representative of the middle years of the
twentieth century in Ireland.

from Christina Nulty (ed.), *Images of the Irish Woman: The Crane Bag*,
Vol. 4, No. 1 (1980), pp 26–30.

NOTES

1   Ian Barbour, *Myths, Models and Paradigms* (London, SCM Press,
    1974).
2   *Ibid.,* p. 27.
3   cf. Dinneen, *Foclóir.*
4   I should like to record my appreciation to Professor Jerome
    Murphy O'Connor O.P., of the École Biblique for drawing my
    attention to what he considers its inescapable evidence. I am
    indebted to him also for directing me to a little known article in the
    Harvard Theological Review on 'Virgines Subintroductae' (Vol. 61,
    1968, pp 552–566).
5   *Revue Celtique,* Vol. 47, 1926.
6   cf. *Harvard Theological Review,* Vol. 61, p. 558 for a discussion of Ó
    Faoláin's translation.
7   *Ériu,* 3, 1907.

8   Lambert McKenna, *Philip Bocht Ó hUiginn* (Dublin, Talbot Press, 1931), p. 169.
9   Ian Barbour, *op. cit.,* p. 6.
10 Larkin, *American Historical Review,* 1972.
11 Sean O'Casey, *Juno and the Paycock,* Act. 2.
12 *Ibid.,* Act 3.
13 Quoted by David Marcus in his introductory essay to his selection of *Modern Irish Stories* (London, Sphere, 1972).
14 cf. *Irish University Review,* Autumn 1979.
15 David Marcus, *op. cit.,* p. 12.

In March and April 1979 the Irish woman went on tour to the United States as a series of lectures organized by Professor Eoin McKiernan, president of the Irish-American Cultural Institute. Over decades Eoin McKiernan had promoted an understanding of Irish culture in America through his 'Irish Fortnight'. The lectures, edited by Eiléan Ní Chuilleanáin, were published by Arlen House and the book was intended in a broad sense to partner Women in Irish Society: The Historical Dimension. *Visibility and celebration, but also dependency and experience of hardship run as themes through individual essays and give cohesion to the overlying design.*

In giving my essay a place in the scheme of the lectures, Eoin McKiernan and I originally agreed that the series needed a historical perspective on the position of women in the long view of what constituted 'image and reality', and that it should endeavour to weave together in a coherent theme some of the issues which other contributors addressed as particular strands. Thus, in considering the position of women over centuries, I postulated that it had not gradually improved as we approached the present time. Prevailing laws and customs affected the status of women at different eras and consequently they possessed greater or lesser opportunities at various times.

Long out of print Irish Women: Image and Achievement *was interdisciplinary in character which compensated for an unevenness of treatment. It was a bold and imaginative attempt to integrate women into the fabric of the country's past and went beyond the conventional limited range of sources.*

The Irish literary imagination has, over centuries, stored certain images of women which exercise a powerful pull on the behaviour patterns of Irish society and resonate at many levels of Irish nationalism. Tracing these images back over the centuries, a 'type' of woman emerges, though the image has been shaped and remodelled by the changing Zeitgeist. W. B. Yeats evoked her as the *cailleach*, one of the stock figures of early Irish literature, whose age conceals her immortality.

Sometimes the etymology of a word is as significant as its literal meaning. *Caille*, denoting a veil, made its way into primitive Irish no later than the fifth century. It is not clear how it became assimilated into the word *cailleach* which from then onwards signified a 'nun' in the growing christian society, while retaining in secular mythology its original meaning of 'old hag', and carrying with it overtones of the sacred. Thus in Frank O'Connor's 'The Old Woman of Beare' which he places in the ninth century, the old woman becomes a nun in a Christian community at the close of her long life as a goddess of love. Yeats, however, linked the image of the *cailleach*, or old hag, to that of the *spéirbhean*, the vision-woman dear to eighteenth-century Gaelic poets as a female image of captive Ireland seeking a male protector. With the dramatic presentation of his play Cathleen Ni Houlihan, Yeats perpetuated into the twentieth century the femaleness of Ireland, linking with her destiny that of men ready to die to free her:

> Peter: Did you see an old woman going down the road?
> Patrick: I did not: but I saw a young girl, and she had the walk of a queen.

How far does the historical imagination deal with the subject of women in Irish history? What stores of memories are allowed to seep through into the upper layers of consciousness either at folk level, or into the accepted version of our past? Making visible hidden elements in the total experience of a country's history is largely a question of perception, a kind of intellectual consciousness-raising. It is rare for historical research to accomplish the task of getting a society to contemplate its own identity without the help of literature as an auxiliary. The clues to the position of women in Irish history are invariably present in the literature of a particular phase of Irish history.

The significance of the idea of the femaleness of Ireland has not escaped the attention of scholars of early Irish history and of Celtic mythology over the decades. 'It would be hard to exaggerate the importance of this idea of the land and its sovereignty conceived in the form of a woman', remarks Proinsias Mac Cana in his study of women in Irish mythology.

From the beginning of history and before, until the final dissolution of the Irish social order in the seventeenth century, traditional orthodox thought was dominated by this image of the *puella senilis*, the woman who is literally as old as the hills yet endlessly restored to youth through union with her rightful mate. She outlives not only men but also tribes and peoples.

Furthermore the goddess is the symbol of the land and only by uniting with her can the ruler become acceptable to his people, and she, joined with the rightful ruler, becomes young and beautiful once more. Mac Cana, turning to the historians, puts the question succinctly:

> ... it is nevertheless reasonable to ask whether a society which in its literature attributes such independence to its women characters as does much of early Irish literature would on the other hand deny it or rigidly curtail it in real life.[1]

Women in Early Irish Society

Even now it remains true that the history of women in Early Christian Ireland is largely unwritten. Though the sources are abundant, they remain scattered. In his contribution to *Women in Irish Society* Donncha Ó Corráin examined the position of women before the law in early Irish society. Women had extensive rights in marriage contracts, over property, in divorce and marital arrangements, and in their responsibility towards their children.[2] According to the earliest law-tracts it would seem that by the beginning of the eighth century women had progressed from a situation in which they had little independent legal power to one of equality with their husbands. A serious study is now required of that first period reconciling the discrepancies that suggest the presence of female power in the sagas set in the historical period of the seventh century, and in the hagiographical material surrounding the lives of female Celtic saints, notably Brigid, with the evidence of women's legal incapacity in the earliest of the law-tracts. Liam de Paor, in an unpublished paper which he delivered to the Dublin Historical Association in 1975, and D. A. Binchy, in his *Studies in Early Irish Law* (Royal Irish Academy, 1936), buttress the conviction that early Irish society was patriarchal in the sense that politics and law were governed by men. Binchy suggests that the influence of the Christian Church may have helped to bring about the change noticeable in the eighth and ninth centuries. Yet another point of view is expressed by Eoin MacNeill when he suggests that the women in early Irish society enjoyed a fairly decent status in literature and in life which may have derived from the customs and legal sagas of pre-Celtic peoples which, over time, influenced the law-tracts of their conquerors.[3] Writing on the development of women's rights in the ninth and tenth centuries, Ó Corráin notes that the privileges of 'the woman of equal lordship' were by that time extended to the wives of a lower grade, thus extending it to the majority of married women. In general the property laws were equitable to women and men and the rights of children were safe-guarded by a legal designation of responsibility between fathers and mothers.

Politically, the woman who in literature is closely associated with the sovereignty myth did not inherit power, nor did she govern as an independent sovereign. Nevertheless there is similarity between Medb (Maeve) of the Táin Bó Cuailnge whose sexual indulgence conceals her primary function as a goddess of sovereignty, and the christianised Brigid, founder of the great monastery of Kildare which, under her rule and that of her successors as abbesses, laid claim to a wide parouchia of over thirty churches around AD 630. Though Brigid was under the authority of the Church as a consecrated nun, her jurisdiction over the local Church in Leinster was undisputed at a period when the organization of the Irish Church was far from complete. Not only did she assume spiritual responsibility for the Christian people around the monastery that she founded in Kildare, but the seventh century *Life* by Cogitosus speaks of 'her See ... episcopal and virginal', and the Book of Armagh invokes her: 'O Brigid, your parouchia within your own province will be reputed as your kingdom'. John Ryan remarks:

> This seems to suggest that the abbess of Cill Dara wielded 'monarchial' authority over all the churches and church lands attached to her monastery within the Kingdom of Leinster. It would appear, also, that with the approval of the primates of Armagh later abbesses of Kildare, if not St Brigid herself, exercised some kind of jurisdiction at Kildare and elsewhere ... From the evidence there seems to be no doubt that Brigid's

successors exercised some of the functions more generally restricted to bishops.[4]

Brigid's capabilities can be measured by the near contemporary testimonies to her skill as a chariot-driver, her ease in the company of men, and her achievements as the founder of a large double monastery where celibate men and women attended vast numbers of the sick and weary.

Brigid's Kildare was founded towards the close of the fifth century, and its rise coincided with a period of transition in the Irish Church in which a number of female Irish saints came to be important Christian leaders in their local communities. Saint Íte of Kileedy in County Limerick was a hermit of the heroic dimensions we associate with the Egyptian desert hermits: in her case she communed with God rather than wrestled with devils. Saint Moninne of Sliab Cuilinn (Killeevey) was the leader of her community on the borders of Louth-Armagh and was a friend and collaborator of Brigid's. Patrick, according to his biographer Tírechán, initiated his missionary policy by placing women in leadership roles whenever the occasion required it. A more detailed scrutiny is now required of the part played by women saints in the age of transition after Patrick and later in the *Célí Dé* movement under the influence of Samthann, abbess of Clonbroney (c. 730) in order to understand what they possessed in terms of prestige, power and authority – and how much was lost in the centuries following the decline of Celtic monasticism.

Women in the Viking and Norman Period

Ó Corráin detects a major rise in the political status of women by the middle of the tenth century, consorts or wives of kings then assuming the title of queen. History and propaganda are deeply intertwined in this middle period. Gormlaith, for instance, ex-consort of Brian Boru, persists in Irish folklore as a strong political woman of the eleventh century, and An tAthair Peadar Ó Laoghaire, in his historical saga *Niamh* (*Celtica* 1907), revived for nationalist readers of the early years of the Gaelic League a story of the Viking period which, though simplistic and tedious, juxtaposes two women, one from the Viking world, Gormlaith, and the other, Niamh, from the Celtic world as imagined in the late nineteenth century. Gormlaith deserves to be reset in Irish history and rescued from the pro-Brian propagandists of the twelfth century. What is clear is that the position of high-born women in early Irish society was in comparatively high profile: wielding influence and power, they possessed a freedom before the law quite astonishing in comparison with the stunting imposition of feudal and later English law upon the position of women in society.

What women lost in Norman Ireland in the way of legal rights and freedoms in the areas of marriage and divorce was partially offset by their admittance into a larger European milieu. It was a high price to pay. The position of women in western Europe was diminished after the Crusades. Claude Lévi-Strauss puts it pithily, reviewing the effect of Islam on the western world at the time of the Crusades: 'it was then that the west lost the opportunity of remaining female'. Whatever the reasons, Anglo-Norman Ireland, in its legal attitude to women, curtailed their freedom both as wives and daughters. The Anglo-Normans operated a system of customary law which was a reflection of prevailing feudal practices and was to become over centuries the corpus of English common law. Among the restrictive practices, it gave the husband complete control of his wife's property, and he became his wife's sole guardian. It gave parents the authority to arrange a marriage for their daughter without her consent. This was particularly poignant in the case of child-marriages, and the Church sought to ameliorate the harshness of secular law by insisting on the 'free will' clause when both parties came of age. The marriage of Aoife, daughter of the King of Leinster, to the Norman invader, Strongbow, has always been regarded as significant in the course of Irish history. In Norman law she became an heiress, thus allowing her husband to claim as her property the lordship of Leinster. In political terms, she was a captive princess handed over as part of the spoils of war, and the marriage marked a decisive change in the position of women in Norman Ireland. As Katharine Simms remarks:

> Anglo-Irish husbands might have masterful wives, but since in law they had no independent control of their property, the women had to exercise their influence indirectly by putting pressure on their menfolk.[5]

It was as a dowered widow with a life-interest in one-third or half of the property of her late husband that the Anglo-Norman woman enjoyed a measure of independence. But the Anglo-Norman world in the late middle ages in Ireland was one of hazardous exploitation for the heiress marrying into an Anglo-Norman lordship.

In contrast, in those parts of Ireland where Gaelic law and rule prevailed, the wife of the Irish ruler preserved financial control over her dowry, and was entitled to certain rents and taxes from her husband's subjects. Notably in the sixteenth century, the political power of the Irish woman administering either her husband's business while he was at war – as with Iníon Dubh, mother of Red Hugh O'Donnell, or her own estate, as in the case of Gráinne O'Malley – was an exercise of customary right, hallowed by tradition. She was expected to participate in council in times of war, to negotiate hostages, and even to determine succession to the throne. The sixteenth century is, par excellence, a century of Tudor women in Ireland. Queen Anne Boleyn, with her Irish background of Ormonde-Butler connections, was eclipsed by her vigorous daughter Queen Elizabeth I. She was matched by an unparalleled gallery of Irish women, challenging, haughty, toughly negotiating for their menfolk and for retention of their territory: Joan Butler Fitzgerald, the war-torn wives of the Maguires and the O'Donnells, Catherine Magennis, who accompanied the Earl Hugh O'Neill in his exile to Rome after 1603, and many more awaiting discovery. It was a great century for women in Irish history, and a terrible one in the aftermath of their eclipse. Living in genteel poverty on the continent as the wives and daughters of Wild Geese in the following century, we catch a glimpse of their indomitable spirit in the figure of Lady Rosa O'Doherty, the energetic wife of the military commander Eoghan Roe O'Neill.[6]

One other aspect of the position of these high-born ladies is to be noticed. The wider orbit of European influence associated with the Normans introduced into Ireland cultural themes which are brought together in the collection of poetry known as courtly love. As a literary genre this body of erotic poetry written in fourteenth- and fifteenth-century Irish has received due attention from Robin Flower in *The Irish Tradition* (Oxford 1947) and subsequently in an outstanding work by Seán Ó Tuama, *An Grá in Amhráin na nDaoine* (Dublin, An Clóchomhar, 1960). The same poetry which Flower and Ó Tuama scrutinise for the impact of the Provençal literary forms and style upon Irish poetry yields evidence of social attitudes in what was essentially an aristocratic expression crossing the boundaries of Anglo-Norman and Gaelic. In Ireland there was no Albigensian heresy to isolate the poet and his mistress. Rather there was a teasing pre-occupation with the external delights of the beloved. Female beauty is stereotyped in these poems much as Hollywood imprisoned the notional (as distinct from the ideal) in the mid-twentieth century. Some of the poets were women but they belonged to an aristocracy and took their part lightheartedly in the witty exchanges about the nature of jealous love:

> If he kill me through jealousy now
> His wife will perish of spite,
> He'll die of grief for his wife
> Three of us dead in a night.

– 'A learned Mistress',
Frank O'Connor, *Kings, Lords and Commons*

In a different mood, the satire and 'praise' poems of sixteenth-century Ireland carry overtones of inclusion and exclusion, a whole world of approval of women by men, in this case the *filí* or poets, which still awaits an interpretation.

Women in Transition

Even a cursory glance at sixteenth-century Gaelic society suggests a female-male complementarity and some presence of female autonomy, as in the evidence of women participating in decision-making procedures; the marriage of older women to younger men; female support among in-laws (as in the Geraldine conspiracy of c. 1539); and the presence of women's quarters in the tower-houses. Subordination of women became a reality in the following centuries. With the destruction of the medieval Gaelic and Anglo-Norman institutions by the Elizabethan conquest, Ireland entered into a period of colonisation from which it did not emerge until the early twentieth century. In the seventeenth century plantations – the Plantation of Ulster (1609), the large-scale Cromwellian settlement in mid-century and the final phase at the end of the century – linked with a penal code of legislation connected the subduing of the native population to the particular subjugation of women.

The conquest and plantations of the sixteenth and seventeenth centuries transformed the political, social and economic structure of Irish society. From then until the great Famine of the mid-nineteenth century there are only three general statements which can with any confidence be made concerning the role of women in that society. Firstly, they were totally without formal political rights; secondly, their property and inheritance rights, both within and outside of marriage, were now governed by English common law; and thirdly, theirs was a subject and subsidiary role to the male, and it was performed, for the most part, within a domestic context.

Thus Gearóid Ó Tuathaigh begins his investigation of the role of women under what he terms 'the new English order'. Ó Tuathaigh's essay is concerned with the role of women in those centuries, mainly seventeenth and eighteenth, in the social and economic spheres, and he looks at the residual cultural differences between planter and Gael, and sees the role of women as above all else 'a function of class'.[7]

Implicit in his examination is the background of colonisation. Colonisation in seventeenth-century Ireland, while it differed in certain respects from that of the new world for historical reasons, bore the same general characteristics which have marked it everywhere, that of a stratified state won by military conquest. There was a growth in state bureaucracy as plantation and settlement by foreigners succeeded in utilising the country's resources in what amounted to a structural transformation of the older, pastoral economy. The consolidation of wealth in the hands of great landowners resulted in the emergence of an aristocracy whose power was buttressed by force and legislation. Throughout the seventeenth century there was the painful emergence of a minimally consuming class of producers who, by the beginning of the eighteenth century, can be discerned as the labouring poor at the bottom of a class pyramid whose upper layers of nobility, administrators, churchmen, army officers and great merchants appropriated their labour and produce.

Eighteenth-century Ireland remained a pre-industrial stratified society whose wealth was based on landownership and the management of great estates. The severity of the Penal Code (1691–1715) which stripped a subdued conquered population of the right to ownership was, in the case of Ireland, discriminatory on the grounds of religion. In particular the Roman Catholic and Presbyterian small leaseholders suffered. Those groups or individuals who could alleviate their exploitation tended to take advantage of the unjust system, and the emergence of farming and commercial interests in eighteenth-century Ireland, while it brought prosperity to some classes, did not bring about a collective resistance to colonial oppression. The spiral towards a rising population, particularly at the lower end of the social scale, quickened alarmingly in the last decades of the eighteenth century and hastened the disastrous Famine of 1846–1852. Then a country which had tried to support eight million people faced the breakdown of a rural economy unable to cope with the numbers.

The effects of colonisation on women cannot be disassociated from the effects on society as a whole. English law was introduced from the beginning of the seventeenth century. All the Churches after the Reformation placed women in a subordinate position within the family and the patriarchal nuclear family became the ultimate model in colonial systems. In Ireland, women became virtual minors before the law, 'privatised' in their life-style, and admonished by the Churches to be obedient to their husbands.

Native Irish poetry reflected this quenching of womanly graces and spirit. In general the poets wrote bitter-sweet poetry about the decline of the old order, and in the memorable 'Cill Chais' (c. 1720) the unknown poet made reference to the lady of the great house now in ruins:

> Her company now must lament her,
> Who would give yellow money and white
> But who'd never take land from the people
> But was friend to the truly poor.
>
> – Thomas Kinsella, trans, *An Duanaire*

Within a generation the major poets were writing of the captive *spéirbhean* who was a figure of unliberated Ireland needing to be rescued by her 'prince' across the waters of Europe. Occasionally she was depicted in bondage to the powerful John Bull, who emerged as the symbol of England after the campaigns of Marlborough and in the early eighteenth century. The *aisling* or vision poetry of this period simultaneously projects for the listeners the ideal of the 'passive' beautiful young woman. If she appears supernatural as in Egan O'Rahilly's 'Brightness of Brightness', she does not possess the powers of the ninth-century hag of Beare. Those men who wrote *aisling* poetry spoke to a rural population, conveying through the poems feelings of helplessness, sorrow and pathos. The folk-songs of this period, however abundant and varied, reflect in many cases the passivity and powerlessness of the lovers.

In stark contrast to the powerlessness of the eighteenth-century *spéirbhean* as depicted in the *aisling* poetry, the lament for Art Ó Laoghaire composed by his wife, Eibhlín Dubh Ní Chonaill, is a splendidly sustained work sparkling with anger and grief over the murder of her husband. Apart from its merit as a social and historical document, this fine poem has a distinction of form and theme and well deserves the honourable place it holds in Gaelic literature to the present day. It orchestrates all the wordless grief that the 'keening' women uttered over the bodies of the dead in rural Ireland, and its preservation in the oral tradition of the people of Cork and Kerry established it securely as one of the great laments and love poems in the Gaelic tongue.

> My love and my mate
> That I never thought dead
> Till your horse came to me
> With bridle trailing,
> All blood from forehead
> To polished saddle
> Where you should be
> Either sitting or standing,
> I gave one leap to the threshold,
> A second to the gate,
> A third upon its back,
> I clapped my hands,
> And off at a gallop;
> I never lingered
> Till I found you lying
> By a little furze-bush.

– 'The Lament for Art O'Leary',
Frank O'Connor, Kings, Lords and Commons

Irish women in the colonial world of eighteenth-century Ireland responded to their condition by establishing their own coping strategies. Recognition of being oppressed does not preclude recognition on the part of the oppressed that they are capable of acting to influence their own destiny. Young women began to emigrate to the new world, and later to Australia, first incidentally in the 1790s, and then in growing numbers in the early nineteenth century, and eventually in a steady stream throughout the following century to a world where they could hope to better themselves and their relatives. A study of Quaker women reveals their social awareness and activity right through this period. They were in the forefront for reform.

Among the Roman Catholic population, the most consistent expression of women prepared to defend the collective interests of their people was the rise of women's religious orders. In particular the native sisterhoods, such as the Presentation Sisters founded by Nano Nagle for the education of poor children, the Irish Sisters of Loreto founded by Mary Ward to provide home-based schooling for the daughters of the rising middle classes, and the Sisters of Mercy founded by Catherine McAuley, devoted to the alleviation of human suffering and misery wherever they found it, became the clamant voice of the oppressed.

As for the women of the ascendancy in eighteenth-century Ireland, they too emerged from the shadows cast by the class-pyramid and made their contribution in places like Carton House and its rival Castletown House. Emily, Duchess of Leinster, though an Englishwoman by birth, ranks with those Irish women who understood the currents of freedom that were awakening in the colonies of North America and Ireland in the 1770s. She was the mother of Lord Edward Fitzgerald, and had given him a liberal education which he was later to use in imbibing the ideas of the French Revolution; he joined the United Irishmen in 1796 and was fatally wounded a year later while evading arrest. His aunt, Lady Louise Connolly of Castletown, made heroic efforts to reach him before he expired. The ladies of Ireland's great demesnes, though they came from different traditions and of non-native stock, identified with the landscape and possessed an affinity with the Butler gentlewomen who presided over Cill Chais. The aristocracy feature in the fiction of Maria Edgeworth, and Yeats describes the women of a later gentry:

> The light of evening, Lissadell,
> Great windows open to the south,
> Two girls in silk kimonos both
> Beautiful, one a gazelle.

Into Modern Times

The experience of women throughout the nineteenth century was one of gradual awakening, first to their condition, and their economic plight, and then hesitantly to their educational and legal rights. In 1825 there appeared a work of over two hundred pages from the pen of Cork-born William Thompson, *An Appeal of One Half of the Human Race, WOMEN, Against the Pretensions of the Other Half, MEN, to Retain Them in Political and Thence in Civil and Domestic Slavery*. This well-written and impassioned tract was probably inspired by the situation of Thompson's friend, the spirited Anna Wheeler, god-daughter of Henry Grattan, who endured twelve years of matrimonial misery in Limerick before gaining her liberation in London and becoming a remarkable personality, urging on Daniel O'Connell and his circle the notion of women's equality with men.

Thompson's work deserves to be remembered: it was a sharp rebuttal of James Mill's argument in his 'Essay on Government' that women did not need formal political rights as they were adequately represented by their menfolk. Thompson reduced Mill's specious logic to absurdity and presented the argument of political rights for women so cogently that it exerted a strong influence on Daniel O'Connell who frequently asserted that the equality of women was irrefutable.[8] Both men cited Mary Wollstonecraft as one of their mentors.

Mill's son, John Stuart Mill, made amends for his father's austere views on women in his own famous essay 'The Subjection of Women'. John Stuart Mill also presented the first women's suffrage petition to the British House of Commons. That petition was signed on behalf of Irish Women by Anna Haslam from Youghal. Of Quaker stock she, with her husband Thomas, formed the first Suffrage Society in Ireland. In turn they influenced Hanna Sheehy Skeffington and her husband, Francis Sheehy Skeffington, who, with a group of women and men, brought political equality a step further by their agitation about the Vote for Women issue with the Home Rule Party from 1910 onwards. Simultaneously James Connolly and the Larkins concerned themselves with the economic rights of Irish women workers overtaken by the severity of factory conditions in Belfast and Dublin, and by the general oppression of poverty and servile work.

There was then a broad current of liberal thought about the emancipation of women flowing into the revolutionary atmosphere of the early twentieth century. Many factors contributed to its vigour, most notably the education of middle-class women in Ireland from the 1830s onward. With the securing of catholic emancipation, convent boarding, schools for catholic girls sprang up all over Ireland: the Ursuline, Loreto, Dominican and Sacre Coeur orders all established schools which survive into the late twentieth century. In the older schools founded in the 1830s and 1840s cultural and moral instruction was accompanied by the teaching of music, needlework, art and elocution in a curriculum that was not part of the State system. The task of turning young girls into young ladies was effectively accomplished through the teaching of christian values and social aptitudes. The founding of Alexandra College in 1866 for the 'higher education of girls' marked a distinct step forward in the aspirations not only of the protestant girls for whom it generally catered, but also for catholic girls who aspired to university education. The establishment of the Dominican College for girls at Eccles Street and Loreto Abbey in Rathfarnham, in particular, sharpened the perceptions of girls' education at a time when the late 1870s threw public examinations open to girls and women. For the first time, girls' schools in Ireland could participate in public examinations and avail of entry into careers and professions. The effect of the 1878 Intermediate Act on Irish women cannot be over-estimated. It achieved a major revolution in their economic and educational aspirations which brought Irish women in the late nineteenth and early twentieth centuries under the spell of the liberalising influences of the feminist movement in America and Britain. Thus it was that higher education for middle-class Irish women brought them not only economic freedom and university honours, but in the early twentieth century brought them, by various routes, into the revolutionary experience that led to the founding of the Free State in the south in 1922.

James Connolly's words on the conditions of the working-class woman in the early twentieth century were also valid for much of the previous century:

Driven out to work at the earliest possible age, she remains fettered to her wage-earning, a slave all her life. Marriage does not mean for her a rest from outside labour ... she has added the duty of a double domestic toil – completing each day's work, she becomes the slave of domestic needs of family.

The rising aspirations of Irish society, observable by the second decade of the nineteenth century, did not continue to be favourable to the condition of working women, whether on farms or in the cities and towns. The catastrophe of the Famine (1846–52) had far-reaching effects on women, some of which escape historical research.[9] J. J. Lee puts the historical phenomenon succinctly when he observes: 'The great Famine drastically weakened the position of women in Irish society ... economic circumstances therefore conspired to make Ireland an increasingly male dominated society after the Famine'.[10]

The falling status of women and the predicament of the unmarried daughter in rural Ireland had its counterpart in the urban centres. Though status in post-Famine Ireland was not determined by gender, the emergence of single women as a large group – 43.3 per cent of the total female population in 1861 – is in itself a significant commentary.[11] Within that substantial group – by 1911 it was up to 48.6 per cent – there were class groupings with structurally differential access to resources and even subsistence. It is possible to differentiate between rural and urban women and to make distinctions between the working-class woman and the middle- and upper-middle-class woman, but the overall choice of women was between being married and by law the property of their husbands, and remaining single and in a vulnerable economic and social role, whether on the farm or factory floor.

The majority of Irish women were left largely unaffected by the early industrial revolution and the loss of status experienced by Irish women throughout the century was matched by their diminishing representation in the workforce. The same census of 1861 recorded 29 per cent of women employed. By 1911 only 19.5 per cent of women were employed. Mary E. Daly, in a wide-ranging paper delivered to the Irish Labour History First International Conference, noted that trends in women's employment have never paralleled their role in Irish society. Undoubtedly there was under-representation of women in the recording of the workforce, in the farm household and even in dressmaking. She concluded:

> ... the typical working woman was either a domestic servant, a low grade textile or dress-making worker, or an agricultural labourer. Such women worked, not as a means of self-fulfillment, but simply because they had no real alternative.

The centrality of women to the Irish revolution of 1916–21 can be interpreted in a number of ways. Mainly their participation is seen as that of women engaging in a war of liberation with their menfolk. The role played by Cumann na mBan, the paramilitary organization which was founded in the wake of the Irish Volunteers, still awaits a historian.[12] The presence of a woman, Countess Markievicz, in the 1916 Rising and her assumption of command of one of the fighting positions in Dublin city was repeated in subsequent wars of liberation of the twentieth century. Perhaps it required a poet to kindle the imagination of an apathetic people; the sensitivity of W. B. Yeats in catching the resonances of the female presence in the events of the historic years of the Irish revolution was atavistic in its reminder of a Celtic past. More insistent for the historian now is the theme of women's resistance to colonisation, which finds its form in action that represents a struggle against oppression instead of an accommodation to it. As such, the participation of women in the revolutionary movement in Ireland may be seen as a fore-runner of the unified action of women and men in Third World revolutionary movements of the twentieth century.

What then was the reality for the Irish woman in the decade following Yeats's romantic projection of her female presence in Irish nationalism? The participation of women in the national struggle was a short-lived phenomenon. Overtaken by the forces of counter-revolution (again, a familiar pattern in Third World revolutionary uprisings in the twentieth century) Irish women retreated into a secondary role with the setting up of the northern State in 1920 and the Free State in the south in 1922. Around Irish women, as in a cage, were set the structures of family life and women were assigned a home-based, full-time role as housewives, whose talents and energies were devoted to looking after husband and children.

Historians have tended to explain the illiberal legislation and stifling provincialism of the post-Civil War decades in the Irish Free State by referring to the value system of a tradition-minded, rural-orientated society. Rarely, if at all, is allusion made to the total exclusion of woman from public life, and from responsibility for public morality. Woman's place was in the home. The sanctity of the marriage bond and the indissolubility of marriage were upheld, civil divorce being ruled out by a Dáil motion of 1925. The Juries Act of 1927 virtually excluded women from jury service. Legislation on aspects of censorship was passed: in 1923 films 'subversive of public morality' were cut and refused a licence by a male censor; six years later the

Censorship of Publications Act empowered a board of five men to prohibit the sale of any book or periodical it considered 'indecent or obscene' or 'advocating the unnatural prevention of conception'. In 1935 the sale, advertising or importation of contraceptives was prohibited by Section 17 of the Criminal Law Amendment Act. In 1927 the catholic hierarchy had issued a joint pastoral entitled 'The Evils of Modern Dancing' which deplored the destruction of 'the characteristic virtues of our race', and listed the dance-hall, the bad book, the film and immodest fashions in female dress as contributing to the general decline of public morals. The Public Dance Halls Act 1935 gave discretionary powers to District Justices to restrict and regulate local dances. In 1937 the new constitution declared in Article 41.2: 'In particular, the State recognizes that by her life within the home, woman gives to the State a support without which the common good cannot be achieved'.

A deep perplexity about their true identity as citizens was felt by many women. The anomaly of married women being constrained not to work by State policy was compounded by the extension of State responsibilities for the provision of health and childcare services into the home, thus ultimately diminishing her status. Nor is it fanciful to read into Brian Merriman's great poem, 'The Midnight Court', written in Irish at the end of the eighteenth century and translated by Frank O'Connor in the twentieth century (and promptly banned by the Censorship Board) a sense of the poet's dismay at the lack of harmony between the sexes: colonisation always creates antagonism between men and women, and in such a situation their interests do not always coincide.

On a wider canvas it seems probable that the twentieth century will be seen as the century of the 'feminine mystique' in the context of women's history. All the major problems for women appear at one time or another, such as their questioning of war, their economic independence and their psychological liberation. The issue of birth control is one of profound interest to the Irish woman from the Famine onwards, but it was to remain an unresolved area of Irish family life. The majority of Irish women north and south view the two decades after 1921 as crucial to their experience of being female in Ireland. Self-determination was to come tardily, but it was to come surprisingly to the older woman as well as to the young, to the widow as well as to the married woman, to the woman in paid employment as well as to the woman working at home. And the debate was to be about equality of opportunity.

from Eiléan Ní Chuilleanáin (ed.), *Irish Women: Image and Achievement* (Dublin, Arlen House, 1985), pp 37–50.

NOTES

1 Proinsias MacCana, 'Women in Irish Mythology', *The Crane Bag* Vol. 4, No. 1 (1980), p. 7.

2 Donncha Ó Corráin, 'Women in Early Irish Society', in Margaret Mac Curtain and Donncha Ó Corráin (eds), *Women in Irish Society: The Historical Dimension* (Dublin, Arlen House, 1978), pp 1–13.

3 Eoin MacNeill, *Early Irish Laws and Institutions* (Dublin, Burns, Oates and Washbourne, 1934), pp 64–6.

4 John Ryan, S.J., *Saint Brigid of Cill Dara* (Dublin, Irish Messenger Publications, 1978), pp 8, 9.

5 Katharine Simms, 'Women in Norman Ireland', in *Women in Irish Society, op. cit.*, pp 14–25.

6 Jerrold Casway, 'Irish Women Overseas, 1500-1800', in Margaret Mac Curtain and Mary O'Dowd (eds), *Women in Early Modern Ireland* (Edinburgh, Edinburgh University Press, 1991); 'Rosa

O'Dogherty: a Gaelic Woman', *Seanchas Ard Mhacha*, Vol. X (1980–1), pp 42–62.

7   Gearóid Ó Tuathaigh, 'The Role of Women in Ireland under the New English Order', in *Women in Irish Society, op. cit.*, pp 26–36.

8   Professor M. O'Connell, editor of The O'Connell Letters (I.M.C), has kindly drawn my attention to this aspect of Daniel O'Connell's relationship with his wife.

9   The incidence of depression among categories of Irish women is currently being researched and links with emigration of whole households of children from maternal roof is a case in point.

10 J. J. Lee, 'Women in the Church since the Famine', in *Women in Irish Society, op. cit.*, pp 41–2.

11 Mary E. Daly, 'Women in the Irish Workforce from Pre-Industrial to Modern Times', *Saothar*, Vol. 7 (1982), pp 74–81.

12 Margaret Ward, *Unmanageable Revolutionaries: Women in Irish Nationalism* (Dingle, Brandon; London, Pluto, 1983) examines the role of Cumann na mBan.

MARRIAGE IN TUDOR IRELAND

Theorising marriage in sixteenth-century Ireland is a trap for the unwary. None of the usual stereotypes prevail. It was not a patriarchal society in the post-renaissance understanding of the connections between kinship, dowry and arranged marriages. It was not a century of exceptional royal heroines and helpless victims. Romantic love which infused Gaelic poetry of the late middle ages found its way into real life among the ruling groups by the beginning of the sixteenth century. The ethos of the warring and factional society at odds with the centralising policy of the Tudor state was permissive around sexual practices. The Reformation and the Counter-Reformation, backed by the government of Queen Elizabeth I, endeavoured to make public, regularised, christian marriage the norm for marital relationships in the last quarter of the sixteenth century, penalising clandestine and secular marriages and upholding sacramental and church marriages. For most of the century marriage, and to some extent, divorces and re-marriage were shifting zones around the contours of women's lives, particularly in the areas of property and family.

The destruction of the public records office of the chancery courts of that period in the 1922 burning of the Four Courts in Dublin places obstacles in the path of the researcher eager to establish patterns of marital behaviour through wills and chancery pleadings. It is possible, however, to trace the changes in marriage practice by examining how older law codes such as the Brehon and Gaelic law tracts, were brought into line with a centralised legal system that reflected English Common Law practices. The concern for uniformity was visible also in catholic church courts, for by the end of the Council of Trent in 1563, many of the ambiguities in canon law in regard to marriage had been settled and monogamous marriage as one of the seven sacraments was re-affirmed.

The essay, 'Marriage in Tudor Ireland' was one of a series of talks delivered to the Dublin Historical Association during the session 1983–4. Revised for publication in Marriage in Ireland *(Dublin, College Press, 1985), in consultation with the editor, Professor Art Cosgrove, it concentrated on the legal considerations that affected the lives of women and men in sixteenth-century Ireland.*

Most of the major issues concerning matrimony were discussed in the Irish parliament throughout the Tudor period – the binding force of the affinity impediments; solemnisation of marriage; conditions of divorce and remarriage; legitimation of offspring and disposal of property at a time when wives held property in their own right. It was the century when reformation and counter-reformation alike sought reform of doctrine, faith and morals; so by the end of the sixteenth century marriage was transformed into a formal ecclesiastical institution. For Ireland the process was delayed for a variety of reasons, among them the inability of church and state to enforce registration of marriages on couples entering the state of matrimony.

Change is the one constant in sixteenth-century Ireland. The successful attempts of the Tudors beginning with Henry VIII to establish their ascendancy over the entire country affected religion, landownership, legal systems, and shook the institution of marriage to its foundation. Given Henry VIII's interest in the subject of marriage, the expectation is bred in the researcher that the king's pursuit of marriage found echoes in the minds of his subjects. Nor are those expectations disappointed. In the last decades of the reign of Henry VIII marriage was a subject of intensive and far-reaching legislation reflecting the constitutional changes that took place in the relationship between Henry and Ireland.

Whatever point of time is tested in the 1530s, crisis is visible, whether it was the Kildare rebellion and the liquidation of the family, or the religious and constitutional changes that followed Henry VIII's decision in England to assume headship of the church in his dominions. Our examination begins at that period of pause when the old medieval institutions of the Irish church were whirled away in the religious and land-owning changes enacted in the Irish parliaments of 1536–7 and 1540–1.

Any consideration of the legislation of the Henrician parliaments of the years 1536–41 yields surprising revelations. Dr Brendan Bradshaw has masterfully analysed the ecclesiastical legislation that confirmed government policy about the dissolution of the Irish monasteries and achieved what he claims was a constitutional revolution in the relationship between England and Ireland.[1] What is of interest here is to study the secular enactments of the two parliaments, in particular the parliamentary legislation concerning marriage and its dissolution at the period when the subject of marriage was an issue in the Henrician reformation.

Tudor sensitivity on the question of marriage is reflected in the legislation of their intermittent Irish parliaments.[2] It has not been situated in any remarkable way in the locus of issues which achieved the transformation of Ireland from a loosely connected lordship into a kingdom with a visible constitution. The rivalries between the Butlers and Fitzgeralds, the process of gaelicisation in lordships whose rulers were Irish, the emergence of a Pale group of Anglo-Irish 'reformers' – these, and considerations of a military nature, have traditionally supplied the framework for understanding the changes which took place in Ireland during the last decades of Henry's life. Some key-ideas of Henry's reign may have been under-written by others; but in the area of his marriage problems, in particular that of his first marriage, its dissolution and subsequent legislation, Henry VIII was demonstrably the prime-mover. All the more interesting then is it to endeavour to chart the sea-changes that his subjects suffered in the context of Irish parliamentary affairs.

The intricacies of canon law held no terrors for the educated lay-minds of Thomas More's generation. Henry VIII's difficulties concerning the nature of affinity as a diriment impediment to his marriage with Anne Boleyn was a real one. The canon law on affinity in his lifetime, starting from the principle that husband and wife are two in the one flesh, considered the marriage of one party with the relations of the other as equivalent to a marriage with his or her own relatives. Theoretically, just as all blood relations were forbidden to intermarry, so were all those related by affinity. The 1215 Lateran Council reduced the extent of the impediment to the fourth degree and this remained the computation in Henry's time. A further complication for Henry VIII was the ruling, by church law, that affinity arose also *a coitu* even outside marriage, thus constituting an impediment to marriage, and if it arose after marriage, made the use of that marriage unlawful. Even apart from the bond already existing with Catherine of Aragon, his brother's widow, should Henry have previously contracted a sexual relationship with Anne Boleyn's sister – as was asserted – there was then an impediment of affinity to his contemplated marriage with Anne.[3] And Henry's subsequent marriages also encountered some difficulties.

The Irish parliament of 1540–1 passed the 'Act for marriages' based on an English statute of the previous year. It provided that from 1 July 1540 a solemnised and consummated marriage should supersede an unsolemnised and unconsummated prior contract. Under the terms of canon law a contract freely entered into by words in the present tense *(per verba de praesenti)* was considered binding even if not followed by consummation. This, presumably, was 'the unjust law of the bishop of Rome' to which the act referred, and the stated purpose of the act was to safeguard 'true matrimony' against any challenge from alleged prior verbal commitments. The real reason for the enactment was to protect Henry VIII's marriage with Catherine Howard against attempts to impugn it on the grounds of pre-contract by either party. In 1549, two years after Henry VIII's death, the provisions of the English statute relating to pre-contracts were repealed on the grounds that they had encouraged people to break contracts in order to satisfy bodily lusts.[4] A similar repeal occurred in Ireland in the parliament of 1557–8.[5]

The same act also raised the issues of consanguinity and affinity. In 1537, again following an English act of the previous year, dispensations to marry within the degrees specified in Leviticus 18 (as interpreted by Henry VIII and his advisers) were prohibited. Anyone so married was to be:

> separated by the definitive sentence and judgement of the archbishops, bishops or other ministers of the church of this your said land of Ireland, within the limits of their jurisdiction and authorities …[6]

In other words, no one had the right to dispense from impediments laid down by God's law.

The act of 1541 went further and enacted that only the prohibitions contained in Leviticus 18 were to be observed in the future. Papal regulations on consanguinity and affinity were condemned as having no sanction in God's laws and, it was alleged, dispensations were issued by popes 'all because they would get money by it and keep a reputation to their usurped jurisdiction'. In future no challenge was to be permitted to any marriage 'without the levitical decrees'.[7]

Consanguinity in its widest sense is the bond between persons descended from the same stock. By the thirteenth century the prohibition was reduced to the fourth degree by the Lateran Council of 1215. This meant that everyone descended from the same great-great-grandfather was prohibited from marrying anyone similarly descended. It was not until the reformed churches and governments introduced wide ranging changes that the law of nature as the basis for the regulations concerning consanguinity began to be re-evaluated. For the catholic church, as we shall see, such concessions came slowly: in fact the Council of Trent's decree, *Tametsi*, established exact norms for marriage which remained practically unchanged to the twentieth century. For catholics one result of the protestant reformation was a new impediment to marriage, that of mixed religion.

In Gaelic Ireland marriages between kinsfolk were quite acceptable in what Kenneth Nicholls describes as 'Celtic secular marriage', resulting in an easy tolerance of divorce, clandestine marriages where no outward ceremony was needed, and a rapid succession of spouses.[8]

Among the Anglo-Irish, too, it could be difficult to find a marriage partner who was not related within the forbidden degrees. A statute of 1541 recited how consanguinity and affinity were widespread among the king's obedient subjects in Ireland:

by reason that they are inhabited in so little a compasse or circuit, and restrayned by estatute to marrie with Irish nation and therefore of necessity must marrie themselves together …'[9]

Papal dispensation was required for the diriment impediments of affinity and consanguinity. Apart from the expense, the difficulties created by canon law in a society based on family membership such as that of Ireland, ensured the perpetuation of problems in this sphere well into the sixteenth century.

With the enactment of the statute, 'An Act of the succession of the King and Queen Anne' in the 1537 session of the Irish reformation parliament, marriage and its dissolution assumed a dimension of public significance foreign to the great majority of the legislators, who were only too familiar with the underlying impediments outlined in the act, and who had been accustomed over time to transgress them as did their Gaelic Irish peers by contracting secular and clandestine marriages, that is, marriages not solemnised by the church, or by contracting forms of mutual consent involving no public civil ceremony. According to Lodge, writing in the middle of the eighteenth century in his *Peerage in Ireland,* William Brabazon was responsible for getting the Act of Succession through the Irish parliament and we can only speculate about where the opposition, that Lodge asserts was present, came.[10] Queen Mary had the act repealed in her Irish parliament, 'An Act declaring the Queen's Highness to have been born in a most just and lawful matrimony, and also repealing all acts of parliament and sentences of divorce had and made to the contrary.' Elizabeth, of course, made sure to re-instate her legitimacy in her Act of Supremacy 1560.

Anne Boleyn had once been designated by Henry VIII to marry Piers Butler and so end the feud between the Boleyn and Butler families over the title to the Ormond earldom. The dispute intensified in 1532 as Anne Boleyn's father, the earl of Wiltshire, gained more influence in Henry's court, leaving Piers Butler, earl of Ossory, to find what allies he could, while Wiltshire openly supported the Kildare faction. Titles as well as lives were short-lived in those turbulent years. The same Irish parliament that welcomed Anne Boleyn as queen to King Henry and recognized her daughter as legitimate legislated for the execution of the Fitzgerald family. There is a wryness in the way the two statutes follow each other in that 1537 session. Dr Brendan Bradshaw has examined the links between these reforming impulses of Thomas Cromwell and his selected administrators drawn from the Pale nobility in the months before the Geraldine rising of Silken Thomas. One of Dr Bradshaw's conclusions was that the Fitzgeralds were brought down by what he terms 'the exigencies of reform'. Thomas Cromwell, he claims, and not the anti-Kildare forces master-minded their extinction. 'The Fitzgeralds were victims, therefore, not of their enemies but of their own refusal to adapt to a new political era'.[11]

There are some curiosities about the 'Act of the attainder of the earl of Kildare' which beg questions about the motives of those present in the Dublin sitting of 1537, and which shed light on their pre-occupation with marriage legislation in both that and the 1540 parliament. The act is a long-winded one and drops certain innuendoes about the Kildare women which demand a more thorough investigation than the purpose of this essay allows.

The Fitzgerald women were drawn not only from the ranks of the Pale families, but were the daughters of Gaelic lords whom the Fitzgeralds wished to draw into alliance with themselves, thus contravening the Statute of Kilkenny. In the 1520s, perhaps even earlier, a group of kinswomen of the ninth earl of Kildare, Gearóid Óg, began to consolidate his supporters in the Pale and pave the way for the eventual outbreak of hostilities between Thomas and King Henry's officials in Dublin. According to the act, Alice Fitzgerald, wife of the baron of Slane and daughter of Gearóid Óg, was credited with getting the eventual conspiracy off the ground. She was the only woman cited by name in the act and was found guilty of high treason, and a careful distinction is made between her and the wives of the listed conspirators who actually received back their inheritances. Apparently they were free to take possession of their lands again:

> And more-over be it enacted and ordained by the said authority, that every of the wives of the said persons now living, by this act attainted and unhabled, and every such women, such as was the wife of the said person now dead, and were convicted and attainted of treason ... shall freely enjoy, have and possess after the death of her husband all her own inheritance to her and to her heirs other than be attainted.

Evidently much more went on behind the scenes of the Irish reformation parliament than meets the eye of the scholar eager to see signs of reform in the gentlemen of the Pale. The haste with which Sir Thomas Cusack married Maud, widow of Richard Fitzgerald, sixth son of the eighth earl, Gearóid Mór, and uncle of Thomas, was unseemly. He had applied for and got a divorce on grounds of consanguinity from his wife, Joan Hussey, the decree being granted in chancery on 6 July 1537, and his marriage to Maud took place shortly after. Maud had been implicated in the murder of her first husband by her second husband and obtained a pardon, (presumably by the efforts of Sir Thomas Cusack) the following year.[12]

Turning to an act closely connected with the Kildares and their rebellion, the following phrase titillates historical curiosity:

> It was thought that the said Sir Walter and James were partly ruled and counselled by the said Sir Walter and Jenet Eustace, then his wife, in all their traitors' purposes.

It is when familiar source-material is examined from a different perspective that a fresh historical problem demands attention. The marital status of women in sixteenth-century Ireland was closely bound up with property and dowry. Consequently the term 'wives' in the statutes assumes an autonomy not present a century later when plantation certificates eliminated much of the land-holding significance of a wife's position before the law. The Eustace women are a case in point and they are presented here as a sample that is capable of being tested in an examination of any number of womenfolk in the Pale married into or out of families such as the Dillons, Luttrels, Marwards, Taaffes, Dowdalls, Nettervilles, Cusacks, Aylmers, Delahydes, Barnewalls and a host of others bound to each other and to the Fitzgeralds by ties of marriage.

The Eustaces with the earls of Kildare and the Desmond Geraldines were active supporters of the Yorkist kings, Edward IV and Richard III, and though they accepted the Tudor Henry VII, they continued to support the Yorkist interest in Ireland. Alison, daughter of Roland Fitzeustace, Baron Portlester, became the wife of Gearóid Mór, eighth earl of Kildare. Lodge's *Peerage* bears quoting here as it artlessly reveals the network of marriage alliances engaged upon by the Pale families such as the Fitzgeralds and the Eustaces. Gearóid Mór, eighth earl of Kildare:

> married to his first wife, Alison, daughter and co-heir of Sir Roeland Eustace of Harristown, in the county of Kildare, baron of Portlester and by her, who died of grief 22 Nov 1495, during his confinement in England and was buried in the monastery founded by her father, he had Gerald his successor; and six daughters, Elinor, first married to Donald Mac Finin Mac Carthy Reagh, prince of Carbery: and secondly, to Calvagh O'Donnell lord of Tyrconnell and the whole county of Donegal; Margaret to Pierce, the eighth earl of Ormond; Elizabeth to Christopher Lord Slane, treasurer of Ireland, and by him who died 2 August 1517, had James Lord Slane who married the Lady Alice Fitzgerald his cousin – german, Alison, Eustachia and Joan, of whom there is no further mention than that one of them was married to Con Ó Neale, her first cousin, who, in 1480 was naturalized by Act of Parliament.

A nephew of the earl Gerald, Sir Maurice Fitzgerald, married Anne Eustace in 1519. We find Rose and Janet Eustace were members of the intimate family circle around the ninth earl and his son, Silken Thomas, in the final years before the rebellion. Much later Elizabeth I restored Jane Eustace, daughter of Sir Christopher Eustace and wife of Nicholas Taafe 'in blood and name to inherit as to any of her ancestor's lineal or collateral'. The Eustaces were one of the great families of fifteenth- and sixteenth-century Ireland and they flit in and out of the major conspiracies of those centuries. They were part of the Geraldine league to protect the young half-brother of Thomas from his pursuers after the latter's execution. Still later the Eustaces were implicated in the Baltinglass rising against Elizabeth I.[13]

One of the deficiencies in Irish legal scholarship is the paucity of information on issues concerning women's position in the holding of property at certain key periods. In sixteenth-century Ireland all the evidence points to the presence of wives as a sub-group holding property in their own right – a right that was gradually whittled away towards the end of the century by attainder, plantation schemes and by the exclusion of inheritance for women in the common law courts. Elizabeth I was generous in her endeavours to restore property to wives of attainted rebels:

> any land tenements or hereditaments with their appurtenances, that the wife … had in her own right in use, possession, reversion, remainder, or otherwise, in estate of inheritance, or to any land, tenements, or hereditaments with their appurtenances, that were ensured by any conveyance to his said wife, or to any to her use …[14]

There is every reason to support Kenneth Nicholls' view that marriage-contracts involving the exchange of property were central to sixteenth-century marriage alliances whether they were contracted in the Gaelic parts of the island or among the Pale families. They all had benefited from the dissolution of the monasteries. Whatever other characteristics Tudor marriages possessed, for the nobility of Ireland (and England) the business side of marriage was one of conveyancy, estate-management, inheritances and wardships. Married women of the nobility and gentry class administered large properties during the greater part of the century by way of widow's dower, by being co-heirs, and by marriage contracts. They also learned the ways of buying and selling property and became skilled in the ways of executing deeds of settlement and trusteeship.[15]

But they lost steadily throughout the century despite the goodwill of Elizabeth I. They lost to the new plantation schemes in the harsh atmosphere of the common law courts. Gradually by the end of the sixteenth century dowry as marriage goods was in the ascendancy. For example, in the marriage articles of Murrough O'Brien, baron of Inchiquin and Mabel, daughter of Christopher, baron of Delvin, the following style was adopted. The date was 25 June 1591:

> Lord Delvin binds himself to Lord Inchiquin 'in marriage goods with the said Sir Christopher's daugher Mabill Nugent, whome by the grace of God the said Muraghe shall marrye ... fyve hundrethe pondes sterlinge curante money of England'.
>
> On his side Lord Inchiquin agrees, in case he dies before begetting issue male by the said Mabill, to leave her a jointure of £100, made up out of his lands held in fee simple.
>
> (*Apud* Nugent Papers, Nugent Registry, p. 9)

In the original paper which I presented to the Dublin Historical Association entitled 'To Marry or Not to Marry: Wives, Nuns and Tradeswomen in Sixteenth-Century Ireland' I explored facets of the position of women before and after the reformation. One question I raised in the paper was that of divorce Irish-style at a time when Henry VIII was dissolving his own marriages with the rapidity of a conjuring trick. Henry VIII always went for the process of nullity and procured annulments. During his reign in England divorce remained a matter for the spiritual powers rather than the temporal courts and the church courts were brought directly under royal control.[16] Moreover the 'Act in restraint of appeals' both in the English reformation parliament and the subsequent Irish parliament decreed that all appeals concerning matters which were normally heard in church courts were to be determined within the realm of England and not in Rome. The Irish statute runs thus:

... instead they shall have, take or use from the first day of this present parliament, their provocations, appeals and such like process to the king of England and lord of Ireland, his heirs and successors or to his or their lieutenant, deputy, justice or other governaur ... to his or their court of chaunceries within the same realme of England or land of Ireland and the Chancellor of England, or Keeper of the Great Seal for the time being, shall grant a commission or delegacy to some discreet and well learned person of this land of Ireland or else of England ... for the final determination of all cause and griefs, contained in the said provocations and appeals ...[17]

In Ireland it is clear from the legislation that follows and from the 'great volumes of chancery findings' which Kenneth Nicholls mentions that the court of chancery played a major role in transforming the legal and land system of Ireland in the sixteenth and seventeenth centuries. (The question which an investigation of divorce in the middle decades of the sixteenth century raises is in the nature of an historical 'whodunnit'). Did the court of chancery, and in particular the chancellor, undertake the dissolution of marriages in the Pale between the reformation legislation and the setting up of the ecclesiastical courts that accompanied the Elizabethan settlement in those areas which were sympathetic to the reformation?[18] During the period, about twenty years, the ecclesiastical law ceased to be the canon law of the medieval universal church and became incorporated into the law of the monarch as head of the church. As such, matrimonial law was to be treated by the ecclesiastical courts of the Church of England, and presumably by the Church of Ireland. Both the Act of Appeals and the Act of Faculties directed that appeals and dispensations no longer go to Rome but instead that the 'granting be given for the time being to the archbishop of Canterbury', adding that they must be enrolled in chancery. A further rider directed that 'the chancellor of this land and all persons appointed by this act to have the same authority as the chancellor of England'.[19]

Then who was the final ecclesiastical authority in Ireland? Henry VIII had encouraged doctors of civil law to take over the functions of the ecclesiastical lawyers, in particular the clerical canonists, and in practice civilians presided over the church courts. The exact extent of the transition is still not clear but the evidence points to a subordination of the church courts to the law of the land. Is it then tenable to suggest that in Ireland the chancellor exercised a quasi-ecclesiastical role in determining appeals which were normally heard in church courts, even matters such as judicial separation leading to re-marriage? Occasionally the career of an administrator describes the function of his office and Sir Thomas Cusack merits closer scrutiny than he has received from Tudor historians.[20]

Sir Thomas Cusack was the eldest son of John Cusack of Cushinstown. His mother was Alison Wellesley. In 1522 he was admitted to the Inner Temple to study law. In 1533 Thomas Cromwell bestowed on him the office of chancellor of the Irish exchequer. The following year he was appointed second justice of the common bench. Thereafter his promotion was rapid. As M.P. for Meath, he assisted in the preparation of legislation both for the dissolution of the monasteries and the king's supremacy in the church during the Irish reformation parliament. He became successively speaker of the Irish house of commons, master of the rolls (1542) and keeper of the great seal. Personally known to the Tudor monarchs, he was appointed lord chancellor of Ireland in 1550 and though active in promoting the reformation, Queen

Mary retained him in office. Elizabeth, too, was favourably disposed to him and, though she did not re-appoint him, he remained an influential member of the Irish privy council until his death in 1571. In the matter of divorce his presence was discreet, indeed intangible, and were it not for the evidence of chancery decrees, he would remain unnoticed. Surprisingly for a man who possessed large properties as a result of the dissolution of the monasteries, he died poor and was habitually in debt during his life.

One of the really tantalising problems in the period is chasing the effects on a property-conscious landed class on the fluid situation occasioned by the legislation of the Irish parliament concerning marriage and divorce which accompanied that of the dissolution of the monasteries – and endeavouring to gauge the time-lag before taxation and due process of ecclesiastical law caught up with them! Unlike England there appeared in Ireland with increasing visibility by the second decade of Elizabeth's reign a landed gentry, swollen by their augmentations of monastic lands, who dithered between the competing claims of the protestant Tudor reformation and the catholic counter-reformation.

With Martin Luther's treatise, *Concerning Married Life* (1522) the reformation theology of marriage was developed. Marriage according to Luther is ordained by God and is a *bonum,* a good, a 'school for character'. The home became, above all, the area for the exemplification and cultivation of the meek christian virtues: love and tenderness, sharing of goods, humility, reconciliation and the bearing of one another's burdens. Each of the major reforms developed its own doctrine of marriage. *The Book of Common Prayer,* 1552 (Cranmer's second edition), with its beautiful marriage ritual gave to the Church of England, and that of Ireland, a spiritual legacy which had and continues to have a strong impact on the social order. Its rite of marriage accepted the holiness of marriage and linked marriage with liturgy rather than sacrament. Thus 'marriage in the face of the church' or solemnisation of marriage was insisted upon as a means of bringing marriage under the authority of the monarch as head of the church and eventually much later, of the state. Nevertheless clandestine marriage remained popular with the laity until 1753 when the British parliament outlawed the practice.

'The reformation' remarks Dr Schillebeckx, 'compelled the Council of Trent to go thoroughly into the question of marriage'.[21] The Council of Trent recognized the sacramental nature of marriage as one of the seven sacraments. It confirmed the indissolubility of the contract of monogamous marriages and asserted the church's right to define the impediments that made a marriage invalid. The introduction of an ecclesiastical form as the normally valid form of the marriage contract had far-reaching consequences. This was the famous *Tametsi* decree of 1563 in the closing session of the Council of Trent. It decreed that a marriage between baptized christians was from then onwards to be regarded as valid only if it had been contracted in the presence of the parish priest (or priest authorised by him) and in the presence of at least two witnesses. 'The main purpose of the priest's intervention and of the church's solemnisation of marriage in public *(in facie ecclesiae)* was to ensure control of the impediments to marriage' concludes Dr Schillebeckx in his study of marriage in the history of the church.

Motivated by pastoral concerns the Council of Trent's purpose was to remove the dangers of clandestine marriage by insisting on the publication of the banns of marriage and the registration of contracted marriages in the church records. The Council of Trent, then, refined the juridical apparatus of the catholic church and defined explicitly its doctrinal and legal position on marriage. Its decrees gave the local bishop within the diocese a power of jurisdiction reflected in the re-vitalisation of diocesan marriage tribunals. On the continent diocesan tribunals to examine marriage cases and dispense separations or decrees of nullity began to function as early as the late 1550s; the diocese of Constance near Freiburg in Germany was a prime example.[22] In Ireland because of the political situation and the imposition of a penal code in the following centuries, marriage tribunals as part of the normal functioning of the catholic post-Tridentine diocese did not come into effect, and for the remainder of the sixteenth century in Ireland marriage remained problematic both as to its solemnisation and to the enforcement of correct procedures for dispensations and annulment.

Elizabeth I took her position seriously as head of the Anglican church. For the Tudors religious orthodoxy was as much part of their church policy as was uniformity. The same year that the Council of Trent drew up its *Tametsi* decree, Elizabeth caused the Thirty Nine Articles to be promulgated and the *Book of Common Prayer* was re-affirmed in its usage. It was no accident that she brought the consanguinity regulations into line with christian practice in Europe even as she, too, like her sister Mary, repealed the 1541 'An Act for marriage' with its obscure inconsistencies concerning divorce. Henceforth the ecclesiastical model of marriage was the chosen alternative to clandestine and secular marriages.

Customs die hard in Ireland. The inability of the post-Tridentine catholic church and the Church of Ireland alike to ensure the registration of marriages delayed reform. For decades to come endogamous secular marriages remained acceptable to the Irish laity. Thirty four years into the new century Wentworth writing confidentially to Archbishop Laud made the following observation:

They are accustomed here to have all their christenings and marriages in their private houses, and which is odd they never marry till after supper and so to bed ... This breeds a great mischief in the Commonwealth which is seen in this – that because these rites of the Church are not solemnised in the Public and open Assemblies, there is nothing so common as for a man to deny his wife and children, abandoning the former and betaking himself to a new task. I conceive it were fit these particulars should be reduced to the Custom of England.[23]

By the time of Lord Deputy Wentworth a new factor had entered the marriage scene in Ireland, brought to these shores by the planter and legislated against by Wentworth in the 1634 parliament – bigamy, thus shifting the emphasis to a much broader segment of society than we have examined in sixteenth-century Ireland.

from Art Cosgrove (ed.), *Marriage in Ireland* (Dublin, College Press, 1985), pp 51–66.

NOTES
1   Brendan Bradshaw, *The Dissolution of the Religious Orders in Ireland Under Henry VIII* (London and New York, Cambridge University Press, 1974); *The Irish Constitutional Revolution of the Sixteenth Century* (Cambridge and New York, Cambridge University Press 1979).

2   The citation of the Tudor acts of the Irish parliament which I have grouped and quoted from are taken from *The Statutes at Large, Passed in the Parliaments Held in Ireland* (Dublin, printed by B. Grierson, printer to the King's Most Excellent Majesty, 1786–1801). Eighteenth-century parliamentary sources on Tudor Ireland supply many missing clues.

3   A. F. Pollard, *Henry VIII* (London, Longmans, Green and Co., 1905), p. 187. For an excellent analysis of the impediments cf J. J. Scarisbrick, *Henry VIII* (London, Eyre and Spottiswoode, 1968), pp 163–97.

4   Ralph Houlbrooke, *Church Courts and the People during the English Reformation* (Oxford and New York, Oxford University Press, 1979), pp 66, 72.

5   *Stat. Ire.,* i, 277.

6   *Ibid.,* 78–79.

7   *Ibid.,* 181–83.

8   K. W. Nicholls, *Gaelic and Gaelicised Ireland in the Middle Ages* (Dublin, Gill and Macmillan, 1972), pp 73–77.

9   *Stat. Ire.,* i, 179–80.

10 John Lodge, *The Peerage of Ireland,* revised, enlarged, and continued to the present time by Mervyn Archdall (Dublin, J. Moore, 1789), 7 Vols. Indispensable as a starting-point for basic structures of Tudor family history.

11 Brendan Bradshaw, 'Cromwellian Reform and the Origins of the Kildare Rebellion, 1533–34', *Transactions of the Royal Historical Society,* 5th series, Vol. 27 (1977), pp 69–73.

12 H. Gallwey, 'The Cusack family of Counties Meath and Dublin', *The Irish Genealogist,* V (1979–80), pp 591–600.

13 J. Kingston, 'Catholic families of the Pale', *Repertorium Novum,* Vol. 2, No. 2 (1959–60), pp 245–56.

14 *Stat. Ire.,* i, 375. For a similar concession to the wife of the attainted White Knight, *ibid.,* p. 388.

15 K. W. Nicholls, 'Some Documents on Irish Law and Custom in the Sixteenth Century', *Analecta Hibernica,* Vol. XXVI (1970), pp 103–29.

16 Houlbrooke, *op. cit.,* pp 65–72.

17 *Stat. Ire.,* i, 146–47.

18 I am indebted to Dr Art Cosgrove for drawing my attention to Cardinal Pole's dispensations, in his capacity as legate (1555–6) to couples who were married within the forbidden degrees 'at the time of the schism'. (TCD MS 557, xiii, 71–75).

19 *Stat. Ire.,* i, 91–93.

20 F. Erlington Ball, *The Judges in Ireland, 1221–1921* (London, John Murray, 1926), I, pp 200–02.

21 Edward Schillebeeckx, *Marriage, Secular Reality and Saving Mystery* (London, Sheed and Ward, 1965), II, 168ff.

22 T. M. Safley, 'Marital Litigation in the Diocese of Constance, 1551–1620', *The Sixteenth Century Journal,* Vol. XII, No. 2 (1981), pp 61–77.

23 Wentworth to Laud, 31 January 1633/4 (Letter Book 6, Strafford MSS in Sheffield Public Library, p. 20). My thanks to Nuala Murphy who retrieved this extract for me.

In the mid-1980s women's studies moved from the periphery of the women's movement to the centre as the main provider of theory and research into feminist issues. It was tempting for women's history to take a satellite position in the range of subjects that constituted the core of women's studies, and women historians were prepared to teach history as a component of women's studies and to direct research at post-graduate level. However the goal of integrating the new discipline of women's history with mainstream surveys of history was still perceived in the early eighties as an attainable objective in the near future, so women historians were stretched to the utmost limits in meeting competing demands. It was a time of great energy, and women's publishing houses, Arlen House, Irish Feminist Information, Women's Community Press, Attic Press and Women's Education Bureau facilitated the spread of ideas by publishing women's research and creative writings; all this at a time when the country was racked with radical, and at times extreme ideological and religious divisions.

'Moving Statues' was a curious episode that subsequently found its own niche in the cultural and religious topography of the 1980s. Sightings of statues of the Blessed Virgin Mother, swaying and changing appearance, in rural grottoes countrywide were reported throughout the summer and early autumn of 1985, and drew large crowds to view the paranormal occurrences. A paradigm of traditional catholic piety was shifting, and a familiar system of catholic representation, the Marian wayside shrine, became the vehicle for interpreting the moral anxiety that engulfed catholic believers in the aftermath of the angry exchanges that accompanied the 1983 Eighth Amendment to the Constitution. Dubbed 'the war of the womb' the referendum

required citizens to vote on protecting the unborn life of the child by enshrining a clause to that effect in the Constitution amidst acrimonious debates.

The essay originated in an interdisciplinary seminar organized by the Women's Studies Forum in University College Dublin towards the end of 1985. It was published in Studies *special issue,* Woman Alive! *(1987).*

Introduction

It rained all through the summer and early autumn of 1985, and the statues moved at Ballinspittle, Mount Mellery, Asdee, Ballydesmond, Courtmacsherry, and over thirty small Marian shrines in different parts of the country. There were reports of moving or speaking statues, ones that showed visions of heavenly light during that untowardly long spell of unceasing rain in July, August and September. By October the statues had become stationary again and the coach firms, the burger vans, the temporary benches and car parks around the grottoes gradually disappeared.

What was the spirit saying to the Irish catholic church? Can it even be assumed that the Spirit of God was speaking through a series of events? A number of journalists, some theologians and churchmen, and a group of psychologists gave the subject serious attention. The media, both Irish and British, including a remarkable photo-book taken during the last week in August, *Ireland: A Week In the Life of a Nation* (Saunders and Shelton, 1986), covered the crowds at the different shrines intent on encapsulating the out-of-the-ordinary. Canon Denis O'Callaghan, parish priest of Mallow and former professor of moral theology at Maynooth College, addressed audiences on the subject, neither dismissing the crowds' eyewitness accounts superciliously nor yielding to any pressures to sanction their alleged authenticity.

The observers from the Applied Psychology Department of University College Cork offered a substantial explanation at the phenomenological level. They claimed in relation to the Ballinspittle statue of the Blessed Virgin (which attracted unusually large crowds during the night hours) that it was a problem of eye focus where the onlookers were unable to fix a bright object against a dark background. Staring at the statue fixedly gave the onlooker the experience of seeing it shimmering or moving backwards and forwards. This mass experience they termed the 'Ballinspittle syndrome', but they did not address the question why the power of the imagination to form such images occurred just then.

What the Journalists Thought

Journalists probed the reality of the phenomenon with acuity. Some had attended the gatherings as spectators in Ballinspittle or elsewhere, writing for newspapers and periodicals throughout Ireland and Britain. Colm Tóibín, at the time a freelance journalist, assembled in book form the impressions of a group of journalists and invited other writers to contribute by analysing what was occurring on a cultural level to draw some inferences. Of the four women who contributed to the book *Seeing is Believing* (1985), two, June Levine and Isabel Healy, had gone to Ballinspittle and they narrate the effect on the bystanders and on themselves of the moving, five-foot-eight statue of Mary, placed high up above the road. The other two women, Mary Holland and Nell McCafferty did not visit the shrine. In their contributions they endeavour to situate the reported sightings of the statues within the context of female experience in Ireland in recent years. For Nell McCafferty the moving statues of the Virgin Mary were symptomatic of 'the desolate situation of Irish women'. In Mary Holland's estimation: 'The crowds at Ballinspittle are a salutary reminder of how divided our society has become'. With the trained ears of sensitive journalists they sensed that the occurrences were in a subliminal way connected with issues that affected women's lives in the area of what Nell McCafferty termed 'the war of the womb'. Both referred to the aftermath of the 1983 Eighth Amendment to the Constitution, the incorrectly-styled Abortion Referendum. Both listed a series of tragic incidents connected with unwanted pregnancies, singling out the Kerry Babies Tribunal, which had occupied the media for months in 1985, as an example of the public humiliation that women in this country had to undergo. Both situated the moving statues of Mary in the context of female oppression in Ireland. For Nell McCafferty the occurrences were a predictable superstitious reaction; for Mary Holland:

> The crowds at Ballinspittle dramatise the problem facing the Church ... for the yearning after the old certainties goes beyond religious practice to reflect an unease with the quality of life in Ireland and with a society which, it now seems to many people, has failed them materially as well as spiritually.[1]

The stranger to Irish politics could well suppose that in the mid-eighties our society was traumatised around women's issues, and that large sections of that society were caught between the competing claims of catholic morality and secular modernisation of our civil legislation in the areas of birth-control, illegitimacy, marriage and divorce.

Not the Full Explanation

For other contributors to *Seeing is Believing*, explanation of the phenomena went wider. Notably in the essay by folklorist Dáithí Ó hÓgáin, 'A Manifestation of Popular Religion', there is an effort to place the sightings in the context of iconophily. He reminds the readers of the role statues have played in pre-christian culture and traditions as heroic images, as representations of deity, as oracles that spoke or moved. After the death of Christ, the place of Mary in iconography of the mother-symbol, and the almost sacred character of the Icon and the 'Luke' portraits were firmly established in western religious consciousness. Parallel to the statues, in pagan and christian memory, was the notion of prodigies, signs, portents foretelling disaster, signs associated with the Apocalypse of John, indicating a popular perception of some approaching catastrophe. Because of the historical circumstances, statues in Ireland were a fairly recent introduction in catholic worship associated with the building of churches from the mid-nineteenth century onwards, thus the phenomenon of moving statues, well-documented in western European religious history, is not familiar to the Irish psyche. Ó hÓgáin concludes his observations by noting:

> It would seem to be of far greater value if we searched for the underlying causes which lead people to notice such things at some times and places rather than others.[2]

Something certainly happened at the level of religious and psychological experience in Ballinspittle and found a response in men as well as women. Even if it can be decided that it was the imagination playing tricks on the crowds that gathered nightly, such an acknowledgement – that the imagination of hundreds of people was exploding in tantric or semi-magical images – allows us to comment on the event in a less dismissive way than if we approached it with an uncompromisingly scientific explanation. After all, the episodes were communal events, and many people who came there experienced simultaneously a sensation of a Marian statue swaying or dissolving into other images, such as St Joseph, Padre Pio – for June Levine, a young rabbi. Not everyone was bewitched; but those who went realized that the social happening they witnessed had a significance that so far has defied a totally satisfactory analysis. To explain away the phenomenon in terms of a diagnosis consonant with 'normal' secular views of mental health is to miss the nuances. Some kind of fuse ignited the imagination around an object of popular devotion during those weeks, and there occurred a disjunction of spiritual vision, or a suspension of conventional faith. It took place in the context of lay devotion. No catholic rituals, no masses, no official presence of Church authorities occurred at the grottoes. The statues that moved were of Mary, a woman, in a year that had not been kind to Irish women.

My purpose in the following pages is to follow the line of investigation opened by the women journalists and to examine what has been happening to the spirituality of Irishwomen as they encountered the challenge of secularisation and feminism.

Irishwomen in the 1980s

In 1969 the women's movement was entering consciousness all over the world. In Dublin a number of women met regularly in a support group whose goal was to launch the movement upon a society more open, more liberal than at any previous period in the twentieth century.[3] The 1960s had been a buoyant, optimistic decade in Ireland, north and south. The closing of the

Second Vatican Council in 1965 with its call for *aggiornamento,* had released spiritual energies among priests, laity, and religious women and men. The catholic church was seen to be part of the contemporary world. The weekly radio discussions of Seán Mac Réamoinn from Rome and the television exposure of large sections of Irish society to the minds of the world's finest theologians contributed to a new awareness among Irish people. Irish society was about to take its place among the member-states of the European Economic Community and it was to face, among other challenges, the hitherto unknown one of secularisation.

For many Irish catholics there was perplexity. To a society as highly sacramentalised as the catholic Irish new demands of vernacular liturgy resulting from a changed model of Church caused bewilderment. There was a sense of loss which affected devotional practice and religious observance alike. It is in this period that Professor J. A. Murphy, a specialist in twentieth-century Irish history, perceives 'a collapse of the kind of solid catholic church-going practices that were there up to 1960 or so'.[4]

The women's movement inserted an added tension into the Irish woman's faith-life. The splendid mutterings of the Latin Mass became the vernacular whose language was, to ears sensitized by consciousness-raising exercises, disconcertingly sexist. Confession was, throughout the 1970s, supplanted by the therapies – gestalt, co-counselling, psychosynthesis – and never regained its old ascendancy. As the decade moved on, the catholic church in Ireland began to be considered by groups of women, religious as well as lay, as unattractively male-dominated. Two alternatives presented themselves to women: they closed ranks around the Church they loved and clung to their familiar devotional practices; or they embraced the ideology of the women's movement wholeheartedly, and identified with feminism.

The Search for Feminist Spirituality

In her 1985 *Studies* article 'Secularization: A Healing Process', Ursula Coleman examines the effects of dualistic thinking upon our experience of the sacred and the secular, sealing them off from each other. She applies her methodology to the women's movement in contemporary Ireland and arrives at the conclusion that feminism is, at this point in time, perceived to be opposed to religion because it is identified with secular philosophy. She traces the growing polarisation which has occurred since our membership of the European Community. There is a better deal for women in paid employment, social welfare, equal work opportunity but, she adds:

> In the really contentious issues ... the discussions relating to contraception, sex education, unwanted pregnancies, pre-marital sex, the abortion trail to England, the need for civil divorce, Irish people have divided.

As she views it the women's movement has become part of that divide, finding itself at odds with the catholic church. 'It was seen to be waging war against what was sacred. The response, therefore, was a defensive one. The catholic church and the women's movement became enemies'.[5] Thus the 1983 referendum was a watershed in attitudes which polarised women among themselves.

Feminism is more than the women's movement, however: it is a way of interpreting life and it has a protean quality in its diversities. There is a radical agnostic, even atheistic feminism which rebels against male authoritarian structures and, unable to contain the critique from within the institution, forces the feminist to leave; or, as Hanna Sheehy Skeffington once declared, 'to read or think oneself out of the Church is a hazard of being a feminist'.

Feminism is also a 'therapy of the soul', to borrow a phrase from James Hillmann, the psychoanalyst, and as such he insists 'it tends to ignore that gender question'. He sees feminism as a structure of consciousness, and like the ecology movement it has much to offer in perceptive insights. The soul, he argues, does not know whether it is rich or poor, learned or ignorant, male or female.[6] Feminism thus understood pertains to men as well as to women and it offers profound insights to the contemporary church in its self–understanding of liberation.

Many Irish women who have left the devotional practices of their youth are now genuinely seeking a spirituality that meets both their search for a god who is not patriarchal, and for a continuing revelation of god's presence in the world not in opposition to past traditions but evolving out of them. In Ireland it is to Celtic models that the feminist search is turning more and more. One such model has been studied as a Leaving Certificate textbook by thousands of Irish women, unaware that in the person and autobiography of Peig Sayers there are to be found clues that lead into the heart of Celtic spirituality, and supply an agenda for becoming a free spirit.

The Faith-world of an Irishwoman
Broadly speaking the religious experience of Irish women is uncharted territory. It may be discovered in diaries, letters, recorded conversations if researched carefully, and it appears in the occasional autobiography

that spans the century between 1870 and 1970, frontier decades for Irish women in their long stride towards self-awareness. 1878 bestowed on them the Intermediate Certificate; 1973 gave them entry into the equality of the European Community.

Following a tentative methodology, I shall endeavour to discover the faith-worlds of the Irish rural woman using whatever personal sources are at hand. Peig Sayers (1873–1958), in her autobiography and her subsequent *Reflections of an Old Woman,* gives us glimpses of the spiritual resources on which she drew, when as a young bride she came from the mainland to live on the large Blasket Island off the Dingle peninsula. It was an Irish-speaking world and she lived on that rocky island for over forty years of the twentieth century as wife, mother and neighbour in a community which her own testimony has rendered famous. For Peig Sayers, her encounter with the supernatural was one in which she sharply differentiated her superstitious world of ghosts and spirits, of which she was a supreme story-teller, from the central mysterious path of her life. For Peig the significant guideline of her actions was always 'whatever God has destined for me, I will receive it': this as a young thirteen-year-old parting from her beloved mother for nearly three years. The note is clearer in the incident of her son's fatal fall from the cliff. Unable to leave the house because of her sick husband, she cannot accompany the boats in their search for the body:

> It was they who were surprised when they found where he was, not hundreds of yards out to sea but high up on a smooth ledge, his exact size, and he was laid out as quiet and composed as if twelve women had taken charge. No living person knew he had happened on that ledge with the blue sea all around. No one but God alone.[7]

Peig's deepest conviction that she was 'a bauble in the hands of the Maiden and her Son' is reminiscent of Teresa of Avila, and another of her sayings is biblical: 'God always opens a gap of support'. When her son, Micheál, is going to the USA she enjoins on him: 'Let nothing cross you that would diminish the love of God in your heart'. Her faith in Mary's powers of intercession with her son was unshakeable; her identification with the Sorrowful Mother complete. She lost four children and her husband before middle-age:

> I remember bending to my work with my heart breaking. I used to think of Mary and the Lord – the hard life they had. I knew I had a duty to imitate them and bear my sorrow patiently.

Celtic Spirituality

Peig Sayers' God was pre-eminently the spirit who infuses nature: she had an intense sense of the presence of God. Her favourite form of refreshing her own spirit was to be by herself looking over the harbour out to sea on a clear day, enjoying the waters that so often claimed the lives of the fishermen. This facility in contemplating God in nature is the essence of Celtic spirituality which John Macquarrie describes thus:

> The sense of God's immanence in his creation was so strong in Celtic spirituality as to amount almost to a pantheism ... But perusal of typical Celtic poems and prayers makes it clear that God's presence was even more keenly felt in the daily round of human tasks and at the important junctures of life. Getting up, kindling the fire, going to work, going to bed, as well as birth, marriage, settling in a new house, death, were occasions for recognizing the presence of God.[8]

On reading her autobiography the reader is left with a sense of a human being who has succeeded in integrating the different strands of her life in a meaningful way. Her ability to observe her own grief and to describe herself and the way of life on the Great Blasket was truly remarkable. She was esteemed by the other islanders for her neighbourliness and for her capacity to enjoy good company and laughter. Her sense of Heaven was that of the conviviality of friends gathered, talking together and telling stories; her concept of God as final judge daringly familiar: he was *An Rógaire*, The Rogue. There is a tenth-century poem called 'St Brigid's Heaven', translated by Seán Ó Faoláin in *The Silver Branch,* which finds echoes in many of Peig's reflections and epigrams:

> I would like to have the men of Heaven
> In my own house;
> With vats of good cheer
> Laid out for them ...
> I would like a great lake of beer
> For the King of Kings.
> I would like to be watching Heaven's family
> Drinking it through all eternity.[9]

Peig Sayers' life, like that of many country women, was of necessity one removed from church-going, frequency of mass and sacrament and from the hearing of sermons. Like her neighbours she lived, when times were bad, in poverty and frugality of food. What, then has she to offer the town-dweller in the way of getting 'to know God'?

The answer is in her life, written and lived. There is a sense in which the quest for feminist spirituality must veer towards the side of the oppressed and the poor if we want to find God. The world of the late-twentieth century, including Ireland, is one of structural conflict in which keeping large masses of people poor is the key element. Women and children suffer grievously in such circumstances. For women there is a growing recognition that the issue of oppression will not go away, has not disappeared, and needs to be confronted daily.

If Peig Sayers on her rocky island has any spiritual meaning for the contemporary Irish woman, it is about finding a knowledge of oneself that comes from within the soul and within the culture, one which steels the will and detaches the spirit from all sentimentality. To be a kindly neighbour sharing house and bread, to be steadfast in the face of loss as great as hers, to remain true to her roots which she discerned had to do with her essential identity, and to add to that, serene old age, and the reputation of being the best storyteller in Ireland: what more salutary antidote to a moving statue could there be than the spirituality of Peig Sayers?

from 'Woman Alive!' themed issue of *Studies*, Vol. 76, No. 302, Summer 1987, pp 139–147.

NOTES

1   Mary Holland, 'Ballinspittle and the Bishops' Dilemma', pp 45–8; Nell McCafferty; 'Virgin on the Rocks', pp 53–8, in Colm Tóibín (ed.), *Seeing is Believing* (Dublin, Pilgrim Press, 1985).

2   Dáithí Ó hÓgáin, 'A Manifestation of Popular Religion in Ireland', *loc. cit.*, pp 66–74.

3   The best account of the early years of the women's movement in Ireland is in June Levine, *Sisters* (Dublin, Ward River Press, 1982).

4   J. A. Murphy, 'What it means to be Irish', *Boston College Magazine,* Vol. XLIV, No 3, 1989, p. 23.

5   Ursula Coleman, 'Secularization: a Healing Process', *Studies*, Vol. 74, No. 293 (Spring 1985), pp 26, 30–3.

6   James Hillman and Laura Pozzo, *Inter Views: Conversations with Laura Pozzo* (London, Harper Books, 1984), pp 70–4. I am indebted to Monica Cullinan for drawing my attention to Hillman's insight.

7   Máire Ní Chinnéide (ed.), *Peig* (Baile Átha Cliath, Comhlacht Oideachais na h-Éireann, 1935), translated by the editor; cf. Bryan MacMahon (trans.), *Peig, The Autobiography of Peig Sayers of the Great Blasket Island* (Dublin, Talbot Press, 1973).

8   John Macquarrie, *Paths in Spirituality*, quoted in Michael Maher (ed.) *Celtic Spirituality* (Dublin, Veritas, 1981), p. 7.

9   W. R. Rogers, 'Introduction', p. XII, in his edition of Peig Sayers, *An Old Woman's Reflections* (Oxford and New York, Oxford University Press, 1978).

FULLNESS OF LIFE:
DEFINING FEMALE SPIRITUALITY
IN TWENTIETH-CENTURY IRELAND

This study was my contribution to a book of essays with a general theme of ways that women in Ireland survived in the nineteenth and twentieth centuries. The editors, Maria Luddy and Cliona Murphy, both trained scholars in the field of women's history, invited a group of professional women historians to offer from their current interests and research an essay on the theme, 'women surviving' examining the situation of women 'living and working amid all the complexities that make up Irish life' in the nineteenth and twentieth centuries. Wherever possible, the editors suggested, an original rather than a conventional topic might be chosen. Women Surviving: Studies in Irish Women's History in the 19th and 20th centuries *was an important publication marking a new stage in the writing of women's history in Ireland. Its bold, provocative introduction set the tone for future discussions on the theory and practice of writing about women in Ireland. The editors' critique of the canon of Irish history was humorous and hard-hitting and their alternative periodisation, one appropriate to social history, gave fresh dimensions to the familiar political contours of nineteenth-century Ireland. They raised the issue of gender history then beginning to assert its presence as a more satisfying way of studying the relationship of men and women in history, but Luddy and Murphy came down firmly on the merits of researching women's history as integral to a new history of Ireland.*

In offering a study of the spirituality of two remarkable, though arguably invisible, women whose lives overlapped in the first half of the twentieth century, I was attracted to the comparative model in which I could identify points of comparison and contrast. The underlying structure of the study was the tracing of life-cycles, a theme popular at that time in the social sciences. The life of Peig Sayers on a rocky, isolated island off the coast of the Dingle peninsula in County Kerry lent itself to a scrutiny of her youth, middle years and old age since she had extensive written and oral records as a noted story-teller. Edel Quinn's battle against tuberculosis in her twenties led her to 'invent' a life-cycle that brought her to a fulfilled and adventurous life in East Africa and public recognition of her role there as a lay missionary.

The essay appeared in Maria Luddy and Cliona Murphy (eds), Women Surviving: Studies in Irish's Women's History in the 19th and 20th Centuries *(Dublin, Poolbeg Press, 1989).*

If one were to speculate on the titles of the three or four most influential books that helped to shape the intellectual mind of Irish catholic women in the final quarter of the nineteenth century, it might well prove a baffling and fruitless endeavour to arrive at the merest consensus. However, if one were to change the terms of reference and the geographical base, altering the emphasis from 'intellectual' to 'spiritual', then few would contest the mainstream influence of the Child of Mary manual, that sober guidebook to the spiritual life of the young catholic sodalist on admittance to the Confraternity of the Child of Mary. Wherever Jesuit-inspired schools at secondary level developed throughout western Europe, including Great Britain and Ireland, the initiation into, and practice of the Sodality, usually referred to as the E. de M. *(Enfant de Marie)*, or the 'Blue Ribbon' signified a mid-adolescent rite of passage into a position of leadership and responsibility in the upper school. Admittance to the ranks of the Sodality conveyed an aura of dignity and conferred status, even privilege, on a class educated into middle-class virtue. It was a serious consideration for a young person to accept the rules of the Sodality and be bound by its simple requirements, to live a chaste life and to perform its daily obligation of prayer.[1]

Equally daunting, as we learn from the young James Joyce, was the challenge of rejecting it and of accepting the consequences that followed the internal conflict set up by such a rejection.[2] It was not so much that the Sodalist became a member of an elite group in the school community and often combined its duties with those of a prefect. For the Sodalist the touchstone of its membership was perceived to lie in its invitation to personal holiness at a period of life when young adolescents were making choices around their future, and with the help of the spiritual director of the Sodality, discerning vocations to the priesthood or to religious life.

For the catholic girl, reception into the Sodality gave an added impetus to the deeply-rooted French traditions of girls' education, a tradition which regarded the societal role of the young girl to be within the family as daughter, wife and mother. Sissy O'Brien, in *The Farm by Lough Gur*, describes the experience with artless candour. Born in 1858, Sissy was about fifteen years of age when the event she narrates took place in her convent boarding-school belonging to the French Order of nuns, the Faithful Companions of Jesus, at Bruff, County Limerick:[3]

> In my third year I became a Child of Mary. I was promoted to the highest table. I was allowed to give lessons on Sundays in the Poor School at the Convent gate. I slept in the Immaculate Conception dormitory,

which had a small chapel at one end. In school I was in the highest form but I was still diffident, mistrustful of myself. Little was done by our teachers to encourage self-reliance and independence ... our timorous outlook was intensified to such an extent that several of my schoolfellows chose to become nuns rather than face the danger and evil of life outside the convent No direct effort was made to persuade the pupils to make this choice, certainly nothing was ever said to me, and though I was wholeheartedly religious, I had no wish to be a nun.

Sissy grew up to become the sensible, intelligent woman who married her neighbour, Richard Fogarty, a prosperous young farmer. Years later she gave Mary Carbery the memories of a farming childhood beside Lough Gur and unself-consciously produced a classic.

Increasingly over the last decade historians have suggested that religious practice in Ireland began to move from a populist, peasant-based native style towards a more disciplined and churchly observance in which there were gains and losses. The change accompanied the Great Famine, 1846–52, which in turn hastened the transition to town-based religious observances. Holy well patterns, wake customs and the superstitious rituals described by Sissy O'Brien disappeared. They were replaced by the new Roman devotions such as Benediction of the Blessed Sacrament, the Christmas Crib, and the annual mission given in the church by a visiting Redemptorist or Vincentian preacher. The laity were encouraged to make devotional visits to the Blessed Sacrament in the parish church. After the Famine, particularly during the period of Cardinal Paul Cullen's ministry as archbishop of Dublin (1852–78), the catholic church gained ascendancy over the minds of its flock. Devotions, more precisely 'imported' devotions, became the familiar vehicle of prayer for the church-goer. In 1878 Ireland was formally consecrated to the Sacred Heart and to the older seventeenth-century devotion was added that of the Nine Fridays with the obligation of confession of sins followed by reception of Holy Communion and attendance at Mass on the first Friday of the month for nine consecutive months. The church-going laity devoutly made the Way of the Cross hung in fourteen pictorial representations along the walls of late Victorian churches and the chapels of boarding schools. The black-covered prayer book appeared, a sign of rising literacy. An anthology of prayers for all occasions, it was packed with invocations to continental saints. The Marian cult had deepened following the Apparitions of the Virgin Mary at Lourdes in the south of France in 1858. The Knock, county Mayo Apparition, 1879, added an Irish gloss to the yearly round of feast-days and May-day processions in catholic schools.[4]

By the death of Cardinal Cullen in 1878, the fundamental changes in Irish society which made its general tone more 'bourgeois' had taken place. For the catholic population the dominant spirituality sprang from the middle class. It was town-based and centred on the 'chapel'. Convent schools for girls reflected these trends. Anne V. O'Connor in an essay 'The Revolution in Girls' Secondary Education in Ireland, 1860–1910' remarks:[5]

> The emphasis placed by many Irish convents on politeness, deportment, good conduct, order, regularity, and application was another striking aspect of the French convent tradition in education at work in girls' schools in Ireland in the nineteenth century ... The Irish convent boarding schools supplied a certain status to their pupils which ensured the survival of these traditions until the mid-twentieth century.

Even more telling is O'Connor's analysis of the pervasiveness of French culture, including the spoken language, in girls' boarding-schools in Ireland. Moreover, the French character of the Irish school found approval from parents eager to promote the French virtues of *la politesse* and *le gout* (politeness and good taste) for their daughters. They enthusiastically endorsed the prevailing French objectives of girls' education: to prepare them for marriage or to become nuns. Refinement of manners was accompanied by character-formation. Training in self-discipline was set off by good handwriting and the cultivation of a literary style for the keeping of diaries and for letter-writing. A sound knowledge of the French language permitted the occasional use of a well-chosen phrase like Sissy O'Brien's *bonne tenue* and Nannie's comment to Sissy, 'That's the French way of making a bed: all the rules are French'.

In any consideration of the history of Irish spirituality, traditional Irish spirituality was, according to Diarmuid Ó Laoghaire, S.J., an incomparable legacy from rural, Irish-speaking parts of the country.[6] It fuelled the devotional lives of the people even beyond Famine times. It continued to flourish in the Irish-speaking regions of the island as well as in the remote rural areas sealed off by lack of communication from Patrick Kavanagh's 'clever villages that laughed at ancient holiness'. We are fortunate in possessing the printed autobiography of an Irish-speaking woman, Peig Sayers (1873–1958), who lived most of her adult life on the Great Blasket Island off the coast of Kerry, where she became a noted story-teller. Elsewhere I have endeavoured to describe the spiritual resources on which Peig Sayers drew when, as a young bride, she left the mainland to dwell for over forty years on the Great Blasket as wife and mother.[7] She was part of an Irish-speaking community both on the adjacent mainland, the Dingle peninsula, and on the rocky island of the Blasket. Though she experienced several years of domestic service in the town of Dingle, she preserved the traditional spirituality which for her was connected with the roots of her essential identity. She could have chosen to emigrate to the United States and she was well aware of the freedom it offered; yet decisively, she accepted the offer of an arranged marriage and the hardship of living on a barren, wind-swept island. By mid-life she had lost husband and four children:

> I remember bending to my work with my heart breaking. I used to think of Mary and the Lord – the hard life they had. I knew I had a duty to imitate them and bear my sorrow patiently.[8]

Peig Sayers was a convivial neighbour who enjoyed late nights of story-telling, a pipe of tobacco, and the company of men, including Oxford scholar Robin Flower. Yet the springs of her humanity were nourished by an intense sense of the presence of God and a delight in creation, the core of Celtic spirituality, according to John McQuarrie.[9]

> The sense of God's immanence in his creation was so strong in Celtic spirituality as to amount sometimes to a pantheism ... But perusal of typical Celtic poems and prayers makes it clear that God's presence was even more keenly felt in the daily round of human tasks and at the important junctures of life. Getting up, kindling the fire, going to work, going to bed, as well as birth, marriage, settling in a new house, death, were occasions for recognizing the presence of God.

Peig Sayers tells us how she liked to withdraw into herself sitting in a solitary place overlooking the harbour out to sea, reflecting on life. There was a maturity inherent in the culture of the Irish-speaking Blasket

Island, a kind of evening incandescence, to be observed also in the writings of her fellow islanders, Tomás Ó Criomhthain, and Muiris Ó Súileabháin. The islanders had the capacity to confront their own isolation and to discover the truth behind the experience of living frugally and dangerously in such an exposed place. Bad weather and treacherous currents cut the islanders off from church-going, and from the comforting rituals of their religion for weeks on end.

Peig Sayers and her co-islanders were a segment of a society that had undergone revolution and civil war. They belonged to a country which had established its political identity as a democracy, the Irish Free State (Saorstát Éireann) in 1922. Their children were given elementary education on the island in a government school and continued to emigrate to the new world, or came to Dublin to work in areas created by the government in its aspirations to revive the Irish language. Wherever they scattered they embraced urban ways. Gradually throughout the thirties the old way of life of the Blasket declined. The school was closed and the last islanders left the island in the course of the next decade. Peig Sayers settled on the mainland in a secluded townland near Dunquin, where she was joined by her son Micheál, on his return from Cambridge, Massachusetts. From there she transferred to the Dingle hospital for the last few years of her life, dying in 1958 at the age of eighty-five years.

There are certain epochs when two separate worlds overlap, yet remain distinct, apart, with currents of communication flowing between them. Peig Sayers never travelled to a city. Even so, the bustling world of North American cities and the gossip of Dingle and Dublin reached her in letters and accounts of relatives and neighbours. In this study the writer has set herself the task of scrutinising the life-cycles of two Irishwomen drawn from those overlapping worlds in order to chart their paths of spirituality in the context of environment and life-style. Drawing on Peig Sayers' published writing and on the collection of stories and anecdotes that held her listeners enthralled over decades and which are now stored in the Archives of the Folklore Department, UCD, it is possible to recognize that her spirituality drew on contemporary devotional practices such as that of having a lamp burning before an image of the Sacred Heart on her kitchen wall, and of invoking the help of Mary, Mother of Sorrows. It is also sustainable, though less demonstrably proofworthy, that the springs which nourished her spirituality reached back to a past unknown to her and to the islanders. Her life-cycles developed imperceptibly from each previous phase and were integrated and permeated by a spirituality that was unstudied, seemingly instinctive, even commonplace and in her own estimation, were she asked about it, unremarkable. In her own testimony, belief in God, in His will, *creideamh*, that elusive Irish word meaning faith or belief, was the rock of her soul.

The second woman, Edel Quinn, came from the other catholic Ireland, a town-dweller from the business community in the first decade of the twentieth century. An intelligent, charming child, as is attested by the extant photographs of her at the ages of four and of eleven, she grew up to become a woman who, in the short span of thirty-seven years, encountered and kept at bay a fatal form of tuberculosis, travelled to East Africa as a lay-missioner, was regarded in her own lifetime as a person of great sanctity, and after her death in Nairobi, has been singled out by the catholic church as someone eminently worthy of being investigated for process of beatification.

Edel Quinn was born in Kanturk, County Cork, on 14 September 1907. She was born into the comfortable world of the banking community in provincial Ireland and she could have married into the pleasant provincial world of France twenty-one years later. The eldest of four children, three girls and a boy, her childhood was passed in a succession of towns to which her father was moved by the National Bank in which he was an official. Edel Quinn's family moved from Clonmel to Cahir in County Tipperary, then to Enniscorthy in County Wexford. She was eleven years of age when the family arrived in Tralee, County Kerry. By then her father had been appointed manager of his bank in the chief town of the county, a well-to-do provincial centre with a brisk business community.

Wherever the Quinns moved they lived a town-life adjacent to bank, school and church. They were, as bank people, expected to live a reserved, well-mannered existence, keeping up the social position of a bank official. Those who recalled Edel Quinn in the first seventeen years of her life commented on her bright looks, 'a good child, intelligent, full of life and fun and at the head of her class', according to one of her Tralee teachers in the Presentation convent school which she attended.[10]

The Quinn household was a kindly one with an unsophisticated religious atmosphere. Edel was close to her parents and recalled later in one of her letters the evening walks that her mother took with the children which invariably included a visit to the local church to pray before the Blessed Sacrament. When misfortune occurred, the Quinns met it with dignity and family loyalty. In Tralee, Mr Quinn infringed the rules of his bank by lending a sum of money injudiciously. It was 1923, in the immediate aftermath of the Civil War. The guidelines concerning the lending of money by a bank to a customer were inflexible; even a half-morning's latitude was not permitted. For the Quinns their loss of status was experienced immediately. Years of financial strain followed, plans for the children's future education disrupted. Edel was obliged to leave school in her seventeenth year. She was then boarding as a student in the convent school managed by the Faithful Companions of Jesus at Upton Hall, outside Liverpool. This was a period upon which she looked back with delight, when she was allowed to round off her education uninterrupted by the frequent removals of the household. Financed by one of her aunts, it gave her, among other skills, an opportunity to develop her talent for letter-writing.

Like Sissy O'Brien in Bruff, Edel was received into the Sodality of the Children of Mary. There, and in the general running of the school, she assumed a leadership role as a prefect. A serious student, she has left a record of her favourite books at this period in her school diary.[11] A promising academic career lay ahead of her, and, though she left the school before her seventeenth birthday, she had acquired the Cambridge School Certificate.

Edel returned home to a new environment, the sea-front at Monkstown, County Dublin, some seven miles from the centre of Dublin city. The family occupied a high, three-storey house in Trafalgar Terrace, overlooking Dublin Bay towards Howth on the far side. Below the terrace, across the road close by the shore line, ran the railway. For the following eight years Edel caught the eight a.m. train at the Monkstown station 'invariably at the last minute', a familiar slim body which flung itself into a receding carriage. Edel was late because she took in morning mass on her way to the city, a not unusual practice in catholic Dublin. In record time Edel had qualified herself in book-keeping and typing as a commercial secretary. She became a wage-earner, securing a position in the office of the Chagney Tile Works in Tara Street and bringing home her weekly pay packet to augment the family budget.

Frank Duff, founder of the Legion of Mary, a world-wide lay catholic association, described her at this stage of her life.

> When she became a self-supporting individual she did not give herself to devotion or to higher pursuits. She indulged in the usual after-work occupation with the extra one of helping in a girls' club.

Frank Duff was making the point that it was the spirituality of the Legion of Mary that transformed Edel Quinn. His reference to 'helping in a girls' club' dates back to her membership of the Sodality of the Children of Mary attached to the Loreto Convent in North Great George's Street which she joined on her return to Dublin. This Sodality operated a social club for working girls, and it was here in an area which was adjacent to the Dublin slums that Edel first encountered the poor of Dublin.

Edel's mother was unshakable in her testimony to her daughter's biographer Cardinal Suenens, that Edel, as a small child, was extraordinarily good-humoured and unselfish. Her sister Leslie, in her sworn testimony to the Process of Interrogation Concerning Edel Quinn's Cause for Beatification (1963) revealed that the young Edel led a hidden life of prayer, was austere in her eating habits.[12] She had admitted to Leslie her attraction to religious life in a contemplative community. Yet Edel's close friend Mona Tierney was sceptical that Edel, at twenty, had the 'makings' of a Legionary when Edel expressed her interest in joining the lay-organization just seven years after Frank Duff had founded it. The energetic tennis-player who enjoyed dancing and was taking tuition in the French language from a young Frenchman who had serious intentions of marrying her, concealed from most of her friends her spiritual quest.

Frank Duff, in founding the Association in 1921, released lay-people into a sense of their role and mission in the church of twentieth-century Ireland. The beginnings of the Legion of Mary were modest. A group of people came together in Myra House in Francis Street, in Dublin, Frank Duff being the convener and leader. Their intention, he recalled later, was to address the spiritual needs of the city using an organizational structure similar to that of the Conference of St Vincent de Paul which had spread from France in the previous century in a church-affiliated movement to assist the practical needs of the poor. Frank Duff's first group consisted of fifteen women, himself and a priest.

It was a time of grave national tension in the country. The War of Independence had just terminated in a Truce and the Treaty between the British Government and the Irish negotiators was in the process of being worked out in London. When the Treaty was subsequently put before the national parliament, Dáil Éireann, in December 1921, the House split on the issue of the oath of allegiance to the British monarchy, and the country found itself plunged in civil war between the pro- and anti-Treatyites. It was a shattering experience for all who had dreamt and fought for a new Ireland and its termination in 1923 left the pro-Treaty Free State government in control of a deeply divided country of twenty-six counties. For the official catholic church, the hierarchy, who had acknowledged the significance of the reality of the Irish Free State with the signing of the Treaty, the civil war challenged them to declare their support for the will of the majority expressed in the Dáil and in the Provisional Government. In so doing they condemned the Republican cause and viewed the young men engaged in its defence as 'unpatriotic'. As for the civil war, in the words of Dr Margaret O'Callaghan, 'the image of the fall, of a descent from heights of nobility was the prism through which the Church insisted on viewing the unfolding tragedy'. O'Callaghan's thesis in her study 'Religion and identity, the Church and Irish independence', that the hierarchy's revulsion against the anarchy and breakdown of social and familial bonds during the civil war was a strong element in determining the shape and ethos of the Irish Free State, leads her to conclude that in the years after the civil war the hierarchy asserted the immense authority of the Church of the majority in the Free State 'in the area that was now their only real domain – the field of faith and morals'. Moreover, their view of Irish human nature was pessimistic as a consequence of the civil war: they were 'suspicious of their people's moral calibre, wary of their inclinations, determined to keep them under control'.[13] Frank Duff's Association was lay-inspired and it had a head-start on the hierarchy's changed outlook after the civil war. Its distinguishing characteristics were its cultivation of the devotional life of the lay-catholic through the cult of Mary as Mediatrix of All Graces, its emphasis on personal holiness, and an open-ended spiritual ministry to others to lift them out of their apathy, indifference or unawareness of God. As a lay catholic organization its self-confidence and autonomy were new experiences in Irish catholicism. To Frank Duff's dismay his Legion of Mary met with coldness, even suspicion from Dublin church authorities, the vicars of the archdiocese withholding formal approval for over two decades and two successive archbishops, Dr Byrne and Dr McQuaid, refraining from wholehearted support despite its enthusiastic reception into dioceses all over the world. Frank Duff's insistence that it was an organization for men and women, and not women only as was suggested to him on one occasion by the vicars as a compromise, may have been a factor in withholding official approval in Dublin. Frank Duff more than once wondered if such was the case.

The full explanation for the success of the Legion of Mary abroad validates its intrinsic merits. In Dublin despite the lack of official approbation it attracted people of all classes. The names and occupations of those early groups reveal its populist character. By the mid-thirties a hundred groups or *praesidia* were functioning in Dublin. In addition to the weekly meetings for its members went the task of rehabilitating the marginalised, organizing one-day retreats for all manner of people, and running hostels for the homeless. Frank Duff was accused of being 'anti-clerical'. He was 'that fellow Duff' who was emancipating the paralysed tongues of the laity. Members of the Legion of Mary were sneered at for engaging on a spiritual level with a stratum of society which was demonstrably beyond redemption. Frank Duff was later to say in a fit of exasperation, 'anyone who wants to work in Ireland will be cribbed, cabined and confined. Religion has become a routine. A terrible conservatism exercises relentless sway, and tells the Irish people they must walk in outmoded ways ... plainly we are looking at Jansenism, and not true catholicism'. Those strictures were wrung from him in 1947.[14] In the first decade after the civil war, the sense of mission in the new state was tangible. The strains within Irish society were not strikingly visible for some time to come.

Frank Duff, in founding the association in 1921 that quickly became the Legion of Mary, created in Ireland a school of Marian spirituality. He found a society ready to accept a central devotion to Mary as developed by the French spiritual writer, Louis Marie de Montfort in the late seventeenth century, but only then gaining ground in catholic devotional circles possibly because of the apparitions of Mary at Lourdes, La Salette and Knock. Frank Duff's *Handbook of the Legion of Mary* was based on a theology of the lay-apostolate not fully apprehended by official church authorities in Dublin though enthusiastically accepted elsewhere. Its influence in the middle decades of the twentieth century has never been fully appreciated though it is now acknowledged as a ground-breaking exercise for the theology of the laity that emerged from the deliberations of the Second Vatican Council, 1962–65.

Edel Quinn joined the Legion of Mary a few months before her twenty-first birthday, six years after it was founded. Her local branch, or *praesidium* (Frank Duff delighted in Latin titles) was bound to a weekly meeting consisting of prayers, spiritual reading and discourse, followed by the minutes of the previous meeting, a report on visitation work undertaken in pairs, and assignment of tasks for the coming week. Doubt had been expressed that the organization would attract Edel. She persevered and in a short time she established herself as a person of perceived gifts. Soon she was spending most of her free time in the activities generated by her Legion undertakings, accomplishing demanding visitations after her own work was finished. At least two hours a week were required of Legion members. Edel went on to devote five evenings a week to hospital visitation, to the lonely in the slum tenements behind O'Connell Street, or, a task she found disagreeable, introducing herself at doors to families to promote devotion to the Sacred Heart. Her own preference was for isolated lonely people, for invalids and for the old.

When she had served for two years as an ordinary member of the *praesidium*, she was appointed president of a group whose work was difficult and sensitive, making contact with prostitutes, offering them alternative living quarters, and restoring to them a sense of their own self-worth and spiritual identity. Despite objections to her youthful appearance and what seemed like her lack of experience, she won esteem and commendation for the manner in which she carried out her complicated assignments. It was through becoming an officer in the leadership cadre of the Legion of Mary that she came to the notice of Frank Duff.

'A process of ultra-refining' was how Frank Duff described the development of Edel's spirituality. She has left no autobiography behind her as did the remarkable Peig Sayers, author of two personal volumes of personal reflections. Edel Quinn, on the other hand, was an excellent letter-writer, and more than two hundred of her letters were kept by various people after her death, the bulk from East Africa between 1936–44, and some fifty to Pierre Jean Francois Landrin. Because of the singular scrutiny to which her life and actions have been subjected by church authorities in Rome as a potential candidate for beatification, the sworn testimonies of those who knew her comprise a large volume of 900 pages, *Summarium, super dubio, ad ejus Causa introducenda sit,* issued in Rome, 1982. There are also a considerable number of people still alive, or who have recently died, who gave oral interviews to Edel's distinguished biographer, Cardinal Leon-Joseph Suenens, Archbishop of Malines-Brussels, in the early fifties. His *Life of Edel Quinn* was first published in 1952 and has been translated into English, Dutch, Chinese, Japanese, Korean and Slavic. Still issuing in steady reprints, it is an important source for examining her life. Archbishop Antonio Riberi, Apostolic Nuncio to China, who had spent some time in the nunciature in Dublin, and later on in Nairobi in East Africa, was familiar with both the Legion of Mary and Edel Quinn's missionary activities. In his Preface to the Suenens' biography of Edel Quinn he wrote:[15]

> I have always hoped that her wonderful life would find a pen capable of presenting it fittingly to the attentive examination of the catholic world … It would be difficult to confide it to a person of greater authority, to a more brilliant writer, to a deeper thinker, to one with more expert knowledge of modern conditions.

Acquaintances who knew her in her early twenties describe her variously: 'she had a distinctive personality … the extraordinary brightness of her face … exquisitely pretty … not robust … what she had to say carried weight … reserved …'. Pierre Landrin had first met her when as a nineteen year old she arrived at the office of the Tile Company which he managed. For two years they saw each other once a week on a personal level, for tea in Jury's or the Savoy Hotel, and again at the weekends for a game of tennis. Pierre was well received at Edel's family home. Those who observed them commented on how compatible they were. Pierre began to teach her French which she had left aside after schooldays. He lent her works written in French and they enjoyed discussing books. She also gave him glimpses of the struggle she experienced at times in the Legion assignments. 'I have to get in two visits to people, the second a horrible ordeal. I hate visiting, don't you?' she commented to Pierre on one occasion. To the surprise of Leslie, Edel's sister, one midday Edel arrived home, grieving, her distress obvious, and confessed to Leslie that she had finally not accepted Pierre's proposal of marriage.[16] Instead she was resolved to enter the Poor Clare contemplative community of Franciscan nuns in

Belfast. Edel had entertained the idea for a long time. In a letter to Pierre she explained her delay in making her decision:

> I know you must wonder why I have not entered before, instead of holding on to office work. Well, when I left school, circumstances intervened which showed plainly that my duty, at the time and since, was to stay with my parents. About the beginning of this year, I believed I was free to follow my vocation. It was then I made arrangements. However, when I told Mother, she said I was still needed at home, and that it would not be right for me to go.
>
> After reflection and taking of advice, I saw my duty was for the present at home, and that being so, I could not conscientiously go away. So that is why I am still where I am. Please forgive, Pierre, this long writing about myself. I would not have spoken, and never have to anyone, about this matter, which is so intimate. But I felt I owed it to you, who have been so frank with me.[17]

A religious vocation always implies choice and decision, and within that choice, a narrowing of choice, no matter how obvious the decision to the observer. The contemplative nun, enclosed and cloistered, is a metaphor of the archetypal symbolisations of the self. Religious life, so called, is a way of containing a developed sense of reflectiveness about the transcendent nature of reality. The individual responds to choosing a way of life that commits her to explore in a structured way what God has been calling her to in the particular mode designated by that impulse. Edel was, untypically, reticent about her selection of the Poor Clares of the Colletine Observance in Belfast and her decision came as a surprise to many who thought they knew her well. From the testimony of one of her closest friends, it emerges how carefully she had prepared for her entry into religious life.[18] She imposed upon herself a strict asceticism. 'She rose every morning at half past five, and Mass, Holy Communion, morning meditation and a very scanty breakfast were her preparation for the day's work'. She also read widely the classics of the spiritual life, Juliana of Norwich, St John of the Cross, the French Carmelites, Thèrése of Lisieux and Elizabeth of the Trinity, Tanquerey's *A Treatise of the Spiritual Life*, *The Imitation of Christ* and the works of the contemporary Benedictines, Dom Marmion and Abbot Vonier. After essaying four chapters of *The Interior Castle* by the mystic Teresa of Avila, she returned it to its owner saying that a treatise of extraordinary graces was not for her. Increasingly she read daily the Scriptures, the Legion *Handbook* and de Montfort's *True Devotion to Mary*. Much later, in a letter to Cardinal Suenens giving his thoughts on Edel Quinn, Pierre Landrin wrote of 'her irrevocable decision of entering the Poor Clare Convent in Belfast'.

Edel planned to enter in the course of her twenty-fifth year. Early in February she became suddenly ill with a suspicious haemorrhage indicating the nature of the malady. A medical examination confirmed that her lungs were in an advanced state of tuberculosis with little hope of permanent cure. On 5 February 1932 she was taken to Newcastle sanatorium, County Wicklow, where she remained eighteen months. Tuberculosis in twentieth-century Ireland awaits its historian. It was for young and old 'the dread disease', the only remedy at that time, quarantine in a sanatorium, preferably at a high, cold altitude. Edel was to become familiar with the clinical interior of the TB sanatorium, not once but several times in her life. Outwardly she remained a cheerful bright person who teased and bantered her way into the affections of her companions, and was called upon by the nurses in times of emergency. Inwardly the Newcastle interlude, one of intense cold and painful treatment, strengthened her will-power immeasurably.

The perceptive Frank Duff stated that the experience 'made her realistic'. Years later, in answer to a question about Edel's ability to evaluate a situation while working in East Africa, he observed: 'she was realistic in her comments, a critic, albeit a constructive one, sharp in her observations'. Of her sojourn in Newcastle he said: 'I do not know the details. She must have spent many sad moments in sanatoriums'.[19]

An illness such as Edel got has more than one meaning. One must look at Edel's story in terms of life-cycle and endeavour to discover what made her succumb to tuberculosis, what levels of significance this may have for women's lives, and what the spectacular prolongation of her life for twelve more years might mean for the life-journeys of other casualties of tuberculosis. When her condition became known, friends remarked with concern how little she ate for years before, her seemingly tireless round of Legion activities, her athletic tennis-playing, the frequent wettings in the damp Dublin evening visits she undertook in the tenements. Concluded Muriel Wailes, a colleague and friend of Edel's: 'though her family was a robust, athletic one, Edel abused her health, fasting, often missing her meals, abstaining from milk, butter and meat'. While she has left no record of what conflicts may have been going on within her during those years or whether her struggle to repress the experiences of meeting Pierre took their toll, her descent into tuberculosis may have allowed her to economise on a psychical effort to have an undivided heart for her religious vocation. It was, on one level, a thwarting of her high purpose by closing off her entry into religious life. It was also a resolution of conflict in the manner in which she made it the prelude to a new life-cycle which was to be brimming with energy, unimagined travelled in Africa, and the period of her greatest achievements.

When Edel discharged herself from the Newcastle sanatorium in 1922 her lungs were not healed, but her health was much improved. One of the reasons why she left was the expense of the 'gold injection treatment' which her family was financing and which had not healed the defective lungs. At that period there were no welfare benefits that Edel could draw upon and two of the younger members of the family were still school-going. The only ostensible change she made in her resumption of activities was her insistence that she occupy a room by herself always lest her tubercular state of health prove a hazard to others. This rule she maintained for the rest of her life. In Eastleigh, Nairobi, the little room she occupied behind the sacristy of the church is still used as a meeting place. It was in that room she died, rather suddenly, on 12 May 1944. She had chosen to live there instead of occupying a room in the small convent close by, lest her racking cough or her proximity to others in the house caused discomfort. The bareness of her little room, its isolation on the compound, speak for her ability to encounter solitude and live with courage in the face of advancing death.

At first glance it seems far-fetched to suggest Edel Quinn as a study in survival strategies. When she was in the sanatorium she joked about her illness although it signified the end of her hopes for entering religious life, and dramatically altered her plans for her future. Pierre Landrin had returned to France and according to his own account had assumed she had departed to the Belfast monastery. She kept her own counsel, declining to be drawn on matters so intimate to her own life. She quickly found other work, this time as accounting secretary to Tallons Motorworks in Westland Row, close to the railway station. When Edel took the decision to discharge herself from Newcastle she was to demonstrate the qualities of a woman whose self-actualisation made her more confident and more authoritative in deciding how she would live the rest of her life. It was not a matter of time, but of maturity. Instead of denying her tubercular state, Edel found acceptable outlets for her own deepest desires and following those deeper wishes, her religious aspirations were released and channelled creatively into the construction of a more humane society. Before we examine how she adapted herself to her changed condition, some consideration needs to be directed to the opinion Frank Duff held of her at this time. It was first expressed to Cardinal Suenens in preparation for the latter's study of Edel Quinn in the context of the lay-apostolate, undertaken five years after her death. Much later Frank Duff, under oath, testified to the Tribunal which was examining her Cause for Beatification and admitted to a friend, León Ó Broin, how meticulously he had endeavoured to be truthful.[20]

Frank Duff was a sound judge of character. A skilled civil servant, he largely drafted the Hogan Land Purchase Act of 1923. He acted briefly as personal secretary to Michael Collins, Chairman of the Provisional Government and Commander-in-Chief of the National Army, until the latter was killed. For over ten years he worked in the Finance and Supply Division of the Department of Finance and when he retired from the Civil Service in October 1934 to devote himself full-time to the Legion of Mary, he was probably even at that early stage the most influential layman in the catholic church in Ireland. His astute and energetic leadership of the Legion of Mary in its formative years was reflected in the kind of officer he personally selected for his organization. It was a mark of his own standing among his colleagues in the Department of Finance that several of them joined his organization and accepted responsibility in the leadership cadre. Thus León Ó

Broin, distinguished man of letters and later secretary of the Department of Posts and Telegraphs, recounts how he met Frank Duff and became a life-long friend and associate of his in the work of the Legion, undertaking the quarterly editing of the periodical, *Maria Legionis,* for ten years as well as being an officer of the organization. Seán Moynihan, secretary to the government and Maurice Moynihan, later to serve as secretary to the Department of Finance, remained, despite onerous public duties, devoted members of the Legion, assisting in the running of the hostels. Celia Shaw, who was recruited as a young graduate to the civil service, joined the Legion of Mary in 1924 and sixty years of close co-operation with Frank Duff followed. Her collection of letters from Frank Duff form an important source of documentation for his life. He had no time for class or sectional interests. Among his first group of Legion officers was the remarkable Elizabeth Kirwan, a New Zealander and an office cleaner, who later became a president of Concilium, the executive group of the worldwide organization. Colette Gill from the heart of the Liberties in Dublin supplied much information on the early members of the Legion. There was Joe Gabbet, 'the man with the fearsome moustache', and Jack Nagle, anchor-man for decades in the headquarters of the Legion of Mary in Myra House in North Brunswick Street. Like Sam Hughes, Jack Nagle was president of Concilium. Sam Hughes was a cycling companion of Frank Duff, from the civil service and was left, after Frank Duff's death, the task of steering the Legion of Mary into the late twentieth century.

There was no obvious strategy of recruitment, yet in a seemingly effortless way, Frank Duff attracted to his organization in those early years men and women of unusual competence who were possessed of a genuine desire to minister to the spiritual needs of Dublin's numerous outcasts. Frank Duff's wholehearted devotion to the 'down-and-outs' to whom he gave a refuge in the hostels off North Brunswick Street found an overwhelming response in a generation who understood his mission and who were themselves in the public life of the new state engaged in articulating and identifying the nature of the enterprise of that new state.

Frank Duff first met Edel Quinn in 1931 and became personally acquainted with her when she was appointed president of a *praesidium* shortly before her sojourn in Newcastle. On her return to active membership of the Legion, she was advised by him to take a less active position working with young people in a children's hospital close to the house her family had moved to in the same pleasant area of Monkstown. Though she had abandoned the idea of religious life, she kept her habit of early rising, morning mass and austerity. In those middle years of the thirties the Legion of Mary was rapidly expanding to America, to England and Wales, and to Africa. Frank Duff's concept of extension work to England, a system of short-term volunteering carried out during a legionary's holidays, was enthusiastically received by hierarchy and parochial clergy alike. The Legion Envoy was a bolder initiative. The notion of offering to a bishop of a diocese a lay-missioner who was prepared to work out a blueprint of which the bishop had prior knowledge and to which he had given his approval proved to be a factor which won the Legion worldwide acclaim. The Legion Envoy, chosen and missioned by the Concilium of the Legion, undertook in whatever part of the world selected by Frank Duff and his executive committee, to establish a cohort of lay-people, bonded by the Legion structures, who functioned within the parish framework. It proved attractive in all missionary countries and in places where the clergy were scattered over a wide region. There was the communitarian element of assembling at a weekly meeting a group of lay-people who undertook the responsibility of spiritual ministry to their own people as well as developing their own spirituality. For a hard-worked missionary priest there was the availability of catechists, and visitors to the sick, the disease-ridden, and those who lived in remote inaccessible villages. The flow of information was invaluable and the reports of Legion Envoys to Concilium form a massive testimony to what León Ó Broin described as 'Frank Duff's organizational genius'.

Edel Quinn was singled out by Frank Duff to go to Wales on extension work. According to Muriel Wailes, her friend and longterm colleague of Frank Duff, he lifted down the map of Britain and pointed out the diocese of Minevia to Muriel and watching the expression on her face, 'looked at her in that serene way he had and said "Do your best, yes, it is a bleak part of the vineyard, but you can count on divine help"'. Edel had offered to use her 1936 holiday time on extension work and he sent her along with Muriel Wailes, secretly scrutinising her for other possibilities. According to Muriel Wailes, Edel was an astonishing success. Her *joie de vivre* and sense of fun, together with her sincerity and conviction brought to many a desire to be reconciled with their God and church.[21] On their return, Edel Quinn suggested to Frank Duff that she move to Chester, find an occupation there and spread the Legion of Mary from there to Wales and England. Hard on the heels of that proposal, Frank Duff recounts, came a request to develop the Legion of Mary in South Africa and he introduced Edel's name for consideration to Concilium. Then Bishop Heffernan of East Africa requested formally a Legion Envoy for his diocese. After serious consideration with the other officers of Concilium, Frank

Duff invited Edel to consider Bishop Heffernan's request. She accepted.[22]

A storm of opposition ensued, dramatically described by Cardinal Suenens in his biography.[23] The ex-general of the Calced Carmelites, a man of considerable authority, shot to his feet. He enumerated in rapid-fire fashion the obstacles and perils that lay in wait there, arguing 'to send Edel Quinn to Africa would be sheer folly, particularly for a woman travelling alone, the deadly climate, the vast distances to be covered under appalling conditions'. And so he went on, 'if someone must be sent, let it be a man of more than average strength, and not a fragile young girl'. When he stopped for breath, Edel arose. 'All those difficulties have been explained to me in detail', she interjected:

> I know what is before me. It is exactly what I am looking for ... I am going with my eyes open. I don't want to go on any picnic.

Her unexpected vehemence disarmed her adversary and so won the consent of that experienced and shrewd assembly.

It was a critical decision and Edel was sensible of the responsibility placed not only upon her, but upon Frank Duff who had put forward her name. She wrote to him on board ship to Mombasa a few months later:

> I would like you to understand always, whatever happens, that I am glad you gave me the opportunity of going. I realize it is a privilege and also that only for you persisting I would never have been sent ... Whatever be the consequence, rejoice you had the courage to emulate Our Lord, in his choice of weak things, in Faith. Any sorrow caused to others was worth it, remember; I know that you felt pretty badly the fact that others were suffering. Have no regrets ... I am glad you let me go – the others will be glad later.[24]

On Saturday 24 October 1936, Edel Quinn sailed away from Ireland, never to return. *The Llangibby Castle* took her from Tilbury docks on Friday morning, 30 October and deposited her in Mombasa, the gateway to East Africa on 23 November. Awaiting her was Bishop Heffernan, there to welcome the new arrivals which included a group of Irish Loreto Sisters with whom Edel was always free to stay. On the bishop's suggestion, she made Nairobi her headquarters, travelling that same day the three hundred miles inland and uphill by train. Her remaining years, ones of spectacular success and of courageous travels into the interior of Africa, form a brilliant climax to her life.

In contrast to her declining health which forced her twice into TB clinics, the last eight years of her life were infused with energy and a richness of experience which lights up her weekly letters to Jack Nagle and Frank Duff. The log-book of her journey to Africa was published in the first numbers of *Maria Legionis*. Its publication brought her presence in Africa and her mission there to hundreds of readers. Her African letters were, in the main, factual reports, written on a typewriter which accompanied her, insofar as it was possible, wherever she travelled. Her correspondence with Concilium in Dublin was extensive, full of information and sharp questions. She wrote with clarity but the reader senses that her letters were written in low-key, unemotional, predictable style which concealed many of her personal reflections.

In the thirties the relationship of Ireland to Africa was one of increasing geographical intimacy, all the more startling because it has never been articulated as a conscious extension of the Irish emigration experience. 'The flight to Africa' in the middle decades of the twentieth century by hundreds of Irish men and women as missionaries intent on christianising that continent goes further than bridging a gap in the historical consciousness. The earlier surge of religious orders to Africa at the end of the nineteenth century was arguably a following of the flag of empire. For Irish Dominican Sisters, Christian Brothers and the Irish branch of the Holy Ghost Order (C.S.S.P.) there was accommodation within British colonial Africa including South Africa. With the founding of the new missionary orders a different kind of impulse brought hundreds of young Irish missionaries to Africa. St Patrick's Society for African Missions, founded in 1932 from Maynooth College, followed the inspiration of Bishop Shanahan, C.S.S.P. in Nigeria 1902–43 in his strategy of developing schools, hospitals – but also farming, irrigation, road-making, tea and coffee plantations. For women the setting up of the Missionary Sisters of the Holy Rosary (Killeshandra) in 1924 also benefited from the inspiration of Bishop Shanahan's Nigerian endeavours. Earlier the Franciscan Missionaries for Africa, under the leadership of Sister Kevin Kearney, pioneered nursing and midwifery skills in that part of the world. Her sisters were clustered mainly in Uganda with a major teaching hospital in Kampala. The founding of Mary Martin's Medical Missionaries of Mary in 1937 opened up a new phase by bringing professional medical services to remote regions of Africa. The rise in religious vocations in twentieth-century Ireland overflowed to Africa in abundance. There was scarcely a townland or village in Ireland in the 1940s that had not some missionary working in Africa, nor a postman who could not locate some far-distant region of that continent by its postage stamp.

Edel Quinn's role was different. She was a young lay-woman in a largely clericalised world of European missionaries. She was an accredited Envoy whose task it was to set up the Legion of Mary wherever a bishop or local priest invited it. According to the testimony of many who came forward to be interviewed for the process of beatification, she was much more. She proved herself a trainer of leaders, a resource person for the parishes, a tactful link between bishop and people. In the Legion archives are outlines of her formidable, highly efficient timetable. She showed the missioner when best to use a catechist, how to acquire an over-all plan of an area. She set goals for herself, she dealt expertly with masses of correspondence which awaited her on her return to Nairobi. She taught a non-literate society to run meetings.[25]

From the beginning Edel Quinn sensed that her core relationship was with the African people and tactfully she receded from the European and Goan communities in Nairobi and Mombasa to devote herself to getting in touch with the Kenyan, Ugandan and other African peoples. In the thirties East Africa was a segregated society. Yet Edel Quinn travelled simply in the matatoes packed tightly with African farm-workers. Most of the Europeans of the White Highlands of Kenya rode in motorcars or on horseback; Edel's simple mode of travel did not go unnoticed. John Omolo, who joined the Legion of Mary in 1939 as a result of meeting her and who later became the Chairman of the Senatus of the Legion in Nairobi, taking over the leadership of the Legion there after her death, believed that the secret of her success was her ability 'to walk with us'.[26] All recall her enthusiasm, the challenging, magnetic blue eyes, the clear face, the laugh, the husky voice, 'bubbling with energy', the 'tough tennis player'. She worked at incredible speed, establishing the Legion securely, conscious that the catholic church in East Africa was a developing one. She became the owner of a dilapidated Ford at one stage and, despite rationing and the hazards of World War II in East Africa, she journeyed through villages, the jungle tracks of Kenya, Uganda, Tanganyika, Nyasaland. A Missionary priest writing to Concilium after her death recalled her itinerary:

> At eleven a.m. she departed for a certain place about sixty miles away, returning the next day at ten a.m. with a message for me from our Bishop. Immediately after this she went off on a trip of about 110 miles ... On her way to our mission she got stuck in the mud and had to abandon the car. After walking ten miles she reached a hotel, where she had a little rest but she took no food. Early in the morning she went with the mechanic for the car ...[27]

Her journeying brought her out to Mauritius where she had received a special invitation to set up the Legion. The alarming state of her health sent her to Johannesburg with a diagnosis of advanced pulmonary tuberculosis and a six month rest in bed in that cool bracing climate. That was 1941. She recovered and resumed her activities. By the beginning of 1943 she was back in Nairobi, directing her Envoy responsibilities through letters and the occasional short stay, invariably returning to her room in Eastleigh in the compound of the Precious Blood Sisters. Though she had not mastered Swahili, she studied it. East Africa was spread before her like an open book.

Edel Quinn died of a heart attack brought on by extreme exhaustion and weakness on Friday 12 May 1944, in the thirty-seventh year of her life. Frank Duff received the news by telegram almost immediately from Nairobi despite the war-situation. Unprecedentedly, another telegram came from the Vatican Secretary of State to the Nuncio in Dublin formally announcing her death. Sadly Dublin heard the news filtered through on newspaper hoardings and in the daily papers. She had become a legend in her lifetime. Eight years later Cardinal Suenens produced his carefully documented biography of Edel Quinn in French. Dr Louise Gavan Duffy, the Irish educationalist and legionary, simultaneously translated it into English. In November 1956 Edel's Cause for Beatification was introduced in Nairobi. In effect it initiated the setting up of a Tribunal, and the process of interviewing witnesses under oath and collecting all manner of data concerning her life. No other Irish woman of the twentieth century has been so carefully documented, or so relentlessly revealed in the testimonials of her contemporaries and in her own letters as Edel Quinn. Her historical presence is assured.

Peig Sayers and Edel Quinn form a unique comparison in the context of Irish female spirituality. Peig Sayers inherited an archaic way of life and her religion, its beliefs and practices, were part of that life. Her spirituality never preoccupied her consciousness nor fired her imagination to achieve any heroic goal of sanctity. Her faith in God, in a life after death, in the humanity of Christ, in her closeness to his Mother Mary was deep and untroubled. Life, however, was destiny for her. Saying 'yes' to God's will was to place trust in her father's and brother's judgment that the made 'match' between them and her future husband was the right selection for her. Moreover, this world was a place of suffering in which she strove against the harsh poverty on a bleak island and became familiar with death which snatched her menfolk early in life. She stands at the end of a tradition of christian living which, centuries before in the estimation of Professor James Carney 'was perhaps the most ascetic that western Europe has known'.[28] Like her Celtic ancestors of the ninth century Peig Sayers sought out and observed Nature in all its manifestations of changing moods. For her, as for them, Nature was the handicraft of God. She does not tell us of her moments of rebellion. She found relief by resorting to humour and drew upon a vast reservoir of stored tales. She celebrated life in the nightly story-telling (the scoraíocht) in her house, in which she was both hostess and entertainer. Well might she echo the ninth-century Hag of Beare's great poem 'Ebbing': she too outlived her loved ones and had passed through the seven ages. In her the natural life-cycles moved inexorably to her own encounter with death in old age. She survives in her two volumes of personal reflection and in the masses of folklore material that were collected by her friend Dr Robin Flower on his summer visits to the Great Blasket. Throughout the greater part of the twentieth century her *Autobiography* and her *Reflections of an Old Woman* have been standard textbooks for the Senior State examination in Irish language and literature.

Edel Quinn contrasts strongly with her older contemporary. She was urban as Peig was rural. There was a generational divide and an educational one. Her schooling with its French emphasis continued to influence her cultural and devotional interests. Her generation inherited 'Independent' Ireland and there was present in her life goals that sense of dedication which women and men brought to the service of country, church and family after the civil war. Looking below the surface of her behaviour, her decisions were taken from somewhere inside and showed a steady inclination to move away from the patriarchal roles which Irish society in that period was bestowing on its womenfolk. The Legion of Mary, in the vigour of its first phase, supplied her quest for self-actualisation with an ideation content, largely of Frank Duff's making. Membership invited her to holiness. It intellectualised her simple piety by drawing her to the classics of the great spiritual writers. It was no accident that she chose as her guide Fr Eugene Boylan, the Irish Carthusian monk, whom she consulted. Central to the Legion spirituality were the writings of the French seventeenth-century Louis Marie de Montfort. Yet another clue to Edel's development, as we know from her letters to Pierre Landrin, was the autobiography of Thèrése of Liseux (given to her in French by Pierre), a volume underlined and pencilled with her own marginal notes. Suenens concludes that Edel was seeking the pure spirit of the Gospels, and at the end of her life the Scriptures had become her main daily reading.[29]

Saints, according to the psycho-analyst James Hillman, become transpersonal figures, ideal beings, beyond the human, 'persons of the imaginal for the soul to remember'. For the weak, the chronically ill, those with a terminal disease, Edel Quinn in that last period of her life demonstrates the ability of the human spirit to house the body and surrender it with courage and dignity. In the history of how women survive this was her greatest achievement, the possibility of inventing a life-cycle of amazing vitality in the face of advancing death.

Peig Sayers and Edel Quinn reflect two paradigms of religious culture in twentieth-century Ireland. To both was given fullness of life and both developed, in quite different ways, strategies of survival. To be able to examine the elements that went into those modes of survival is intrinsically a satisfying intellectual exercise. But when we have acknowledged that contribution to understanding the life-cycles of twentieth-century women, something more remains. It is the reality of glimpsing lives lived to full capacity defying the boundaries of biography.

from Maria Luddy and Cliona Murphy (eds), *Women Surviving: Studies in Irish Women's History in the 19ᵗʰ and 20ᵗʰ Centuries* (Dublin, Poolbeg, 1989), 233–263.

<small>NOTES</small>

I would like to thank Professor Enda McDonagh for his valuable suggestions on the earlier draft of this article.

1   *Manual of the Child of Mary.* Rules of Membership.
2   Richard Ellman, *James Joyce* (Oxford, Oxford University Press, 1983, revised ed.), pp 47–50.
3   S. O'Brien (Mary Carbery), *The Farm by Lough Gur* (Cork, Mercier Press, 1973), p. 140.
4   P. J. Corish, *The Irish Catholic Experience* (Dublin, Gill and Macmillan, 1985), pp 229–30, 233; Kevin Whelan, 'The Catholic Parish, the Catholic Chapel and Village Development in Ireland', *Irish Geography,* Vol. XVI (1983), pp 1–15.
5   Anne V. O'Connor, 'The Revolution in Girls' Secondary Education in Ireland, 1860–1910', in Mary Cullen (ed.), *Girls Don't Do Honours* (Dublin, Women's Education Bureau, 1987), p. 39.
6   D. Ó Laoghaire, 'Traditional Irish Spirituality in Modern Times', in Michael Maher (ed.), *Irish Spirituality* (Dublin, Veritas, 1981), pp 123–34.
7   Margaret Mac Curtain, 'Moving Statues and Irish Women', *Studies,* Vol. 73, No. 302 (1987), pp 139–46.
8   Máire Ní Chinnéide (ed.), *Peig* (Dublin, Talbot Press, 1936); Bryan MacMahon (trans.), *Peig: the Autobiography of Peig Sayers of the Great Blasket Island* (Dublin, Talbot Press, 1973). For evidence of the poverty of the inhabitants of the Great Blasket and of Peig's hardships, see Eibhlís Ní Shúilleabháin, *Letters from the Great Blasket* (Cork, Mercier Press, 1978, reprinted 1988), pp 32–47.
9   Quoted in Michael Maher (ed.), *Irish Spirituality, op. cit.* p. 7.
10 Interview by author with Presentation Sisters, Tralee, 9 March 1984.
11 Original sources written by Edel Quinn, and concerning her work, are now housed at the Concilium Headquarters, Legion of Mary, Dublin. The author brought back two substantial collections of her letters from Nairobi in the course of researching her life in Kenya, July through September 1983. These are now lodged in the Concilium Archives, Dublin.

12 Sworn Testimony of C. Leslie Quinn, 15 November 1963, *Cause of Edel Quinn, Summarium* (Rome, 1982), (proc. reg. Dublinen), pp 301–2.

13 Margaret O'Callaghan, 'Religion and Identity, the Church and Irish Independence', *The Crane Bag*, Vol. 7, No. 2 (1983), p. 71.

14 Leon Ó Broin, *Frank Duff: a Biography* (Dublin, Gill and Macmillan, 1982), p. 9.

15 L. J. Suenens, *Edel Quinn, Envoy of the Legion of Mary to Africa* (Bruges, Desclée, De Brouwer, 1952; Dublin, C. J. Fallon, 1954).

16 *Summarium*, p. 300, Testimony of C. Leslie Quinn.

17 Edel Quinn to Pierre Landrin, 1931 (?), Suenens, *op. cit.*, p. 53.

18 Irish Carthusian Nun [Mary Wall], *I Knew Edel Quinn* (Dublin, Catholic Truth Society of Ireland, 1969), pp 7–8. Mary Wall entered the Carthusian Order in Italy and wrote her recollections anonymously, describing herself in the title page as 'an Irish Carthusian nun'.

19 *Summarium*, p. 307, Testimony of C. Leslie Quinn.

20 Ó Broin, *op. cit.*, p. 43 ff.

21 Interview by author with Muriel Wailes, Dublin, 22 October 1983; Sworn Testimony of Muriel Wailes, 14 May 1964 in *Summarium*, pp 373–4.

22 Sworn Testimony of Frank Duff, 25 June 1964, *Summariwn* p. 382.

23 Suenens, *op. cit.*, p. 79.

24 Ó Broin, *op. cit.*, p. 54; Testimony of Frank Duff, *Summarium*, p. 383 (reference to the letter).

25 Sworn Testimony of: Miss Elizabeth Gannon, Sister Teresa Joseph O'Sullivan, S.L., Fr John Reidy C.S.S.P., Sister Servita Lembach, Sister Arsenia Ackfeld, Isabella de Mello, Fr Tom Maher C.S.S.P., *Summarium* (ex Proc. Ord. Nairobien, 1963–9), pp 15–105.

26 Interview by author with John Omolo, Nairobi, 10 August 1983.

27 Suenens, *op. cit.*, p. 200.

28 James Carney, *Medieval Irish Lyrics and the Irish Bardic Poet* (Mountrath, Dolmen Press, 1985), pp xxi, 28–41.

29 Suenens, *op. cit.*, p. 60; Sworn Testimony of Pierre Landrin, 28 May 1964, *Summarium*, pp 503–07.

The 'Ordinary' Heroine:
Woman into History

I have included this short essay on what constitutes women's history from the catalogue of Ten Dublin Women *which Medb Ruane put together to accompany the exhibition of that title for Dublin's year as City of European Culture in 1991. The exhibition was held in the Dublin Civic Museum and the selection of the ten Dublin women was drawn from an assortment of backgrounds. Written for the 'ordinary' reader, the essay addressed the problem of 'invisibility', and how theoretically women's history advanced from the first stage of recovering what was hidden or seemingly lost, to that of placing women's contribution side by side with that of men in the life of the country. The emphasis on notable women and their achievements is a second necessary step, categorised as 'compensatory'. For example, Constance Markievicz has been the subject of eight biographies, and recently other 'great' women, such as Hanna Sheehy Skeffington and the Parnell sisters, are being written into political history.*

Yet a further level of development was reached when professional historians deciphered the primary sources following the method Jo Murphy Lawless used in her study of midwifery texts in eighteenth-century Dublin's Rotunda lying-in hospital by deconstructing the text, 'to find the evidence behind the evidence'. This third stage is one of the characteristics of feminist history.

This piece is the introductory essay to Medb Ruane (ed.), Ten Dublin Women *(Dublin, The Women's Commemoration and Celebration Committee, 1991).*

Putting women back into Irish history is a challenging task. For many women, the feeling is that they have no history, or even more poignantly, that it is better not to linger on the absence of having no history of oneself, or of one's group. The very idea of producing an exhibition demonstrating the lives and actions of ten Dublin women who have dropped out of sight with the passage of decades is audacious as a contribution to a city of culture. Why should women not know about their past? Our society has a preoccupation with remembering the past and when one considers how ancient this island is, remembrance becomes another form of dreaming. Newgrange is older than the Pyramids: the earliest field systems discovered by archaeologists in western Europe are located in remote Mayo. Ireland, green and grassy, with magnificent scenery and great harbours, has always attracted settlers, some of whom like the Celts, Vikings and Normans belong to a collective sense of ancestry. Others, more recent, like the planters of early modern Ireland, a mere four hundred years ago, have had a reluctant acceptance and yet paradoxically have contributed immensely to the culture and landscaping of the countryside. So, being Irish, or choosing to live in Ireland is to inherit a past that vibrates in the living memory. The cerebral excitement Irish history triggers off in public controversy, the public rituals of remembrance that are scattered throughout the year, all serve as so many ways of touching the sparks that come from connecting with the energy of the past.

What is strange, however, is that in the far past there was a female presence in history and literature which has always been celebrated. Queen Maeve's saga about her efforts to acquire the White Bull of Ulster is our greatest cycle of mythological story, a constant source of creativity for music, drama and sculpture. St. Brigid of Kildare is honoured at the doorway of spring, recognizing pagan and christian. Ancient placenames honour female goddesses, like Scotia's grave in Kerry. Yet when the history of the last eight hundred years is unfolded there is a disconcerting omission of any reference to women. Occasionally the wife of a ruler or chieftain is named, like Dervorgilla who led Dermot McMorrough astray. The only heroine acknowledged publicly is Grace O'Malley, whose exploits as a plundering sea-captain make her seem larger than life. Since the middle of the last century, there has been a great silence concerning women as appropriate subjects for remembering historically. Who knows that Charles Stewart Parnell had two remarkable sisters, or that Nurse Elizabeth O'Farrell was selected by the leaders of 1916 to negotiate the surrender, not just of the GPO, but also of several other buildings occupied by the insurgents in Easter Week? Our history textbooks have glided over any reference to women's involvement in the life of the nation. It is important, then, to retrieve women, to reset them back into our history and into this city, and to celebrate their presence at every period of our national commemorations.

Becoming visible is always exciting to a group, particularly if they have been hidden over a long period. Allowing them to tell their own story is like following a thread in a tapestry that is being restored. Suddenly there it is glowing, then it disappears into the background, only to emerge again, forming a composite part of the whole. To tell a story, 'storytelling' is basic to the functional meaning of history. Human survival demands recording. The strategies used by human beings are the scarlet thread that runs through the story of the past. We live by stories and the longer we live, the more we live through our own stories and those handed down to us by families. Without our story we would be void of memory, of the reasons for celebration. We would not find our place in the present and, sadly, we would remain without anticipation for the future. 'Her' story is part of the storytelling community. To relate women's traditions, women's struggles, successes, sorrows, is to add to the family, national, religious, political and military narratives. Each generation writes its version of the past, and by including 'her' story, we understand that it is an important part of formal or official history.

Contextualising the Past

Recovery of information and focusing on female subjects as an accepted element of past and present are not a minor activity in human storytelling. Without that action of recovery, we are just repeating what went on before, but we are not renewing the fabric: it becomes lifeless, faded. We discard it as dead and are dimished accordingly. The restoration of what was lost, or made invisible, is the first step in engaging a society to think with esteem of its past.

There is a further step that follows on recovery. To focus on female subjects helps to retrieve the fuller context of what happened at a particular period. It is the threshold to constructing women as historical subjects, not just footnotes, or wives of famous men. It goes beyond the simple search for roots, or for ancestry. That second step is about challenging the accepted version of the past, the one that makes it into the textbooks or lingers as the legend of what happened at a certain time. Into this stage of restoring women goes the nature of women's work, how their reproduction affects society, their relationships of family and kinship – mothers and sons, mothers and daughters – the way work between women and men is organized socially and the manner in which women are educated. To accomplish this task is to question the political chronology, what is called the canon of history.

Periodisation

The notion of 'periodisation' is long established, ever since the formal study of history became a school and university subject. Periodisation simply means establishing the signposts and separating sections of the past off from each other, such as the middle ages, the Renaissance, the religious Reformation, the rise of national states. Many of these past movements imposed greater restraints on women than before. For example, the great Reform Bill of 1832 in the British Parliament (which also affected Ireland) extended the vote to a large number of men but rejected the term 'man', as in mankind, for 'male person', which definitely excluded women. The Second Reform Bill of 1867, though still excluding women, allowed 'paupers and lunatics' the vote under certain circumstances, provided they were men.

Turning to Irish history, the textbook chronology is easy to recognize: the Union of the Irish Parliament with the British one in 1801, catholic emancipation in 1829 which allowed entry into parliament without religious discrimination of men and which the Irish history books link with Daniel O'Connell's election to the Westminster Parliament. Then there was the Great Famine of 1846–52, the Land War and Parnell's efforts to get Home Rule for Ireland at the end of the nineteenth century. Next in the chronology comes the 1916 Rising, the War of Independence and the setting up of the Free State and Northern Ireland with the institutionalisation of partition. These are signposts which appear in all school textbooks but their meaning and significance for the women who lived through those experiences have never, until very recently, been investigated. When women begin to be examined as taking part in the activities of a past event, the questions change because women's area of resources in the life of a society are about everyday experiences. An important date for women's history, and also for the social history of Ireland, was the foundation in Dublin in 1815 of the Sisters of Charity who worked among the poor of the city and in the process showed women in general how to engage in practical social work. The winning of access to public examinations by girls opened up all kinds of possibilities, so 1859, the founding of the first college for women in Ireland, the Ladies Collegiate School in Belfast, is significant for women. It was followed by a steady stream of secondary schools for girls across the country. Out of that movement grew the demand for a political voice for women. Mary Hayden and Hanna Sheehy Skeffington were two Dublin women who took that route and became active in the Votes for Women issue at the beginning of the twentieth century. Kathleen Lynn and Louie Bennett took a somewhat different path after leaving school. One became a medical doctor and was Chief Medical Officer in the Easter Rising, taking the surrender in the Dublin Castle area. Subsequently she founded and worked in a children's hospital in Dublin, St. Ultan's. Louie Bennett became a formidable trade-unionist concerned about women's rights in the workplace and later she participated in international peace movements. The criminal status of women in the nineteenth century – and why certain categories of women convicted of petty crimes such as animal stealing, robbing for food and money, working as prostitutes were selected by the Dublin courts for deportation to Australia, provided the women were young and healthy – needs to be set against the exclusion of women of workhouses and prisons.

Incomplete as these examples are, they supply women with clues about their invisibility. They teach women strategies about how to reclaim rights and power. Mary McCarthy was a Dublin street trader. She became a leader among Dublin street traders and her contribution to the life of the city is now gladly acknowledged. Maggie Barrett was a community midwife. How many women know that it was not until the early twentieth century that Irish women midwives could get state certification?

Sometimes what is rendered invisible by a society's historians tells us more than we care to admit. Early twentieth-century Ireland was dominated by politics. To read about that period is to be persuaded into thinking that women were at home knitting socks. Rosie Hackett could very easily be dismissed as a newspaper vendor but when her life is examined she turns out to have led the women in Jacob's Biscuit Factory out on strike in sympathy with their fellow workers across the city during the Great Lockout in 1913. She then retrained as a printer (because Jacobs would not take her back), was amongst those who printed the Proclamation of 1916 and brought the first copy herself to James Connolly. In 1917 she was one of three women who refounded the Irish Women Workers' Union. Kathleen Clarke, whenever she is mentioned in history books, is described as the widow of Tom Clarke who spoke against the Treaty in the famous Treaty Debates, yet what do we find when we look closely? A Limerick-born business woman, a shopowner who became the first woman Lord Mayor of Dublin and was so highly regarded and trusted that she was involved in re-establishing the nationalist movement after 1916, and also acted as a judge in the Sinn Féin Courts, which maintained law and order in the city between 1919 and 1921.

Until very recently, no study of female domestic servants, how they lived, their working conditions and wages, their relationships with their employers, was undertaken. Mona Hearn reconstructed the life of domestic servants between 1880 and 1920.[1] According to her, Dublin had fifty women servants for every 1000 of the population in the early 1900s, and the majority were general servants who, together with the housewife, were responsible for all the work of the house. As a major source of employment in Dublin in the late 19th and early 20th centuries, domestic service was regarded as 'an inevitable part of life for many thousands of girls'. Domestic service appealed to parents as offering a safe career for daughters, in keeping with the ideology of a period which considered the home and the work done there suitable for a girl or woman, despite its isolation and poor marriage prospects. In selecting Mary Lear, who was employed in domestic service for over sixty years, as one of the ten Dublin women, we honour those women who made up 48% of employed women listed in the 1881 census and the 125,783 female domestic indoor servants cited in a special category in the 1911 census.

During all these years, Irish women were expressing themselves eloquently in creative literature. In fact they wrote considerably more than most people realize today, and a selection of their work appears in the bibliography of the *Ten Dublin Women* catalogue. Dublin women are also great talkers and nowhere are they more eloquent than when they are acting, either on or off the stage. In remembering Sara Allgood, we celebrate not just the voice and features of Sara, but the quintessential Dublin woman who can slay her adversary with her witty sallies. Whether in the Coombe Lying-In Hospital or in

Moore Street, or on the boards of the Abbey Theatre, the Dublin woman is rarely at a loss for words.

Women and Identity

Reading and understanding women's history is not so much the task of recovering our past identity as historical subjects, as that of critically examining the scale and magnitude of how women's lives have been monitored and eventually designed by the dominant stories of past and present. The development of new methods of writing women into history has been accompanied by an emerging philosophy concerning the nature of women's history. Mary Cullen, the historian, puts it succinctly in her various essays. Women's history writing has grown and changed from a position of regarding women as victims to a further stage which fitted 'extraordinary' and 'famous' women into the accepted canon of political history. In Ireland this resulted in a cluster of biographies of Countess Markievicz, the revolutionary activist who played a notable part in the College of Surgeons' occupation during the 1916 rebellion. Subsequently after a spell in gaol, she was returned in the 1918 elections from a Dublin working-class constituency and became the first Minister for Labour in the first Dáil. For most women who study her life, she is an impossible model to follow. The other cluster of biographies centre on Maud Gonne whose historical and literary presence owed a certain amount to Yeats' celebration of his obsessive love for her in his poetry. She was, in her own right, one of the important architects of the Irish Republic and one could argue persuasively that Yeats' public discourse diminished her as a major influence on the generation of men and women who participated in the events leading up to 1916. For the majority of Irish people, these two women were the best known, possibly the *only* Irish women who have had any significant historical/political presence in official versions of Irish history. In 'Telling It Our Way', Mary Cullen describes how F. S. L. Lyons in his influential *Ireland Since the Famine* (Fontana, 1973) has only this to say about Markievicz: 'Interested above all in women's rights – it was the suffrage question that first caught her interest' when he makes a single reference to the Irish suffrage movement in his book. Cullen puts it trenchantly:

> A woman like Markievicz may be seen as part of Irish history when she is participating in nationalist or labour political or military activity. She and other women are *not* seen as part of Irish history when they campaign in support of women's claims for civil and political rights.

Turning to the responsibility of the historian, Cullen makes the point that F. S. L. Lyons:

> has made a judgement, whether consciously or unconsciously, that women's rights and feminist movements are not a significant part of Irish history in the sense that he judges nationalism, the cultural renaissance and the labour movement to be.

Since Mary Cullen wrote that essay, women's contribution to historical movements has been further elaborated. In current Irish research, there is a process called getting at the evidence behind the evidence. Anna Parnell's *Tale of the Great Sham*, edited with an introduction by Dana Hearne, provokes questions as to how the efforts of Parnell's two sisters came to be judged unworthy of mention in official history. What process of selection caused the Ladies' Land League to be trivialised and ridiculed in such a way that it slipped into oblivion for nearly eighty years? A similar amnesia occurred about Irish women's contribution to the Irish revolution until Margaret Ward published her study *Unmanageable Revolutionaries,* a title she took from an exclamation of Eamon de Valera when discussing women during that period.

Compensatory and contributory history are important in their own right because they demonstrate that certain women 'earned' a place in official history. All very well, the non-historian may assert, these women form only a minority and they are closely identified with male-dominated organizations. These women could afford the luxury of being whole-time in their political activity, presumably because they were from a wealthy background. Moreover, their involvement in politics established for them a relationship to the political concerns of men. Most women continue to be absent from history and women are still viewed within a 'male-defined conceptual framework'.

How then is it possible to have a legitimate women's history which is neither a post-script nor a footnote to official history – 'textbook' history whose ground rules have been laid down by generations of male historians? There are three lessons to be extracted from *Ten Dublin Women.* The first one is that we must tell it our way. We have begun to write our own stories and they are as captivating written down as spoken. They are authoritative, the evidence is there, it speaks for itself. The second lesson is what Jo Murphy Lawless calls 'the search for a women's history grounded on first-hand testimony, grounded in observations at the crucial level of the ordinary and commonplace'. What she set out to recover was the authentic history of childbirth in eighteenth-century Dublin. In her published study, 'Images of "Poor" Women in the Writing of Irish Men Midwives', she explains how certain images of women are constructed:

Certainly, in relation to childbirth, there is the stark reality that the immediate accessible detail from women of every class is seldom available. Whether one attempts to utilise the descriptions of women that occur in the writings of seventeenth- and eighteenth-century obstetricians which, as Laget states, are mostly what we have left, depends on where, as feminist scholars, each of us stands on the issue of the 'real' and how we define the demand for authenticity in reading women's pasts.

First-hand accounts may not be obtainable, but that does not mean that the historical experiences of childbirth are beyond reach. We may, she suggests, instead be dealing with the problem of how women are represented in the texts of male midwives. An analysis of these texts begs the question of how certain images of women are being constructed and why.[2]

Sources for women's history abound, only women have not been trained to find them. Those sources need to be collected and they demand a repository, a place where the documentary or oral evidence may be deposited: in short we need a women's archive as part of our national archives. Thirdly, women's history, if it is to earn its place in the world of credibility which is not invariably a male world, must continue to develop new methods of examining the ways in which women's identity, work, their modes of domesticity, their categorisation as different but inferior have been constructed, and then relate those findings to a range of specifics such as social organization, political activity and to a particular historic cultural representation.

The ten Dublin women were chosen for their overwhelming testimony to the shared humanity that was experienced in this city of a thousand years. Their distinctive personalities, their contrasting lifestyles are part of 'her' story, each one's story and ultimately of Dublin's story.

NOTES

1   Mona Hearn, 'Life for domestic servants in Dublin 1880–1920', in
    Maria Luddy and Cliona Murphy (eds), *Women Surviving: Studies
    in Irish Women's History in the 19th and 20th Centuries* (Dublin,
    Poolbeg, 1989), pp 148–70.

2   Jo Murphy Lawless, 'Images of "poor" women in the writing of
    Irish men midwives', in Margaret Mac Curtain and Mary O'Dowd
    (eds), *Women in Early Modern Ireland* (Edinburgh, Edinburgh
    University Press; Dublin, Wolfhound Press, 1991), pp 291–303.

WOMEN, EDUCATION AND LEARNING
IN EARLY MODERN IRELAND

Unlike Gerda Lerner who traces resistance to women's inclusion in the world of learning through the centuries in her provocative study, The Creation of Feminist Consciousness from the Middle Ages to Eighteen-seventy *(Oxford University Press, 1993), the problem of women's acquisition of knowledge in past societies in Ireland has remained over years an abiding preoccupation for me. How women acquired knowledge at different levels of class, to what extent women's education was tied to the economics of family funding and property, what did women learn, and what effect had literacy on oral skills of storytelling, these and other questions have exercised me during my teaching life.*

In selecting 'Women, Education and Learning in Early Modern Ireland' for this collection, there is a sense of completion. It grew out of years of teaching and directing theses in the centuries that comprise early modern Ireland, the sixteenth and seventeenth centuries being those of my choice. Great was my satisfaction when Mary O'Dowd and I succeeded in editing a substantial book Women in Early Modern Ireland *(Edinburgh, Edinburgh University Press, 1991) which brought together twenty-one studies written by specialists, women and men, in their chosen field of scholarship.*

The importance of gender in the shaping of family, class and community was an original contribution to conventional approaches to Irish history in those centuries and the demarcation between private and public worlds of men and women became more inclusive as gender and women's culture moved from one site of historical activity to another. Yet in several ways Ireland in that period of conquest and plantation presents the researcher with a lack of evidence about levels of literacy, writing as well as reading, which cannot be attributed to paucity of records alone. Only a very small elite acquired a humanist education and since there was no court life in Dublin, the seat of colonial government, the intellectual world of upper-class women was limited to their homes and family circle. We can assume that in those parts of Ireland where the Irish language was spoken, women of the nobility were patrons of learning and possessed influence with the learned classes, the poets and men of law, but whether that influence was intellectual or that of patronage remains obscure. On completing this study, and a subsequent one for The Field Day Anthology of Irish Writing, IV–V *(Cork University Press) which concentrated more on levels of literacy, my sense of this period is that much more remains to be discovered.*

This essay appeared in Margaret Mac Curtain and Mary O'Dowd (eds), Women in Early Modern Ireland *(Edinburgh, Edinburgh University Press; Dublin, Wolfhound Press, 1991).*

The educational experience of men and women in sixteenth-century Europe was dominated by the effects of the Reformation. Educational attitudes and pedagogic theory which predated the Reformation certainly influenced the reformers but the revolt against priestly office, religious life and traditional forms of liturgical worship at the time of the Reformation outstripped the aspirations of the christian humanists, such as Desiderius Erasmus and Thomas More in making the new learning the basis for lay piety. Thomas More was convinced that humanistic studies, as the new learning signified, must be accessible to women as well as to men.

In a letter to William Gunnel, tutor to his daughters, More wrote:[1]

> Nor do I think that it affects the harvest, that a man or a woman has sown the seed. If they are worthy of being ranked with the human race, if they are distinguished by reason from beasts; that learning, by which the reason is cultivated, is equally suitable to both. Both of them, if the seed of good principles be sown in them, equally produce the germs of virtue.

All Thomas More's children, three daughters and a son, learnt Latin, Greek, logic, theology, philosophy, mathematics and astronomy from an early age. Margaret, his eldest daughter, became a recognized scholar. Apart from her fine classical training, she responded to her father's meditation on death, *The Four Last Things*, by writing her own. Her translation of Erasmus's treatise on the Lord's Prayer, printed about 1526, was of high quality and gained wide circulation.

Christian humanism as it developed in England, France and the Low Countries contained a commitment to religious reform as an inherent part of its content. 'I would', wrote Erasmus, 'that even the lowliest women read the gospels and the Pauline Epistles ...'. Erasmus connected the life of scholarship with the daily life of a christian and he regarded his works on spirituality as guidelines for practical piety. This humanistic outlook was held by many reformers and contributed to giving women new educational possibilities as the Reformation progressed.[2]

At the highest level of society the new learning with its orientation towards reform distinguished the conversations and writings of the female monarchs and women of the aristocracy in sixteenth-century Europe. Marguerite of Navarre, sister of King Francis I of France, was a celebrated humanist and wrote devotional treatises, the characteristic of a christian humanist. Her daughter Jeanne d'Albret, whose education she supervised actively, led the Huguenot movement in France as Queen of Bearn and Navarre. Catherine de Medici and her confidante Jacqueline de Longwy shared humanistic scholarship. Jacqueline's daughter, Charlotte de Bourbon, left her convent in 1571 to take up the Huguenot cause, became a skilled polemicist and married William of Orange. Vittorina Colonna was steeped in Erasmian humanism and in her writings sought to establish a path into mysticism through the study and knowledge of the sacred writings. Catherine of Aragon, Henry VIII's first queen, possessed great erudition. Queen Anne Boleyn, her successor, grasped the essence of the English Reformation intelligently and supported Cromwell in his efforts to push the Reform legislation through parliament. Henry's last wife Queen Catherine Parr was educated in the spirit of christian humanism and wrote a treatise, *The Lamentation of a Sinner*. Lady Jane Grey was no mean rival in learning to the brilliant Elizabeth Tudor, one of the most intellectual monarchs of the period.

In Ireland women had traditionally esteemed learning; and the endowment of monasteries as places of learning by the wives of princes and Gaelic rulers was a test of nobility, worthy of mention in the annals. In the later middle ages and throughout the sixteenth century, women of the upper classes supervised the dwelling-quarters of the elaborate tower-houses, allowing space for a library as in Maynooth Castle and in the Geraldine castles, such as Askeaton and Rathkeale, County Limerick. In the library of the Earl of Kildare were listed 34 Latin books, 36 French, 22 English and over 20 books in Irish.[3]

In the second half of the sixteenth century, as recusancy asserted itself among the laity, secret rooms were built to hide priests. Thus in the spring of 1571, at Turvey House (the country residence of Sir Christopher Barnewall and his wife Marion Bagenal), the distinguished visitor Edmund Campion, according to his own testimony, was furnished with a fine library and an out-of-the-way room. Stowed away there it is reasonable to assume, as Dr Ó Mathúna suggests, that Campion advised on the education of the younger members of the Stanihurst, Barnewall and Bathe families, who were neighbours and close friends. Jane Barnewall, then eleven years old, later married Campion's pupil Richard Stanihurst, in 1575, and when she died in childbirth in 1579 at the age of nineteen, Richard wrote a poignant Latin elegy to her memory.[4] Technically the four shires of the Pale were an extension of the English realms. The presence of English wives brought the new learning to the women of the Pale nobility. The family network of the Kildare Geraldines interacted with the St Johns, the Grays and the Zouches in the English court. Elizabeth Zouche, the maternal great grandmother of William Bathe, the pioneer of linguistic studies in Europe, was saluted by his first cousin Christopher Nugent in his address to Queen Elizabeth:[5]

> In profe whereof men yett lyvinge which knew Elizabeth Zouche, daughter to the Lord Zouche, sometime Countess of Kyldare, do affirme that in shorte tyme she learned to reade, write, and perfectly speak the tongue.

The tongue referred to was Irish. She also encouraged her son Silken Thomas to become a skilled harpist and she was a patron of the arts.

The creation of an indigenous reform movement in the Pale received much of its impetus from humanism. Thereafter the same bedrock accommodated the forces of the Counter-Reformation. Margaret Ball supplies the clues as to what women with a humanist education were experiencing in the middle decades of the sixteenth century. Margaret Bermingham (1515–84?) was the widow of Alderman Bartholomew Ball and the mother of two subsequent lord mayors of Dublin. She operated, with her domestic chaplain, a school for 'good scholars and devoted followers' from her home. She catechised her servants and those of other Pale families in an educational network. When her son Walter went over to protestantism she gathered 'many Catholic bishops, priests and other learned men' to her house to dissuade him. He became instead a committed reformer and as Lord Mayor of Dublin (1580–1) he demonstrated his hostility to recusancy by arresting and imprisoning his mother and her chaplain. She died in prison subsequently. She was described by the contemporary Jesuit Fr John Howlin as a woman 'who trained servants and could read and write'.[6]

When Henry VIII came to the throne of England in 1509, he was an orthodox catholic who regarded himself as defender of the Faith and supporter of the Pope as head of the Church. Before he died in 1547, he declared himself head of the Church in England and in Ireland; he had abolished monasticism, rejected the supremacy of the Pope, and made significant liturgical changes. Moreover he had constitutionally, by an act of the Irish parliament in 1541, been declared King of Ireland. Thereafter the progress of the Reformation in Ireland was inextricably bound up with the Tudor resolution to subdue the country and bring it under royal writ.

It has been noted by historians that Renaissance, Reformation and Counter-Reformation ran together in Elizabethan Ireland.[7] Education was a critical factor in channelling the direction religious reform took in

Ireland. In England the educational revolution was supported by the government and was stimulated by the demand for professional lay administrators. An educated and literate laity emerged from the English Reformation.[8] In Ireland the tardiness of the Tudor government to organize, fund, and control schools allowed the initiative to pass to the Jesuits and other Counter-Reformation activists in the second half of the sixteenth century. Ireland possessed no university. Queen Elizabeth I's foundation of Trinity College Dublin in 1591 came after the pattern of Counter-Reformation schooling and study on the continent had evolved along well-established lines of transportation and acceptance into continental universities such as Louvain, Paris, Salamanca and Coimbra. In Ireland, as in England, the landed classes subscribed to the arguments of the humanists and packed their sons to schools and universities convinced that a gentleman's education required book-learning and enrolment in a European university or at Inns of Court.[9]

In England education was of major concern to government policy. In Ireland education remained a subversive activity, spearheaded by proscribed Counter-Reformation agents: Jesuits, seminary-trained secular priests, laymen from the families of the Gaelic *literati*, and poets who ran bardic schools in remote areas. This was a century when a shift in the perception of family relationships was experienced: children began to be regarded as individuals and the schooling of daughters was included in the new perspective.[10] From Richard Stanihurst's memories it is implicit that the daughters as well as the sons of the Pale gentry were tutored together by a resident chaplain, or priest in hiding. The Barnewall, Bathe and Stanihurst children were schooled together. Increasingly research in convent registers in Europe is bringing to light the presence of young Irish girls as boarders, pursuing the classroom regime introduced by the Ursuline educational reforms which Angela Merici intitiated in 1562. Francis Lavalin Nugent, founder and leader of the Irish Capuchin mission and brother of the Earl of Westmeath, escorted two of his nieces, Mary and Brigid Westmeath, to France to finish their education. Later he undertook to bring out the younger girls and in true avuncular fashion entertained them in Charleville, the headquarters of the Capuchin mission, before committing them to the care of the Sepulchrine nuns at Charleville.[11]

The dislocation caused by the dissolution of the monasteries affected women more acutely than men. Debarred from university education, schooling in the late middle ages for women of the nobility or *haute-bourgeoisie* took place in schools attached to nunneries. Entry into convent life offered to dowered women alternatives to marriage and child-bearing. It provided some professional training in the art of illumination, embroidery and vestment making.[12] With the closing of the convents that accompanied the Reformation many cloistered women were left homeless and though technically in receipt of pensions, an old age of destitution was the lot of those dispossessed inmates of confiscated monasteries. Mary Cusack was one such. The sister of Sir Thomas Cusack, Master of the Rolls and later Chancellor of the Irish Exchequer, she was Abbess of the Augustinian nunnery of Lismullin, County Meath when it was surrendered and dissolved in July 1539. Sir Thomas Cusack, as receiver for the Crown, transacted the negotiations and acquired both the building and its lands. Abbess Mary Cusack was assigned a yearly pension of £16, handsome enough in those times, but decades later she complained bitterly that her brother withheld her pension from her on the subterfuge of 'borrowing' from her.[13] Alison White, Abbess of Grace

Dieu, the Augustinian monastery in Fingal which conducted a renowned school for girls, received £6 a year when Grace Dieu was dissolved and purchased by Patrick Barnewall. Undismayed she moved her convent to the rectory in Portrane but had to close the school.[14]

Sixteenth-century noblewomen in Ireland were well educated. Joan Butler, the mature wife of Gerald, Earl of Desmond and mother of his first cousin, Thomas, Earl of Ormond, corresponded frankly with Queen Elizabeth I on the intractable nature of the dispute between her son and her husband. Letters from Gerald's second wife Eleanor Butler to both Queen Elizabeth and to Pope Gregory XIII survive and demonstrate her well-turned phrase and keen grasp of the war situation.[15] Janet Taaffe, née Eustace, bargained successfully with the Queen for the restoration of her late husband's lands, forfeited during the Baltinglass Rising and received back her own lands. Gráinne O'Malley proved her ability to converse with the Queen in Latin when summoned to answer charges of piracy. Her nautical skills as a sea captain and leader of a fleet down the west coast of Ireland raise tantalising queries about her education.[16]

But these were a vanishing group as they desperately rounded on the legal nets that closed around their property. By the end of the sixteenth century, the aristocratic widow-with-daughter in circumstances of poverty was a persistent client in the petitions addressed to the Spanish monarchs. Lady Ellen O'Sullivan, widow of Donal Cam O'Sullivan petitioned and received 100 ducats each month in Madrid from King Philip III. Out of that not inconsiderable pension she was able to maintain a household of dependent women, including two Irish nuns, and two servants, both illiterate.[17] Almost a century later, Anastasia Dillon, widow of Colonel Alexander Barnewall, an officer in Galmoy's

Regiment, petitioned King Louis XIV for a pension of 1000 livres, to support herself and the schooling of her two daughters in a French convent. Her petition was granted through the mediation of Madame de Maintenon.[18] The women of the wild geese, from the time of the flight of the earls, 1607, had learned the arts of survival from personalities like Rosa O'Doherty, wife of Eoghan O'Neill,[19] and Catherine Magennis (the fourth wife of Hugh O'Neill, Earl of Tyrone) who displayed the self-confidence and resourcefulness of the educated ruling class as Jerrold Casway indicates above.

By the beginning of the seventeenth century, Reformation concerns dominated the lives of people in their personal aspects of home and family. By then theology in all the major churches was reflected in the use of catechesis for ensuring religious conformity and understanding of christianity as differentiated within the doctrines of a particular religious denomination or sect. The Council of Trent had issued its *Catechism of the Council of Trent*, a basic text of instruction for priests and those engaged in instruction of the faithful. It centred on loyalty to the Roman Church, an appreciation of the mass, and on devotion to Mary, mother of God. International Calvinism established its hold by its doctrinal appeal and its firm logical structure based on the pedagogic methods of the Huguenot, Pierre de la Ramée. The Church of Rome and Calvinism had far more in common in their programmes of evangelisation than the Armenian-influenced Anglicanism of the early Stuart period could handle. The battle for the souls of women was appreciated by the competing sets of protagonists; thus Lady Falkland's conversion to Roman Catholicism was regarded with dismay in court circles in London and in the government set in Dublin, where her husband was lord deputy. James Ussher's mother, Margaret Stanihurst, returned to recusancy but did not live to see her son become Archbishop of Armagh in the established church. Lady Eleanor Douglas, wife of Sir John Davies and daughter of the Munster settler, the first Earl of Castlehaven, after receiving a learned education in her youth, became a Puritan non-conformist and in 1625 declared she was 'seized with the spirit of prophecy'.[20]

The seventeenth century paid more attention to literacy than previous ones. The vernacular languages had stabilised their grammars, and printing presses of the period ensured a constant stream of catechetical and devotional writings. The emphasis by the reformers on the reading of the Bible and on meditation upon the texts of sacred scripture channelled the drive for literacy. Calvinism appealed to upper-class women who had leisure and the education to read the Bible. Calvinism also appealed to the artisan class and the spread of Scottish Presbyterianism among the settlers of Ulster in the 1620s is testified by the high number of non-conformist Presbyterians in east Ulster where tithes to the established church were a contentious issue.[21] Women and men were encouraged to acquire literacy to read the contents of the Bible now appearing in the vernacular. Laurence Stone has observed that for the first time in early modern Europe basic literacy made its appearance in English society.[22] In Ireland the kinds of sources Professor Stone used are not available, but the flood of books imported into the country in the seventeenth century has been noted.[23] If letter writing in English, the keeping of diaries, the financial organization of household and convent accounts were an indication of literacy, then seventeenth-century Ireland abounds in such evidence. The correspondence between the Earl of Clanrickard and his two sisters, theirs with the wife of Archbishop James Ussher, the diary of Mary Rich, the writings of Lady Anne Conway and Lady Eleanor

Douglas, the memoirs of Abbess Cecily Dillon of Bethlehem Convent near Athlone town, the spirited address of Elizabeth Preston, Lady Ormond, to Oliver Cromwell on behalf of the Butler estates, all indicate a level of literacy in the English vernacular at the highest level of Irish society.[24] The point is not that they wrote but that increasingly in the seventeenth century their writing was becoming semi-public and worthy of being stored.

One of the striking characteristics of Puritanism was its belief in the value of education as a weapon against the three great evils of'Ignorance, Prophaneness and Idleness'. Godly learning was the climate of the Puritan home. For the families of English and Scottish settlers of Puritan persuasion in Ireland the situation was more volatile as events moved towards the 1640s and the outbreak of war. The early settlers favoured Trinity College Dublin and in its founding decades the Puritan atmosphere of its theology was pervasive. For both native and newcomer in Ireland the laying down of an identity in opposition to each other was part of the formation of a religious outlook. The theological positions of the religious groupings in the country, Roman Catholic, Presbyterian and Anglican, mirrored their perceptions of 'being different' from each other. It was basic to their sense of identity. Professor Corish notes that Tridentine directives in seminary training for priests emphasised the importance of learning theological treatises rather than the Bible. The development of the 'Controversies' model used by the Jesuits and that of the adversarial theology practised in Trinity College in its first decades contributed to the formation of an identity based on taking up a particular theological position in seventeenth-century Ireland. [25]

This cultivation of an identity in opposition filtered down to the masses by way of catechesis, preaching and reading of devotional as well as biblical texts. The atmosphere of the catechism invaded the classroom and provided a rationale for basic literacy. Women, in the retrenchment that followed the earlier intellectual release of the first phase of the Reformation, were excluded from the highest levels of theological decision-making in all the major churches. But they were the target of the catechesis in the home which now became the sphere where the knowledge of God was purified and controlled. Between the ending of the Council of Trent, 1563, and the age of enlightenment in the middle of the eighteenth century, the intensification of patriarchialism is noticeable in monarchies, in church government and within the family structures. The increased authority of husbands and fathers was the reality of the seventeenth-century domestic life, visible in Puritan households like that of Richard Boyle, Earl of Cork, but apparent also in Old English families who adopted a vigorous Counter-Reformation catholicism.

In 1610 an edict forbidding the travelling abroad of the children of gentlemen for educational purposes was issued by the Dublin government. The growth of recusancy was widespread in the first decades of the new century. Sir John Davies noted that in the towns, women had withdrawn from attendance at the divine service which was an offence liable to a fine. A determined government policy closed the private catholic schools of Waterford and Galway in 1615. Yet the suspicion was widespread in government circles that priests were being hidden as chaplains and tutors in the houses of the gentry, and that they were catechising womenfolk and children. The position is summed up in a letter of the bishop of Cork, Cloyne and Ross to Chichester, the Lord Deputy. 'An English minister must needs be beholden to the Irishry; his neighbours love him not, especially his profession and doctrine, they being compelled to hear him'. Not only that, the bishop went on wryly, but the conforming lords and gentlemen of Munster, such as Lord Barry of Buttevant, protected the priests and friars:

> These priests Sir John countenances openly at his own table ... commending them to the world and applauding their profession and manner of life. They be sturdy fellows, well-fed and warm. ..Besides these friars, every gentleman and lord of the country has his priests. Massing is everywhere ...[26]

Nuns, too, made their appearance as a substantial presence among the forces of recusancy in seventeenth-century Ireland. The dispute over an active apostolate for nuns in the decades following the Council of Trent demonstrates the grip that patriarchal attitudes had on Roman Catholicism as it launched its revitalised agenda for seminary training and marriage reform. It was an agenda that ignored women's intellectual formation. The family and the domestic sphere was where she belonged and 'domestic' religion was the norm of female religious practice. Innovation in interpreting women's religious vocations had been attempted by Angela Merici and by Mary Ward, the English woman, in the sphere of women's education; by Louise de Marillac and Vincent de Paul in the field of active social charity outside the convent walls. Angela Merici's Ursuline women and Mary Ward's group of women helpers hoped to found religious orders for the education of girls and to teach the poor. The new nuns wore no religious garb save that of the contemporary woman in modest circumstances. They did not observe cloister or bind themselves to the choir recitation of the Divine Office. From the ending of Trent to the French Revolution most of the papal decrees and curial directives affecting the religious life of women pertained to maintaining cloister. In the aftermath of the great Council of Trent church ministry of a semi-official nature for women such as teaching or nursing was not regarded favourably by Rome. Pope Urban VIII issued a Bull of Suppression, *Pastoralis Romani Pontificis,* on 13 January 1630, against Mary Ward's Institute, she herself being imprisoned in a convent in Munich the following month. Mary Ward's conviction that the unenclosed apostolic religious life should be available to religious women as it was to men received a severe setback from which religious life for women did not recover for over a century.[27]

The Counter-Reformation in Ireland was conservative in character and drew its vitality in part from the massive protest that recusancy as a movement evoked throughout Ireland. Though Jesuits spearheaded the evangelisation of the gentry and became the schoolmasters of their families as part of the process, it was not part of their mission in Ireland to recruit young women to follow their apostolic life of teaching and preaching. The revitalised Franciscans and Dominicans had a similar outlook. Given the Tridentine prohibitions around uncloistered women and the Roman decrees which demanded that monasteries of women always be built or purchased within fortified towns, the Jesuit resistance to Mary Ward's overtures to develop the Ignatian Constitutions for women religious is understandable.

Of the several convents which made their appearance in Ireland throughout the seventeenth century, three (and a possible fourth) were Franciscan of the Rule of St Clare: one in Merchant's Quay in Dublin, 1629, a short-lived foundation which transferred to Waterford from Drogheda in 1642, and the remarkable Bethlehem convent built by the Dillon family on the shores of Lough Ree five miles from Athlone. It housed over sixty nuns during its brief life (1632–45). A Franciscan foundation in Galway was essayed in 1641 but was destroyed during the Cromwellian occupation of the city. The Franciscan nuns returned in 1672 to resume a life of enclosed prayer and asceticism. There are records of one Dominican convent in Galway during the 1640s which suffered the same fate as the Franciscan nuns during the Cromwellian interlude (1644–52). The Dominican nuns returned to Galway in 1686, and to a life of enclosure.

Little is known of the brief history of the Benedictine nuns in Ireland during this century save that a group took ship with James II's ships shortly after the battle of the Boyne.[28] There are no instances of teaching within the cloister during this century. It would appear that seventeenth-century Irish nuns were *oratores*, in the medieval sense of being a category or order, and their presence was a contemplative one, to witness to a people harried by frequent wars and disruption, an eschatological sign of a life beyond the grave. Nuns were also part of a family network in the recusancy movement. Among the names listed in convent registers were Cheevers, Dillon, Nugent, Dowdall, Eustace (Franciscan), Blake, French, Kirwan, O'Halloran, Nolan and Lynch (Dominican).[29]

How educated were the inmates of these Irish convents? We are fortunate in having records of a convent for Irish Dominican nuns founded in Lisbon in 1639 by the Dominican friar, Dominic O'Daly. Continuity with the past rather than bold lines of innovation mark the constitutions he drew up for those exiled Irish nuns, fully cloistered in their spacious well-built convent of Bom Sucesso in Belem, near the mouth of the Tagus. The ability to read and write, the reading of Latin, and the mastery of plain chant for liturgical celebration (often attended by members of the royal family of Portugal) were required of the nuns. Three vernaculars, English, Irish and Portuguese, were used, and the impression of a lively, well-educated community emerges from the early annals.[30]

It was the settler element in Irish society as owners and administrators of newly acquired estates who displayed pragmatism and independence in their approach to schooling and matters of learning. For them the planning of schools as part of the new infrastructure of towns was incorporated into their building schemes. Under the Ulster plantation schemes lands were assigned for a free school in every county. Control was exercised by the bishops of the established church and the right to nominate teachers rested with them, the archbishop of Armagh acting as trustee for school lands. With constant warfare, the profile of such schools only begins to emerge towards the last quarter of the century. Officially such schools were monitored by the state; in reality private citizens like Erasmus Smith or individual planters like William Herbert, or a corporate group such as the bishops of the Church of Ireland built and maintained them.[31] In Ulster a number of the schoolmasters were religious dissidents of Scottish and most likely Presbyterian background. Little is known of these plantation schools as yet. For the settler the education of their sons and the marriage alliances of their children were of primary concern for the perpetuation of their property and the upgrading of their social status. In general they yearned for the civility of the gentrified English society at which they gazed eastward constantly. Nothing was more gratifying than an arranged match between a son or daughter with an English aristocratic connection.

Richard Boyle, 1st Earl of Cork, typifies the successful family cycle of the seventeenth century Irish settler. The younger son of a younger son, with enough legal knowledge to make him a sharp practitioner in land speculation, he made his way to Ireland in the late 1580s and picked up Irish land in the mercurial swings of land sales that followed the first Munster plantation. Boyle accumulated his phenomenal wealth in the second wave of settlement that developed after the Treaty of Mellifont, 1603. He became one of the largest landowners and was estimated the wealthiest man in the king's realms. He acquired a knighthood, then a peerage as 1st Earl of Cork. He became a member of the Irish Privy Council and in the interim between the appointment of Deputy Wentworth and the departure of Falkland, he and Loftus held the reins of government as lords chief justice.[32]

A family man of strict Puritan conviction, he had eight daughters and seven sons. He left behind him a detailed *Diary* and his memoirs, *True Remembrances*. His daughter, Mary Rich, Countess of Warwick and his son, Robert both wrote diaries or autobiographies as they named them. Another daughter, Catherine, became an accepted member of the Great Tew circle, which gathered in the Oxfordshire house of Lucius Carey, son of the Irish Lord Deputy Falkland and the formidably intellectual Elizabeth Tarfield.[33] Catherine gained the reputation of being a leading intellectual, praised by John Milton and by Bishop Burnet, esteemed by her brother Robert whose genius she tended for over forty years as his companion in her widowhood. She retained her own identity as Lady Ranelagh, holding her own gatherings in her Pall Mall residence. The other daughters are recorded for the distinction of their marriages; certainly their letters to their father display a sense of form and at times a witty and wry sense of humour in describing their husbands to him.

From the voluminous correspondence of Richard Boyle and from his *Diary* we learn how the girls in a wealthy *noveau riche* planter's family in Munster were educated.[34] At the age of two and a half Mary Boyle was removed from her home in Lismore Castle to that of Lady Cleyton near Mallow, County Cork, some 20 miles distant. Lady Cleyton acted as foster-mother for some of the Boyle daughters, beginning with Alice, the eldest. Boyle's second wife was the young Catherine Fenton whose father played a prominent role in the Munster war and had acquired lands in Kerry and Cork in the ensuing plantation schemes. Catherine Fenton appears to have been completely dominated by her husband who even decreed her manner of dressing. She had a succession of pregnancies. It was customary for newborn children of upper-class English families to be put out to a wetnurse and returned home after two years. Lady Cleyton of Mallow was childless and Mary Boyle records that 'she took care to have me soberly educated'. Richard Boyle, a man of high intelligence, encouraged intellectual curiosity in his children. Reading was first taught, followed by writing. Boyle presented each of his daughters with a copy of Sir Philip Sidney's *Arcadia*. There is even a hint in his *Diary* that Mary Boyle may have annotated her copy of *Arcadia*. The Sidney connection and, through it, the humanist tradition of the previous century were strong in Munster circles. Mary, Sidney's sister, had married William Herbert, 2nd Earl of Pembroke whose cousin had received a seignory in Castleisland in County Kerry. He remained close to the Pembrokes. Sir Francis Walsingham's daughter married Philip Sidney (Earl of Leicester); both Walsingham and his cousin Sir Edward Denny played a crucial role in settling the forfeited lands of the late Earl of Desmond in north Kerry. Yet another connection was the marriage between Edmund Spenser and Elizabeth Boyle, a cousin of Richard Boyle. Boyle's son Lewis married the scholarly Elizabeth Fielding, daughter of Lord Denbigh.

Richard Boyle recorded his own reflections and encouraged his children to write. His son Roger wrote plays, a six-volume romance and a treatise on the art of war. Robert became an eminent scientist, equally distinguished in chemistry and physics, the originator of Boyle's Law. All the children wrote moral essays; Francis published his. The education of the Boyle children followed a pattern: wet nursing and fosterage, private tutoring at home under their father's eye. The older boys at the ages of eleven and nine went to Trinity College. Their formal education ended with a continental tour. Francis and Robert, the younger boys, went to Eton. Lewis became a sailor and navigator. Richard Boyle was incessant in his surveillance of his wife and children. Fussy and uxorious, he increasingly supervised their wearing apparel, the household accounts, and arranged both their pocket money and their marriages. The virtues he most admired he enshrined on his wife's memorial: 'religious, virtuous, loving and obedient'. Later he was to build himself an incredibly ostentatious monument to commemorate her (and himself) in the eastern end of St Patrick's Cathedral in Dublin. Archbishop James Ussher who authorised the tomb defended it to Strafford, the Lord Deputy, as a 'very great monument to the Church', presumably a hymn in stone to married life.[35]

Mary Boyle was the rebel in the family. Her *Diary* affords us glimpses of the mind of an upper-class girl educated according to the standards of the time, and on her own admission that education was one which allowed her to read romances. Her mentor was the lively

Elizabeth Killigrew who married her brother, Francis, and Elizabeth gave Mary the taste for reading romances. She, too, introduced Mary Boyle to Charles Rich. Mary went against her father's arrangements in order to marry him, refusing her father's choice, James Hamilton, an Ulster settler. Boyle was slightly mollified when Charles Rich fortuitously attained the earldom, but at the beginning he dealt severely with his daughter, cutting off her allowance. It was her father-in-law, the Earl of Warwick, who converted her to Puritanism. She came to revile herself and records in her *Diary* her regret for the 'ill and horribly disobedient answer for a daughter to give her father'. From her *Diary* we receive one of the clearest expositions of the Puritan doctrine of daughterly obedience.[36]

Mary and Catherine Boyle illustrate the almost symmetrical oscillation between autonomy and dependence that women in Puritan England and Ireland experienced. For Mary her acceptance of the prevailing doctrine of obedient daughter signalled the collapse of her rebellious stage; her desire for parental approval triumphed as she recounts honestly in her *Diary.* Catherine Boyle was the most intelligent and lovable of the Boyle girls. Until her records have been sifted through from the Milton and Ranelagh papers we can form only a general impression of a woman with the capacity of making her mark in the most intellectual elite of the times, the Great Tew circle, and of finding a manner of living which gave her a maximum amount of autonomy over her own life. Her father's intense paternalism was redeemed by the regard in which he held this brilliant daughter and his trust in her ability to advise him in his financial and household affairs.[37] John Leake, the Earl of Cork's most trusted adviser and intimate friend of the household described her thus:

A more brave wench, nor a braver spirit, you have not met withal. She hath a memory that will hear a sermon and go home and repeat it after dinner, verbatim. I know not how she will appear in England, but she is most accounted of in Dublin.[38]

She accounted well of herself in London. Separated from her husband of whom John Leake remarked 'all that could be said of him is that he seldom went sober to bed', she became the incomparable Lady Ranelagh to Bishop Burnet who declared that she had cut 'the greatest figure in all those revolutions of these kingdoms for above fifty years of any woman of her age'. She arranged for her sons to be tutored by John Milton, who held her in high regard.

The failure of the age to provide an adequate education for the undoubted intelligence of girls like the Boyle daughters, despite the good dispositions of a benevolent father, illustrates the gradual exclusion of women from virtually all spheres of productive work, including intellectual activity. It was an exclusion that accompanied the growth of capitalism, colonialism and the birth of modern slavery in the seventeenth century. The assertion of patriarchy as the dominant governing model in state and family was part of the general movement of approval for authority and order in that period. There was a desire to restore women to their places in the family and to restore stability by returning authority to the head of the household, the father, a doctrine dear to all the major churches. Women were valued because they were perceived to maintain men's domestic privileged role. The differentiated educational development of men and women in such a society, in the age of absolutism, was ensured through the conviction that it was women, not men, who bore and raised children.[39]

This is a *pis aller,* a gloss on women's education towards the end of the century. Happily it affords us a glimpse of the ordinary woman, the woman of the 'lower orders'. *Párliament na mBan* (the parliament of women) was composed towards the end of the century, 1697 its probable date of circulation. Its author was Dr Donal Ó Colmáin, a priest or a learned layman, and his work is cast in the mould of an Erasmian dialogue.[40] The women's parliament is situated in Cork and though the author surrounds the dialogue with moralising sequences on subjects like prayer, women's dress, dancing, thieving, and the seven deadly sins, in quite unexpected ways the framework of the proceedings of this unusual parliament of 500 women is feminist in tone. Fionuala, the first speaker, deprecates the lack of participation of women in public life, 'remaining always at home, attending to our distaffs and spindles, even though many of us are no good about the house' (II, 295–8). On the second day the education of girls is discussed, and an act passed by which all daughters are to be sent to school till the age of twelve years. Then the more intelligent shall be sent on to learn the seven liberal arts which are listed as grammar, rhetoric, philosophy, arithmetic, astrology, geometry and poetry. A second act decreed that all daughters who are able to should go on to learn divinity, law and medicine as was deemed suitable. Sive, who introduces the enactments, declares: 'I am certain that we will attain public authority as a consequence of these enactments' (II, 636–50). Ó Colmáin's work reveals a refreshing dimension of the commonalty:

> At a feast or in a public assembly the wife of a rustic or of a churl is so bold that she sits down and moves before a lady who is noble on both her father's and her mother's side, simply because she has a little wealth.

Soon there will be no longer any distinguishing marks between one class and another (II, 592–6).

Satire or humanist tract, *Párliament na mBan* was far from the reality of women at the end of the century.

Early modern Ireland was a major transitional period which culminated in the formation of a transformed countryside and system of government presided over by a powerful socio-political group, the landed ascendancy. The education of women cannot be artificially abstracted from the web of social and economic relationships that developed in Ireland during those centuries. It was not merely a matter of divergent predicaments in which women were placed by religious difference, and by loss of property-owning rights. It was also a predicament of different political traditions, and the manner in which particular groups of women perceived their interests. Religious and political divisions, in part, explain the lack of unified resistance on the part of women to their consignment to a privatised, powerless and subordinate position in the household. Women's ability to question the female destiny in the dominant culture of patriarchy faltered as the growth of the public and private spheres trapped them in domesticity. It also stunted their intellectual growth. At a time when christian humanism was encouraging the vision of a new society based on plurality and access to educational opportunity for women, the sixteenth century moved into the warring confrontations of dominant religious and political ideologies. So the environment of women's education changed. Anxieties about the erosion of the traditional stability of the family contributed to the authoritarian climate of the seventeenth century and when the massive profile of the dawning scientific revolution became visible after the restoration of King Charles II in 1660, women had not even achieved a toehold on the beckoning peaks of the new sciences. Yet the very consolidation of the public and the private spheres, of gender and home, created moments of doubt among those women who became increasingly controlled and powerless as is evident from women such as the Boyle daughters. For catholic women the narrowing of their education to catechesis raises another set of questions: the marginalisation of women in catholic culture in the seventeenth century was reflected in what happened to their education. The sharp lesson that a study of women's education in early modern Ireland teaches is that nothing that happened to women and their intellects during that period is safely past.

from Margaret Mac Curtain and Mary O'Dowd (eds), *Women in Early Modern Ireland* (Edinburgh, Edinburgh University Press; Dublin, Wolfhound Press, 1991), pp 160–178.

NOTES

1   Thomas More to William Gunnel, no. 63,1518, Elizabeth F. Rogers (ed.), *The Correspondence of Sir Thomas More* (Princeton, Princeton University Press, 1947), quoted in full in Ruth Kelso, *Doctrine for the Lady of the Renaissance* (Urbana, University of Illinois Press, 1956), p. 62).

2   S. Marshall Wynthjes, 'Women in the Reformation Era', in Renate Bridenthal and Claudia Koonz (eds), *Becoming Visible: Women in European History* (Boston, Houghton Mifflin, 1977), pp 167–91. Richard Marius, *Thomas More* (London, Collins, 1986), pp 64–78.

3   For the library of the Earl of Kildare see Standish Hayes O'Grady, *Catalogue of Irish Manuscripts in the British Museum* (London, British Museum, 1926), Vol. I; Alice Stopford Green, *The Making of Ireland and its Undoing* (London, Macmillan, 1908), p. 251; for Geraldine Castles see Margaret Mac Curtain, 'A Lost Landscape: Geraldine Castles and Towerhouses of the Shannon Estuary', in John Bradley

(ed.), *Settlement and Society in Ireland: Viking and Medieval Times* (Kilkenny, Boethius Press, 1988).

4 Edmund Campion, *Two Bokes of the Histories of Ireland* (Assen, Netherlands, Van Gorcum, 1963), p. 9; Seán P. Ó Mathúna, *William Bathe, S.J. 1564–1614: A Pioneer in Linguistics* (Amsterdam, Philadelphia, J. Benjamins Pub., 1986), pp 34–5. For an excellent background to this period, Colm Lennon, *Richard Stanihurst: The Dubliner, 1547–1618* (Dublin, Irish Academic Press, 1981).

5 Christopher Nugent Delvin, *Queen Elizabeth's Primer of the Irish Language* (Dublin, J.M. Kronheim, undated, c. 1564) for details cf. Ó Mathúna, *op. cit., pp* 148, 167.

6 The fullest contemporary account of Margaret Ball is contained in Fr Howlin, S.J., 'Perbreve Compendium', in Patrick Francis Moran (ed.), *Spicilegium Ossoriense: Being a Collection of Original Letters and Papers Illustrative of the Irish Church from the Reformation to the Year 1800* (Dublin, W.B. Kelly, 1874–84), Vol. L, pp 105–6. For an account of the Ball family, consult Colm Lennon, *The Lords of Dublin in the Age of Reformation* (Dublin, Irish Academic Press, 1989), pp 136, 143, 149, 156, 228.

7 F.X. Martin, O.S.A., 'Ireland, the Renaissance and the Counter-Reformation', *Topic 13: Studies in Irish History* (Washington, Washington and Jefferson College, 1967); Colm Lennon, 'The Counter-Reformation in Ireland, 1542–1641', in Ciaran Brady and Raymond Gillespie (eds), *Natives and Newcomers: Essays on the Making of Irish Colonial Society, 1534–1641* (Dublin, Irish Academic Press, 1986), pp 75–92.

8 Laurence Stone, 'The Educational Revolution in England, 1560–1640', *Past and Present*, Vol. 28 (1964), pp 41–80; Mark H. Curtis, *Oxford and Cambridge in Transition, 1558–1642* (Oxford, Clarendon Press, 1959).

9 Helga Hammerstein, 'Aspects of the Continental Education of Irish Students in the Reign of Queen Elizabeth I', *Historical Studies*, Vol. VIII (1971), pp 137–54; D. F. Cregan, 'Irish Catholic Admissions to the English Inns of Court, 1558–1625', *Irish Jurist*, Vol. V (1970), pp 95–114; 'Irish Recusant Lawyers in Politics in the Reign of James', *Ibid.*, Vol. V (1970), pp 306–20.

10 Thomas More to family, Autumn 1517, in Leicester Bradner and Charles Arthur Lynch (eds), *The Latin Epigrams of Thomas More* (Chicago, University of Chicago Press, 1953), p. 231; Philippe Ariès, *Centuries of Childhood* (London, Jonathan Cape, 1962) for changing attitudes to the education and rearing of children in the past.

11 F. X. Martin, O.S.A., *Friar Nugent: A Study of Francis Lavalin Nugent, 1569–1635: Agent of the Counter-Reformation* (London, Methuen, 1962), p. 265. For the Nugent girls' expenses at school see Transcript of 11.h.l. (5, ii) in Archives de L'Aube in Irish Capuchin Provincial Archives, Dublin.

12 Joan Kelly, 'Early Feminist Theory and the Querelle des Femmes, 1400–1789', in *Women, History and Theory: the Essays of Joan Kelly* (Chicago, University of Chicago Press, 1984), pp 65–109; S. Croag Bell, 'Christine de Pizan: Humanism and the Problems of a Studious Woman', *Feminist Studies,* Vol. 3–4 (1976), pp 173–84; Shulamith Shahar, *The Fourth Estate: A History of Women in the Middle Ages* (London, Methuen, 1983).

13 H. Gallwey, 'The Cusack Family of County Meath and Dublin', *The Irish Genealogist,* Vol. 5 (1974–9), p. 312. For a transcript of Thomas Cusack's letter to his sister apologising for borrowing from her, Public Records Office Ireland, Transcripts of Deeds and Wills from Exchequer Inquisitions, County Dublin, Vol. II, p. 443.

14 Brendan Bradshaw, *The Dissolution of the Religious Orders in Ireland under Henry VIII* (London and New York, Cambridge University Press, 1974), p. 133.

15 Countess of Desmond to Privy Council, 28 June 1580 (P.R.O., S.P. 63/73/67); for a facsimile of her letter to Sir Robert Cecil, see Anne Chambers, *Eleanor, Countess of Desmond c. 1545–1638* (Dublin, Wolfhound Press, 1986), p. 216. Eleanor's letter to Pope Gregory XIII, undated, is located in Nunz. d'lnghilterra I, f. 205 in the Vatican Archives Rome. See also pp 79–80 above and Margaret Mac Curtain, 'Marriage in Tudor Ireland' in Art Cosgrove (ed.), *Marriage in Ireland* (Dublin, College Press, 1985), pp 57–9.

16 Anne Chambers, *Granuaile, the Life and Times of Grace O'Malley. c. 1530–1603* (Dublin, Wolfhound Press, 1979) pp 25, 55, 62; See facsimile of Grace O'Malley's petition to Queen Elizabeth I in 1593 (*ibid., pp* 136–7).

17 M. Kerney Walsh, 'Irishwomen in Exile, 1600–1800, the Eoin O'Mahony Memorial Lecture in Dublin', *The O'Mahony Journal,* Vol. XI (1981), pp 35–48.

18 *Ibid., pp* 44–5. See also pp 117–25 above.

19 Jerrold Casway, 'Rosa O'Dogherty: a Gaelic Woman', *Seanchas Ard Mhacha,* Vol. X (1980–1), pp 42–62; 'Mary Stuart O'Donnell', *Donegal Annual,* No. 39 (1987), pp 28–36.

20 For Lady Falkland, see Charles Richard Erlington and James Henthorn Todd (eds), *The Whole Works of James Ussher* (Dublin, Hodges and Smith, 1847–64), 17 Volumes, Vol. XV, p. 356. For

Margaret Ussher née Stanihurst, see William Ball Wright (ed.), *The Ussher Memoirs* (Dublin, Sealy, Bryers and Walker, 1889), pp 30–42. For Eleanor Douglas, D. Morrissey, 'Never so Mad a Ladie: the Life of Lady Eleanor Douglas', *UCD History Review,* Vol. V (1988), pp 14–7.

21 Raymond Gillespie, *Colonial Ulster: The Settlement of East Ulster 1600–1641* (Cork, Cork University Press for the Irish Committee for Historical Sciences, 1985), p. 77.

22 Laurence Stone, 'The Educational Revolution in England, 1560–1640', *loc. cit.,* p. 70.

23. The author is indebted to Dr D. F. Cregan, C.M. for drawing her attention to this largely unresearched area, but see T. Flynn, 'The Dominicans of Ireland: 1535–1640' (Ph.D. thesis, Trinity College Dublin, 1988) for references to imports of books into Ireland.

24 Clanricarde to Marchioness of Hertford, 30 January 1644; Marchioness of Winchester to Clanricarde, 4 March 1545; Marchioness of Hertford to Lady Ussher, 20 March 1647 in John Lowe (ed.), *Letter-book of the Earl of Clanricarde 1643–1647* (Dublin, Irish Manuscripts Commission, 1983), pp 35, 153–4, 427; T. C. Croker (ed.) *The Autobiography of Mary Rich, Countess of Warwick,* (for Percy Society Journal, London, 1848). The memoirs of Abbess Cecily Dillon form the first section of the Annals of the Poor Clare Nuns of Ireland (Archives Nun's Island, Galway). The author is grateful to Sr McCarthy, O.S.F., for supplying a transcript. For Anne Conway consult Carolyn Merchant, *The Death of Nature, Women, Ecology and the Scientific Revolution* (San Francisco, Harper and Row, 1980). For Elizabeth Preston, ongoing research by author, see *Calendar of the Manuscripts of the Marquess of Ormonde* (London, Historical Manuscripts Commission, 11 vols, 1895–1920).

25 Patrick Corish, *The Irish Catholic Experience* (Dublin, Gill and Macmillan, 1985), p. 105; Hugh Redwald Trevor-Roper, 'James Ussher, Archbishop of Armagh', in his *Catholics, Anglicans and Puritans* (London, Fontana, 1989), pp 120–65.

26 *Cal. S.P. Ire., 1606–08,* p. 133. 27. R. P. Liebowitz, 'Virgins in the Service of Christ: The Dispute over an Active Apostolate for Women during the Counter-Reformation' in Eleanor McLaughlin and Rosemary Radford Ruether (eds), *Women of Spirit: Female Leadership in the Jewish and Christian Traditions* (New York, Simon and Schuster, 1979), pp 131–52.

28 Annals and memoirs of Abbess Cecily Dillon in Archives of the Poor Clare Nuns of Ireland in Nun's Island, Galway; Irish Dominican Archives (women) in Sion Hill, Blackrock, County

Dublin; Archives of Benedictine Nuns of Ireland in Kylemore Abbey, Connemara, County Galway.

29 *Loc. cit,* The surnames of the seven founding members of the Dublin Dominican community of Cabra, 1717 were listed as Bellew, Browne, Keating, Rice, Vaughan, Plunkett, Weever. They opened a boarding school in Channel Row, Dublin in 1719.

30 For constitution of Fr D. O'Daly, O.P. and annals, registers and documents 1639 ff. Archives Bom Sucesso, Lisbon. The surnames of the early nuns are Kavanagh of Borris and Pulmonty, County Wicklow, Burke of Brittas, daughter of Sir John Burke, Anne and Cecelia O'Neill, O'Sullivan Beare, O'Mahony and they form a group in the women of the wild geese.

31 J. H. Simms, 'The Restoration, 1660–85', in T. W. Moody, F. X. Martin and F. J. Byrne (eds), *A New History of Ireland: Vol. Ill, 1534–1691* (Oxford, Clarendon Press, 1976), p. 436. Samuel Wilson to Lord Herbert, 21 May 1678, in W. J. Smith (ed.), *Herbert Correspondence* (Dublin, Irish Manuscripts Commission, 1963), p. 244. Munster had a headstart on other provinces as planters like R. Boyle established schools in Bandon and Lismore.

32 Nicholas Canny, *The Upstart Earl: A Study of the Social and Mental World of Richard Boyle, First Earl of Cork, 1566–1643* (Cambridge, Cambridge University Press, 1982); Alexander Ballock Grosart (ed.), *The Lismore Papers,* of Sir Richard Boyle, Earl of Cork [1566–1643J (London, Chiswick Press, 1886–8), 10 volumes.

33 H. Trevor-Roper, 'The Great Tew Circle' in his *Catholics, Anglicans and Puritans, op. cit., pp* 171, 173, 179, 209. Lord Dacre refers to her as the 'blue-stocking sister of Robert Boyle'. The 'Bluestockings' was a term first used in the 1750s for men and women of wit and knowledge who frequented houses where the social display of knowledge and advanced opinions was cultivated as a fine art. They wore blue stockings, hence the name. Cf. Dale Spender, *Women of Ideas, and What Men Have Done to Them* (London, Routledge and Kegan Paul, 1982), pp 101–12.

34 Nicholas Canny, 'The Family Life of Richard Boyle' in *The Upstart Earl, op. cit., pp* 77–123. R. Meehan, 'Boyle's Daughters' (B.A. dissertation, University College, Dublin, 1987); Richard Boyle, 'True Remembrances' in *The Lismore Papers,* Vol. II, pp 100–17. For unpublished Boyle material see Canny, *The Upstart Earl, pp* 151–2.

35 T. C. Croker (ed.), *The Autobiography of Mary Rich* (London, 1848); B.L. Add. MS 27,351–5; Richard Boyle, 'True Remembrances', *op. cit.;* for Wentworth's remark see, *Works of Ussher,* Vol. XV, p. 573.

36 Charlotte Fall-Smith, *Mary Rich, Countess of Warwick 1625–1678* (London, Longmans, Green and Co., 1901). See also note 35 above.

37 Nicholas Canny, *The Upstart Earl,* p. 181. Professor Canny does not refer to Catherine's affectionate relationship with her father.

38 R. Meehan, 'Boyle's Daughters', p. 14; David Masson, *The Life of John Milton* (London, Macmillan and Co., 1859–80), 7 Volumes, Vol. V, p. 232.

39 Gerda Lerner, *The Creation of Patriarchy* (New York, Oxford University Press, 1986), pp 216–20.

40 Brian Ó Cuív (ed.), *Párliament na nBan* (Dublin, Institiúid Ard-Léinn, 1977), pp xxxi–xli. (For a different perspective see Bernadette Cunningham in *Women in Early Modern Ireland*, pp 155–7.

THE REAL MOLLY MACREE

One of the weaknesses of the revisionist debate concerning the interpretations of Irish history was its failure to read the signs of the times during which it took place. Schooled in the methods of British empirical objectivity, selection of facts and their ordering, trawling through documents and reading the sources, without bias, the apprentice historian who followed E. H. Carr, What is History *(London, 1961) or G. R. Elton,* The Practice of History *(Sydney, 1967) privileged official sources and reconstructed the past by fidelity to the text, and the questions it raised. Many Irish historians trained over the last fifty years were influenced by British empirical methods, mediated to them through the authoritative teachings of R. D. Edwards of University College Dublin and Theo Moody of Trinity College, Dublin. Ciaran Brady in his reflective introductory essay to his revisionist debate collection,* Interpreting Irish History *(Dublin, 1994) contrasts the historical revision which Edwards and Moody introduced to their students with the political overtone the word 'revisionism' assumed in the late seventies and throughout the eighties:*

> *But what seemed in the 1930s to be an unproblematic combination of intellectual practice and public service had, in the highly charged political and ideological conditions of the 1970s and 1980s, come to be seen in some quarters as an unhealthy even disingenuous position. Yet all the while the majority of practising historians failed or refused to see that such a problem existed; and insisted to the contrary that their critics' case was not merely politically motivated, but rested more seriously on a fundamental misunderstanding of what the practice of scholarly history was all about. There was no further room for argument. (p. 12)*

It was during those same decades, the late nineteen seventies and eighties, that post-modernism offered a disconcerting challenge to historical method by its recognition of dominant intellectual discourses, by its linkages between knowledge and power, by the acknowledgement of subjectivity underlying much so-called objectivity. To the historical establishment the threat of relativism was uppermost and the persuasive R. J. Evans, professor of modern history in Cambridge University reassured his colleagues that they had much to gain from post-modernist theory and method:

> Postmodernism in its more constructive modes has encouraged historians to look more closely at documents, to take their surface patina more seriously, and to think about texts and narratives in new ways. It has helped open up many new subjects and areas for research ... It has led to a greater emphasis on open acknowledgement of the historian's own subjectivity, which can only help the reader engaged in a critical assessment of historical work.
> - R. J. Evans, In Defence of History (London, Granta, 1997) p. 248.

In 1992 while teaching Irish history at Boston College I became aware of how postmodernism in its interdisciplinary modes was influencing my thinking. Adele Dalsimer, co-director of the Irish Studies Program invited me to contribute to her book, Visualizing Ireland: National Identity and the Pictorial Tradition. The subject a painting, Molly Macree and its painter, Thomas Jones, and the task, to demonstrate 'how visual materials can be incorporated into our construction of "Irishness" as an ideological concept'. Research and reading introduced me to a new cultural approach to the mid-nineteenth century Famine and to an understanding of how the artist redefines a theme in art which opens up for the reader a text for decoding through a method of interrogation.

The essay appeared in Adele Dalsimer (ed.), Visualizing Ireland: National Identity and the Pictorial Tradition (Boston and London, Faber and Faber, 1993).

Charles Baudelaire, in a celebrated essay 'The Painter of Modern Life', distinguished between 'mere trivia dressed up for effect' and the artist's obligation 'to have the present in his mind's eye'.[1] He commended 'those exquisite artists, who, although they have confined themselves to recording what is familiar and pretty, are nonetheless, in their own ways, important historians'. Thomas Alfred Jones would be astonished to find that his watercolour of Molly Macree, executed in the 1860s, became a favourite reproduction of purchasers in the National Gallery of Ireland sales department. Furthermore, as a dedicated president of the Royal Hibernian Academy of Arts for twenty-four years (1869–93), he would have expressed satisfaction that one of his own paintings would be such a discreet and steady source of revenue for the cause of art in his native country. Jones would not have demurred when Baudelaire called for an art 'based upon the forms, costumes, actions, even facial expressions of his own day'. In choosing to exhibit a series of paintings titled *The Irish Colleen* in the second half of the nineteenth century, Jones was attesting to his perception of his own world and, in a subliminal way, challenging the conventional sensibility of his circle. Making an Irish peasant girl the subject of a painting in which the rural landscape became the background contravened the tradition of Irish topographical watercolouring. Jones and artists like Michael Brennan presented the innovation to the Dublin academicians of the period, and if Jones moved on to specialize in painting portraits of his contemporaries – and monopolize the field – he returned several times to paint such subjects as *Limerick Lasses* (1872) and *Connemara Girls* (1880), which added to his earlier studies of the 1860s, such as *The Colleen Bawn* (1861), *The Colleen's Toilet* (1864), and *A Limerick Lass* (1865); and, shortly before his death, Jones painted another version of *A Limerick Lass* (1892). Jones gave the genre a place in Irish art that has grown rather than diminished over time.[2]

On the continent and in Britain, the painting of the rural labourer was a popular subject in nineteenth-century art. Depicting peasant life, the artist could suggest the shifts in sensibility that were taking place around the changing role of the cottier. In literature Honoré de Balzac had turned the French peasant into a loutish fellow and Karl Marx despaired of ever making a revolutionary out of what he fretfully called 'the barbarian within society'. Nineteenth-century artists saw the peasant as a subject associated with a receding but passionately remembered scene: the haywagon, the communal harvesting of the crops, the patient figures with bowed heads reciting the Angelus – all the romantic evocations of a countryside before the railways swept peasants into the noisome, crowded ghettos and factories of the Industrial Revolution. Even the word 'peasant' got lost and was replaced by 'the laboring poor', and later still by 'working class'.

Representations of the peasant woman were an important statement of this shift in sensibility. Professor Linda Nochlin has analyzed the connection between peasant and working woman in nineteenth-century European art, and in her study *Women, Art, and Power* (1988) she examines further aspects of the assimilation of the peasant woman into the rural landscape and, more significantly, into the realm of nature.[3] Nochlin, referring to paintings as different as Giovanni Segantini's *Two Mothers* and Jean-Francois Millet's *The Gleaners*, argues that this association of women with nature gave rural poverty an acceptable face and used the farm woman's backbreaking toil to sublimate her destiny and translate it into the sphere of religious piety. Moreover, she cites the idealization of the peasant girl, as depicted in the

'Molly Macree'
Thomas Alfred Jones (1823–93)
41 x 33.2 cms
gouache with varnish on paper
Photo © The National Gallery of Ireland

paintings of Jules Breton, particularly in *The Song of the Lark*. The young peasant girl, invariably striking in form and posture, helped to formulate her gender role in nineteenth-century art, as signifier of earthy eroticism and unconscious sensuality.

The representation of 'natural mother', Nochlin suggests, was communicated in the juxtaposition of mother and child, cow and calf in *Two Mothers*. Add to this iconography that of peasant woman as symbol of religious devotion, as in Wilhelm Leibl's *Peasant Women in the Church*, and the viewer receives the image of the elemental, fertile earth mother who conveys overt messages of submissiveness. Thus, like christian madonna and child paintings, the representation of nineteenth-century peasant woman in art becomes a cliché of a supratemporal, eternal feminine construct. According to Nochlin a biblical setting removed the stooped figures of *The Gleaners* – among the poorest and humblest of rural society – from their stark actuality and placed them in the 'suprahistoric context of High Art'.[4]

Did Thomas Jones deliberately link the young Irish girl with the emerging image of the Irish Colleen, immortalized by his contemporary, James Lyman Molloy, in the popular lyric 'The Kerry Dances'? The archives at the National Gallery have a collection of paintings in the Irish Colleen genre. A group of the artistic elite in Ireland communicate upwards what popular culture was mediating in street ballads like 'The Kerry Dances' and 'The Rose of Tralee'. The popular opera of the time Bendick's *Lily of Killarney* gave Don Bouciault's play, *The Colleen Bawn*, a new lease of life.

O, the days of the Kerry dancing, O the ring of the piper's tunes
O for one of those hours of gladness gone alas! like our youth too soon.
Was there ever a sweeter colleen in the dance than Eily More?
Or a prouder lad than Thady, as he boldly took the floor?

'Lads and lasses to your places; up the middle and down again'
Ah! the merryhearted laughter ringing through the happy glen.
O, to think of it, O to dream of it, fills my heart with tears.

James Molloy recalled his own boyhood in those nostalgic verses putting aside his memories of the Great Famine (1846–52), the scourge of the generation he had enshrined in that charmed past.[5]

The historian rarely understands completely the sophisticated nuances of a work of art and is always in danger of taking art too literally, believing that an overview of the paintings of a particular artist can expose virtually the entire course of that artist's career. This is a misconception of what art is, which the historian is apt to share with the public in general. Thomas Jones was a prolific portrait painter and the historian can all too easily fall into the trap of interpreting his personal life through those visual texts. Jones is a more complicated artist than he appears. He was a deserted child, his parents unknown. The Archdale family reared him in a large house in fashionable Kildare Place, off St. Stephen's Green, in upper-class Dublin. The Archdales were an influential family, well known for their philanthropy. They supplied the foundling with everything, including his name; he himself added 'Alfred' later. He was educated carefully, entering the Royal Dublin Society's school in 1831, and was sufficiently talented to exhibit a picture, *Vision of the Kings, a Subject from Macbeth,* in 1841. In the matriculation register in Trinity College, Dublin, he was entered for 14 October 1842, but he left without taking a degree. He was abroad when the Famine struck parts of Ireland. Returning to Dublin, he demonstrated a cosmopolitan training influenced by pre-Raphaelite technique and continental themes. In 1849, once settled in Dublin, he sent two drawings to the Exhibition of the Royal Hibernian Academy, one of which was the study of *Italian Peasants*. He exhibited again in 1851 (subject unknown), and in 1856 he submitted *Daughter of Erin,* which Holl engraved later that year. Thereafter he was a regular exhibitor and in 1860 was elected associate and then, in the same year, a member of the Royal Hibernian Academy. Nine years later he was elected president. Popular and industrious, he was knighted in 1880 by the Lord Lieutenant, the Duke of Marlborough, for his services to the Dublin art world – the first president of the academy, founded in 1823, to receive that honour.[6]

His oil paintings are numerous, some still hanging in institutions such as the Royal College of Physicians in Dublin, the King's Inns, various banking halls up and down the country, and the Belfast Public Library. Many of the great landowners of Ireland sat for him. Poorly painted, without great artistic merit, his portraits satisfied their subjects. His self-portrait hangs in the Council Room of the Royal Hibernian Academy. Jones was tireless in advancing the interests of the Academy, an indefatigable fund-raiser right through his time of office. Maintenance of the building was not government assisted, save for one instance in 1871 when the Board of Works repaired the roof of the academy building for £400. Jones's commitment to the teaching dimension of the Academy was realistic. He personally donated £1000 towards the construction of a room for the life school in the academy in the late 1870s. During his term as president the academy prospered: Dublin had two art schools and two annual exhibitions.[7] This was a singular achievement for a city whose artistic institutions were established in the post-Union period, after 1801, and much of the credit goes to Thomas Jones's period as president of the Royal Hibernian Academy.

Despite his success as a portrait painter, Jones continued to paint subjects that have proved more permanent as contemporary social commentary. In 1872 he exhibited *The Emigrant's Prayer,* and among the Conyngham Collection that Christies disposed of in 1908 was *The Emigrant's Departure,* which the Marchioness of Conyngham had acquired. The painting *Molly Macree* dates from the 1860s but its provenance was for nearly eighty years somewhat of a mystery. The artist gave it to M. A. Halligan, and she gave it to the National Gallery of Ireland in 1947. It is not listed as having been exhibited in the 1860s, but the picture belongs unmistakably to the Irish colleen genre, made familiar to Irish viewers by Jones after the fashion of European painting.

Jones's portrait has the brilliant colouring of the pre-Raphaelite movement. It is a finely executed and stylish painting. Every detail is painted in a series of tiny brush strokes. The striking juxtaposition of the clear reds, blues, and greens of the shawl against the stained apron achieves a realism that remains with the viewer as a tantalizing question. Confidently, Jones has placed Molly Macree right up against the picture plane so as to evoke a kind of stage or backdrop. Seeming to lean out of the picture, she lightly props her head on one hand, and behind her, the wind-tossed sky and rain-sodden field bespeak the presence of natural forces greater than human ingenuity. By the 1860s the Irish Colleen and Molly Macree were favoured themes of balladeer and musician. Unlike the Colleen Bawn, the Irish Colleen was not associated with tragedy; on the contrary, she was treated as a sweetheart capable of bringing joy to her lover. On one level, Jones treats her allegorically, and the longer one looks at the painting, the more obvious becomes its political statement. As a composition, it is disconcertingly direct, but its iconography expresses what is unrepresentable, disturbing truths that lurk below the surface of this text of an Irish peasant girl in the years after the Great Famine.

The steep rise in population from a little over four million to eight million recorded in the fifty years before the 1841 census was checked dramatically by the Famine years. The shrinkage occurred visibly between 1845 and 1851, when 800,000 died and over a million fled the country. Those statistics represent the poorest rural groups, the cottage dwellers and the tenant labourers. The Famine precipitated the decline of the rural labouring man, leaving him in a precarious and landless position with little prospect of marrying. The corresponding rural woman was left with no prospect of advancing her status by marriage or acquiring respect by paid work. Most historians concur that women lost out in the aftermath of the Famine. They did, insofar as women with small children, the old, and the feeble always suffer in times of disaster. Long before the Famine, however, there was a slump in women's occupations as the cash-paying domestic textile industry gave place to the centralized shirt-making factories of County Derry and the linen and cotton factories of northeast Ulster around Belfast. The fragile, dual-wage economy of the Irish peasant had been greatly weakened before the Famine landed its final blow. Mary Cullen, in an examination of the family budgets of labourers in pre-Famine Ireland, has demonstrated the extent to which women contributed to their households and, apart from their direct contribution to farmwork, how they supplemented the family wages by weaving and spinning. Her analysis of the 1835 Poor Inquiry shows conclusively that the women of destitute families in the 1830s were reduced to begging for survival.[8] As if in anticipation of disaster, the Poor Law Act of 1832 authorized the building of workhouses in 163 zoned districts to deal with the massive wave of poverty and homelessness among families that had relied on the woman's earnings to pay the rent. Between 1841 and

1851, three of every four spinners of wool, linen, and cotton disappeared without trace from the work scene. The new workhouses began to function in the early forties: handsome enough in their stonecut design, totally alien in the Irish countryside, which they dominated. Capable of housing eight hundred inmates, they were planned as short-term shelters for 'the deserving destitute'. The Famine quickly transformed them into refugee compounds, in which the geography of the buildings separated men from women and both from children. Twenty-five percent of all workhouse inmates were able-bodied females over fifteen years of age. Even in the 1860s, twenty years after the Famine, the Cork Union recorded that over half the total population of its workhouses was made up of young, as well as aged and infirm, females. After the Famine one estimate reckoned that 3.3 percent of the adult female workforce was listed as beggars, brothel-keepers, and prostitutes.[9]

The narrative in *Molly Macree* is a silence, the unspoken constituting the discourse underlining almost every individual image of woman in art. The worn apron which partially covers the brown frieze skirt was the uniform of the young Irish woman in the decades after the Famine. Reading the painting as a work scene, we see it as a document in which the public informs the private. Domestic service became a major employment pool for young girls after the mid-century. It was an economic necessity and, in a warped way, also an apprenticeship for the burgeoning domesticity that was increasingly defining the position of women. Puttiug a daughter 'in service' was a safe option for parents, in tune with the ideology of Victorian Ireland, which considered housework and care of the farmyard suitable employment for young women. Urban employers hired indoor servants, preferably young country girls. They became an essential element in the creation of the new bourgeoisie, whose private realm was ordered by the mistress of the house and by the relationship of woman to woman in the tight constraints of domestic bondage. Isolating in its working environment and an impediment to marriage prospects, domestic service provided a precarious sanctuary for the docile. It also allowed more independent young women to leave home and move from domestic service to other kinds of work, an exodus as decisive in its way as emigrating or entering religious life in one of the many new convents in Ireland.

Perhaps it renders a disservice to Thomas Jones to take apart a painting of such charming proportions and careful artistic integrity to exercise a kind of historical deconstruction upon a text so plain to read. The shawl is richly patterned in strong focal tones of blue and red against a cream background. It is fringed with a skillful blend of floral arrangements that picks up the differing browns of the skirt and the somber landscape behind. On the left shoulder is an unusual Celtic design, and the shawl is folded into a patterned crimson belt not unlike an Aran Island *crios* (girdle). Is the artist suggesting that a change was taking place in fashion, fashion here meaning 'that which is worn', that a new concept of fashionableness had arrived as cheaper manufactured textiles supplanted the hand-knitted shawl? The question begs an investigation of how changes in external dress signalled a new self-consciousness in the wearer, connected with the transition from homemade to manufactured goods. The shift was accompanied by the network of railways bringing the ready-made garments to the expanding shop-keeping middle classes of the country towns. Laying aside the traditional cloak and petticoat was as much related to market pressures as it was a gesture of farewell before embarking for another life beyond the island. From the folds and details of

Molly Macree's shawl, the eye is drawn to the face above, a face saved from being 'pretty-pretty' in the Baudelarian assessment of a poor portrait, by the fine, widespread, grey eyes and the spacious brow over them. The hair, brown and wavy, is drawn back in an oddly mature style for so young a face. The expression is serious, though the mouth is smiling. It is the face of a calm, intelligent girl of perhaps sixteen years of age.

By the 1860s literacy and schooling had become an important goal for Irish girls. The national schools, set up by government orders thirty years previously to provide free education, required voluntary attendance only, yet a perusal of existing roll books reveals that female children were attending school in accelerating numbers from the 1860s onward. The growth and spread of towns were economic incentives for the building of schools, and convent schools dominated the country towns and the cities in many areas.[10] Literacy, defined as the ability to read and write English and to be numerate, was the desired objective. In the west and southwest of Ireland, spoken Irish declined and the connection between startlingly high school attendance rates among both sexes and work-related emigration is obvious. Irish girls looked upon emigration as an escape, one sanctioned by their parents. They were, in fact, the first to depart, in clusters of siblings or quite often alone, to regions where spoken and written English were proven qualifications for seeking positions. Literacy was the key to a better life. Schooling replaced powerlessness with a command of one's own destiny, of being able to access a life overseas. Willy-nilly, despite the ugly reality of destitution, life after the Famine, from the 1860s onwards, became more diversified than census returns and their rigid classifications indicate.[11] Survival after a harrowing ordeal is always a barometer of a society's will to live, and the strategies that its women develop provide significant clues about the values of that society. Will those who survive want to re-construct the past and repopulate the landscape? Or will they purposefully set their faces to a future that is unknown, intimidating, but withal emancipatory?

Celibacy, the notion of *le celibat definitiif* as developed by the French social historians, emerged as a choice and lifestyle after the Famine. It contrasted sharply with the early marriage patterns of the previous hundred years. The Irish population rose from an estimated 4 million in 1780 to 6.8 million in 1821 and 8.2 million by 1841. The most obvious features of that dramatic rise were the early age at which marriage was entered into, the universal popularity of marriage, and the average size of family, generally between ten and fifteen children. After the Famine of 1846–52 (during which nearly one million died), the flow of emigration has been estimated as the chief factor in bringing the population down to 4.4 million by the end of the century. Marriage as an institution in post-Famine society became rigid, and for marrying men, the timing was largely determined by succession to land, and by the arrangements around dowry. The distance in age between the late-marrying farmer and his much younger wife perpetuated a structure of strong paternalism. Consolidated by the central position of the widow in family decisions, it in turn postponed the heir's inheritance and eventual marriage. Parental authority wielded significant control over adult children's behaviour and desires, achieving within family considerations a precarious balance between marriage and celibacy. A rigid code of sexual morality imposed uneasy relationships between the unmarried man and woman in both town and country. In a study of marriage in post-Famine Ireland, Dr David Fitzpatrick observes:

For women, the moment of marriage was less tightly tied to their parents' aging process. Nevertheless, the marriage ages of men and women followed quite similar patterns. Parents were reluctant to release one fortune far in advance of receiving another, and encouraged their daughters to remain in service either at home or as hired workers during the years of peak strength following puberty.[12]

Made marriages, the 'match', and the payment of dowries gave daughters little manoeuverability in that period when claims to land among siblings or compensation for waiving a birthright placed restrictions on the size of a dowry and the appropriate moment of inheritance. The dowry, which formerly was paid in land or animal stock, became a cash settlement capable of being commandeered during family crisis. Fitzpatrick concludes that by the beginning of the twentieth century, restrictive marriage arrangements were well in place: 'With the aid of massive emigration, the post-Famine Irish managed to build themselves a drab but functional way of life not too unlike that of their parents'.[13] Demographically Ireland became a notably 'celibate' society with a high proportion of bachelors and spinsters. In his appendix of those who had never married, among those between ages forty-five and fifty-four, Fitzpatrick does not classify those who remained celibate in the service of the catholic church. Between 1851 and 1861 the average age of women entering convents and becoming nuns was 26.2 years. The average amount of a dowry for a choir sister was £500 in the 1860s. For the dowerless girl, religious life offered the role of lay sister whose work and station resembled those of a domestic servant. She was expected to engage in household chores, take charge of the convent farm and garden under supervision of a choir sister, and be content to live without an 'active' voice in convent elections for leadership positions. Her story, largely unexplored, had to do with personal autonomy, with security, and with the exercise of informal power in kitchen, farmyard, and laundry. Judging by the numbers who applied for admittance, convent life, either as a choir sister or a lay sister, was an agreeable choice in the 1860s. The census of 1861 shows 68 percent more nuns in Ireland than there had been ten years previously, when there were an estimated 1552 nuns. Entry to convent life, like emigration, continued to rise for women in Ireland throughout the nineteenth century and well into the twentieth.[14]

Life for working women in the 1860s was drab. Physical desire was muted and death from tuberculosis struck often, sparing neither young nor old. To be an unmarried daughter without dowry affected status within the community. In a patrilineal family dominated by property arrangements, daughters were commodities. Fortunately emigration and the convent provided escape routes that could be negotiated between parents and children. Molly Macree looks out at the viewer from her seated position in a ditch of rain-sodden ferns. Behind her, trees, river, and cornfield are suffused with an atmosphere of bronze-gold light, the sky overhead threatens more flooding. Her posture is composed, even serene. Confidence informs her body and her expression. Her world was far removed from the seventeenth-century aristocratic captivity of Róisín Dubh, idealized in the male-filtered images of the elite poets of eighteenth-century Ireland who wrote in Irish and could not have anticipated that language's decline in Molly's lifetime. She is not a celebratory figure and yet she is a window into that epiphanic world that Yeats created in his invocation of Ireland as Cathleen Ni Houlihan over forty years later. Aodhgán Ó Rathaille, the great Gaelic poet of the previous century, would have recognized her 'brightness of brightness I saw in a lonely place'.[15]

Clearly, Thomas Alfred Jones merits a more detailed study as a painter and as a personality of some weight in Dublin artistic circles. As president of the Royal Hibernian Academy, his judgment was critical in the admittance of new members and in giving fresh directions to the frequent exhibitions. In 1871 the Watercolour Society of Ireland, founded by six women, held its first annual exhibition, providing a respected outlet for the amateur artist. The annual exhibitions of the Royal Hibernian Academy, which showed the works of many foreign artists, throve under his administration. More than 35,000 viewers attended the 1880 exhibition. From 1884 to his death, Jones was professor of painting, an honoured position in the academy. In 1991 the editors of the fine catalogue that accompanied the Irish watercolours and drawings exhibition at the National Gallery of Ireland chose *Molly Macree* for its frontispiece.

In the catalogue entry, Adrian Le Harivel places her in the context of a post-Famine inconography when 'such images of Ireland were understandably popular and part of the received imagery of the countryside'.[16] What the historian would now request from the art historian is a study of the ideological in the Irish Colleen genre of that period. Class and gender are quite overt in *Molly Macree* and generally so in representations of the Irish colleen, but as Le Harivel suggests, a further coded message in *Molly Macree* renders the painting an image of Ireland. After the Famine public discussion of Irish nationalism gradually assumed the proportions of a major ideological discourse, communicated at a popular level through broadsheets, ballads, pamphlets, new forms of journalism, and artistic iconography. Ideology finds avenues to express itself in a variety of texts and the visual image is a powerful conveyor of the political text. It is only by the viewer's ability to decode and interpret – as well as respond to – the artist's composition that new modes of recognition surface. Tastes change over decades and the art historian explains what is taking place at a particular time, guiding the public beyond the constraints of present-day fashion to better understand the narrative and the techniques of a painting, as well as the issues that spoke to that society through the artist.

from Adele Dalsimer (ed.), *Visualizing Ireland: National Identity and the Pictorial Tradition* (Boston and London, Faber and Faber, 1993), pp 9–21.

NOTES

1   Charles Baudelaire, 'The Painters of Modern Life', in P. E. Charvet (ed.), *Selected Writings on Art and Artists* (London, Penguin, 1972).

2   Walter G. Strickland, *A Dictionary of Irish Artists* (Dublin, Irish Academic Press, 1989). Two volumes with an introduction to the reissue of the original two vol. work (Dublin and London, 1913) by Theo J. Snoddy, pp 560-65.

3   Linda Nochlin, *Women, Art and Power and Other Essays* (NY, Harper and Row, 1988). In her key essay, 'Women, Art and Power', Prof. Nochlin refers to her previous work for the Courbet Colloquium and incorporates some of the insights into this essay, pp 1–35.

4   Linda Nochlin, The *Cribleuses de blé*: Courbet, Millet, Breton, Kollwitz and the Image of the Working Woman', in Klaus Gallwitz and Klaus Herding (eds), *Malerei und Theorie: das Courbet-Colloquium 1979, Städtische Galerie im Städelschen Kunstinstitut Frankfurt am Main* (Frankfurt, Die Galerie, 1980), pp 49–74.

5   See reference to James Lyman Molloy in Hasia R. Diner, *Erin's Daughters in America: Irish Immigrant Women in the Nineteenth Century.* (Baltimore and London, Johns Hopkins University Press, 1983), p. 24.

6   Royal Hibernian Academy of Arts, I, A-G. Index of Exhibitors and their works 1826–1979, compiled by A. M. Stewart with a Summary History of the R.H.A. by C. de Courcy, x–xxiii (Dublin, Manton Publishing, 1985).

7   Walter G. Strickland, *op. cit.* pp 560–62.

8   Mary Cullen, 'Breadwinners and Providers: Women in the Household Economy of Labouring Families 1835–6', in Maria Luddy and Cliona Murphy (eds), *Women Surviving: Studies in Irish Women's History in the 19th and 20th Centuries* (Dublin, Poolbeg, 1989), pp 85–116.

9   Caitríona Clear, *Nuns in Nineteenth-Century Ireland* (Washington, DC, The Catholic University of America Press, 1987).

10 Tony Fahey, 'Nuns in the Catholic Church in Ireland', in Mary Cullen (ed.), *Girls Don't Do Honours* (Dublin, Women's Education Bureau, 1987), pp 7–30.

11 Mary E. Daly points out that the census returns are an inadequate representation of the role of women in the economy. The under-recording of women in agriculture and, in the later nineteenth-century returns, the invisibility of dressmakers, washer women, small shopkeepers, and hucksters blur the census figures for women's work. 'Women in the Irish Workforce from Pre-industrial to Modern Times', *Saothar: Journal of the Irish Labour History Society*, 1981, pp 74–82.

12 David Fitzpatrick, 'Marriage in Post-Famine Ireland', in Art Cosgrove (ed.), *Marriage in Ireland* (Dublin, College Press, 1985), pp 11–31.

13 David Fitzpatrick, *op. cit*, p. 129.

14 Anne V. O'Connor. 'The Revolution in Girls' Secondary Education in Ireland, 1860–1910', in Cullen (ed.), *Girls Don't Do Honours, op. cit.*, pp 31–54.

15 Aogán Ó Rathaille, eighteenth-century poet, wrote a celebrated poem on the vision woman, a many-layered theme in the *Aisling* (literal meaning 'vision') poetry of that period. Ó Rathaille's poem, *Gile na Gile, Brightness of Brightness* may be found in several versions. Cf. Thomas Kinsella and Seán Ó Tuama (eds), *An Duanaire, 1600–1900: Poems of the Dispossessed* (Mountrath, Dolmen Press, 1981).

16 Adrian Le Harivel, 'Molly Macree 1860s', *Irish Watercolours and Drawings* (Dublin, National Gallery of Ireland, 1991) p. 98. The author is grateful to Dr Brian Kennedy, former Assistant Director, National Gallery of Ireland, for suggesting possible sources for details of Thomas Alfred Jones's life.

LATE IN THE FIELD:
CATHOLIC SISTERS IN TWENTIETH-CENTURY IRELAND AND THE NEW RELIGIOUS HISTORY

The nuns' story is integral to the history of women in twentieth-century Ireland. It contains all the elements that have made the recovery of women's history a discipline that challenges the official canon of political history. Excluded from the clerical hierarchy of church authority, the presence of nuns in the social and religious life of the country was visible in the spacious architecture of convents in towns and cities throughout the country, and in the daily interaction of 'the Sisters' with children and adults. Regarded as agents of the patriarchal control of the Roman Catholic Church in some quarters, nuns were to many who came in contact with them, 'the Sisters', familiar shapes in their long, sweeping garments and their antiquated head-dress as they paced the classroom, hospital ward or unfashionable streets.

As a category, nuns (sisters, religious women, the terms are interchangeable) provide a map to guide the ignorant through the unexamined landscape of where and how women occupied the religious, cultural and economic space assigned to them in twentieth-century Ireland. Their definition as a group has been well documented in several scholarly studies of their emergence in, and contribution to the formation of modern Irish society. Caitríona Clear's work, Nuns in Nineteenth-Century Ireland *(Dublin, Gill and Macmillan, 1987) led the way for Jacinta Prunty's examination of the Holy Faith Sisters' work in the inner-city,* Dublin Slums 1800–1925: A Study in Urban Geography *(Dublin, Irish Academic Press, 1998), and Mary Peckham Magray's investigation,* The Transforming Power of the Nuns: Women, Religion and Cultural Change in Ireland, 1750–1900 *(Oxford, Oxford University Press, 1998). Nuns sit* comfortably into the configuration of a century marked by the Irish Famine in mid-century. Their growth was phenomenal in the decades after the Famine.

Turning to twentieth-century Ireland there is a puzzling complexity about the place they occupy. Powerful as negotiating tools in the state's educational and welfare plans, south and north, they became in reality pawns in the struggle for control between church and state, between bishops and departments of government. Why that came about is largely unexplored. Mary Peckham ends her analysis of religious women and cultural change on the threshold of the twentieth century with a wry comment:

> Victims of their own success, it was perhaps only to be expected that the relative independence that early leaders of Irish convents fought to maintain during the pre-reform period was lost with the devotional revolution. It was a loss that some convent leaders at the time regretted very deeply and that some still mourn today. The irony is that as the creators and enforcers of a new, modern Irish catholic ideology that idealised meek and docile women, Irish nuns themselves helped to create the very conditions that ultimately robbed them of their autonomy (p. 130).

The recent past is more elusive to capture in a historical framework than the world of one hundred years ago. The 'modern' Ireland of 1900 promised much to Irish women; higher education and a career open to talents, the vote, an invitation to collaborate in the founding of a new state, recognition of literary work. Twentieth-century Ireland was not an age of progress for Irish women. Much of the century was marked by a growing inequality between men and women, and it was not until the middle of the 1960s that gender imbalance began to be adjusted, aided by the Republic of Ireland's entry into the European Economic Community in 1973. Change also challenged the Sisterhoods in the 1960s and their responses, whether conserving of the past, or risk-taking into an unknown future have over thirty years *indicated their acceptance that the enterprise they were engaged on for many decades has ended. As a group they showed themselves to be capable of courageous deconstruction; reconstruction of religious life belongs to the history of the new century and a new millennium.*

The essay 'Late in the Field: Catholic Sisters in Twentieth-Century Ireland and the New Religious History' was read at the twenty-first Conference of Irish Historians held at Queen's University Belfast in 1993. It was subsequently published in Mary O'Dowd and Sabine Wichert (eds), Chattel, Servant or Citizen: Women's Status in Church, State and Society. Historical Studies XIX *(Belfast, The Institute of Irish Studies, The Queen's University of Belfast, 1995) pp 34–57. The essay also appeared in a special edition of* The Journal of Women's History, *Vol. 6, No. 4/Vol. 7, No. 1 (Winter/Spring 1995) and in Joan Hoff and Moureen Coulter (eds),* Irish Women's Voices: Past and Present.

The most significant development of the 1980s has been the emergence of women's history. Its acceptance by the professional history establishment is evident from the theme of this, the 21st Irish Conference of Historians: 'The history of women'. Its entry into, and its reluctant acceptance by the world of academia in Ireland have given rise to new ways of looking at primary sources, innovative methods, and an interest by a reading and listening public that is unprecedented, certainly in my long span of recollection.[1] No summer school, no third level or university department of history can afford to ignore the treatment of women as an important field of studies. Yearly the volume of new scholarship angled on women accelerates as graduate schools take on the task of guiding theses in women's history, often without the training and specialised skills needed for this rapidly expanding field. High on the list of new tools is the issue of gender as a category of analysis and to it may be added in the 1990s those of class and ethnicity in the redefinition of 'difference'. A feminist analysis of power yields a different configuration of the past and in general, according to Linda Gordon in a recent survey of women's history in the United States, 'most women's historians consider themselves social historians, focusing more on private than on public experience, more on informal than on official sources of power'.[2]

Turning to catholic sisters, the chronology of writing twentieth-century nuns into Irish history is full of surprises. A cluster of studies in the first years of the twentieth century focused on subjects such as Foxford and its woollen mills founded by Agnes Morrogh-Bernard, Mother Arsenius,[3] and Irish convent industries including lace and linen weaving.[4] Then, somewhat later, Helena Concannon wrote several studies of the Poor Clare nuns of Ireland establishing securely the spiritual traditions of contemplative nuns in Ireland.[5] Her work contributes in a scholarly method to a history of Irish female spirituality. Two major biographies of foundresses, one by Roland Burke, S. J., *A Valiant Dublin Woman: The History of George's Hill* (1940) and one by Thomas. J. Walsh, *Nano Nagle and the Presentation Sisters* (1959), exemplified the tenets of catholic historiography of the mid-century: namely, that historical biography, especially of those who were leaders, was 'the key to unlocking the past, and the object of this exercise was to understand more fully the history of the institution'.[6]

In 1964 Angela Bolster published her Ph.D. thesis *The Sisters of Mercy in the Crimean War*, a revisionist study that upset admirers of Florence Nightingale. Bolster, with her emphasis on documentary sources, went on to edit *The Letters of Catherine McAuley* and she has been one of the main influences behind the steady stream of postgraduate studies of Mercy Sisters since the seventies.[7] At least fifty post-graduate theses dealing with the role or activities of Irish religious women in the twentieth century have been researched in various university departments over the past fifteen years. Of these, five dealt with the Mercy Sisters in different regions of Ireland: four with the Presentation Order of nuns, three with the Loreto Institute, two with the Sisters of the Holy Faith, one each with the Dominicans, Ursulines, Sisters of St Louis, Poor Clare teaching sisters. Several more theses, including the Ph.D. dissertation of John Coolahan, professor of education at Maynooth College, treated the catholic sisters in the context of training colleges, and several more examined catholic sisters in their involvement with workhouses.[8] Biographies have appeared in the 1980s of Mother Kevin Kearney, founder of the Franciscan Missionary Sisters, Mother Marie Martin, foundress of the Medical Missionaries of Mary in 1937, and the nun of Calabar, Mary Charles Walker.[9] At undergraduate level sixty or more special studies have examined aspects of sisters' ministry, such as the work of the Salesian Sisters in Limerick; the St Louis teaching ministry in rural domestic economy schools; the Hospice Movement; and the Little Company of Mary.[10]

Then come critical published studies of which Joseph Robbins' *From Rejection to Integration: A Century of Service of the Daughters of Charity to Persons with a Mental Handicap* was a narrative study based on primary sources, whereas Mavis Arnold's *Children of the Poor Clares: The Story of an Orphanage,* looked at the darker side of orphanage life and care in the mid-century in a case-study of the fire disaster that consumed the lives of young orphans in an Irish country town.[11]

Given the solidity of the research which this author has sketched in a rudimentary fashion, a new perspective of how to record what has happened to catholic sisters in the twentieth century is coming into focus: the present and next generation of scholars are asking different questions of the past and are looking for wider sources and new methodologies in an attempt to answer questions, free now from the burden of writing apologetic and promotional church history (which was what the old approach required). What has changed in the last decade is the perspective of the trained historians of women using new as well as old tools of research.

The origins of the new religious history are linked with the developments of the 1970s. Great changes within the history profession reflected the growing acknowledgement of new methods and approaches to doing history. This was mainly brought about by the refinement of analytical, theoretical methods and with the introduction of computer technology and more efficient means of assessing quantitative material. Latterly with the techniques involved in information systems research, the use of multiple, qualitative methods for a particular research problem is at hand for collecting data. The work of Dr Eileen Trauth, business historian, in her exposition of the methods used for assessing the role of societal factors in Ireland's progress from an agrarian to an information society combines data collection methods, documentary analysis, and skills for designing a questionnaire and a set of questions for oral interviews based on triangulation and reflexivity. These tools of research, which can now be performed with the aid of computer analysis, may sound depressing to the older historian like myself but as Dr Trauth observes: 'the underlying assumption ... is that the research problem should drive the choice of methods used'.[12]

The creation of the Social Science History Association in the 1970s in the United States does not have a counterpart in Ireland which may explain why influential studies analysing religious belief and behaviour such as Dr Máire Nic Ghiolla Phádraig's analysis of church-going practices;[13] Dr Tom Inglis's study *Moral Monopoly: The Catholic Church in Modern Irish Society*;[14] Dr Tony Fahey's Ph.D. dissertation, 'Female Asceticism in the Catholic Church: A Case Study of Nuns in Ireland in the Nineteenth Century', are coming from the discipline of social science.[15] At this point of time, it is generally acknowledged that the rise of feminist history and the parallel study of gender history in the 1980s has influenced historians to seek connections between religious and non-religious variables. A feminist approach to a historical problem studies the group, the life-cycle, the recurrent. For example, Caitríona Clear in her *Nuns in Nineteenth-Century Ireland* took a sample of nine convents and examined nuns as women in their social and economic contexts.[16] Dr Jacinta Prunty, in her study of Holy Faith Sisters and their ministry of the poor of Dublin moves the scrutiny away from an individual as dramatic as Margaret Aylward, foundress of the Holy Faith Congregation, and examines the forces and interest-groups of women involved in the struggle for children's souls and welfare with some pertinent analysis of population and housing trends.[17]

Professor Margaret Susan Thompson, historian of American catholic nuns, author of many monographs and of the eagerly-awaited book, *The Yoke of Grace: American Nuns and Social Change 1808–1917*, distinguishes the new feminist religious history from traditional historiography by the following characteristics: 'its critique of patriarchy, its analysis of the connection between ordination and power, its recognition of the pervasiveness and importance of unordained ministry and the roles of the laity, and fourthly its identification of transdenominational patterns'.[18] This is a challenging list for Irish historians schooled in the empirical pastures of the formal document. How does it work in practice? Keeping within the framework of 'new' religious history the problem of sources presents itself. Linda Gordon in her essay 'What's new in women's history' suggests that 'the question of what counts as evidence is far more substantive than methodology'. She continues in tones reminiscent of Marc Bloch: 'I consider as evidence material once thought of as outside history – gossip, menstruation, latrines'. She is, of course, in that essay arguing that rather than indulging in a tolerant acceptance of difference, historians 'integrate that experience as part of our whole approach to the study of women'.[19]

Of its nature, the new religious feminist history requires inter-disciplinarity. It cannot rely only on quantitative methodology or statistical data. Not only are these less available for women than for men but ecclesiastical archives in general preserve information on men and tend not to record women unless they have transgressed canon law. The reports of Margaret Anna Cusack, the nun of Kenmare that repose among the Kirby papers in the Irish College Archives in Rome are a prime example. The depositions concerning her eccentric behaviour and actions as filed in Propaganda Fide Archives in Rome have been examined by Sr Avril Reynolds and have proved to be incomplete, if not one-sided.[20]

When finishing doctoral research on aspects of the Irish Counter-Reformation thirty years ago, this author had to make a case for the validity of convent archives, setting them apart from the authoritative state archives and ecclesiastical archives used: the Public Records Office in London, the archives of the various ministries of foreign affairs in Madrid, Paris and Lisbon, Simancas in Castille and the Archivio Segreto Vaticano in Rome. The convent archives appear small and unimportant in the description of sources used. Yet at the oral examination of the completed thesis, the archives of Bom Sucesso Convent in Lisbon, founded in 1639 for Irish-born nuns exiled from Ireland was the area that aroused most interest.[21] The archives of religious congregations possess records of unique value for the historian. All convents are obliged by ecclesiastical law to appoint an annalist who may also be the archivist of the community. Many communities have an unofficial or even a published history of their convent. Convent annals are mainly a chronology of the major events that occur in the life of that community: they also chronicle personal details of the sisters and their relatives, benefactors, distinguished or unusual visitors to the convent. Where a convent is responsible for the management and staffing of schools, asylums, custodial institutes, hospitals, hostels and halls of residence, occasionally letters and less formal observations find their way into convent archives. A second category of material in convent archives is correspondence. Mary Peckham, in the course of her research on the re-emergence and early development of women's religious orders in Ireland from 1700 to 1870,[22] described for the summer school of the Association of Religious Archivists in Ireland the kind of source material she came across:

I have found contemporary accounts of such major historical events as the near landing of the French in Bantry Bay in December 1796, of the exile of women religious from nineteenth-century France and their search for new homes in Irish convents, of Irish emigration, of the founding of missions throughout the world and moving accounts of the great Famine ...[23]

The 1989 *Draft Directory of the Irish Religious Archives* compiled for the members of the Association, lists the material available in the archives of religious houses.[24] In the present century, Irish congregations of religious women worked with the Irish and British governments and with governments and civil service departments throughout the world. For much of this century the involvement of female religious orders with state projects, education, hospitals, social welfare has been of staggering proportions: the closing in 1986 of Carysfort Training College in Dublin managed by the Irish Sisters of Mercy was the closing of a chapter of intense collaboration between the state and religious women.[25] Elites and power players have not been examined to any great extent in twentieth-century Ireland. Leaders of women's religious orders were both, but that is not the stuff of feminist history. As Caitríona Clear remarks:

> The archives of religious congregations have much to offer the history of women, the history of work and work practices. They throw light on the history of the family in Ireland: it is notable that several siblings very often entered the religious life, often the same congregation.[26]

From the historian's angle, one of the most significant developments has been the changed attitude on the part of many religious communities towards the preservation and administration of religious archives. Over the past decade the summer courses organized by Miss Ailsa Holland and Mr Seamus Helferty of the Archives

Department, University College Dublin, have effected a dramatic transformation in the preservation of religious archival material. According to David Sheehy, archivist of the Dublin archdiocesan archives, religious archives have been the leading growth area in the Irish archival profession over the last decade.[27] In practical terms it means the historian no longer has to justify convent archives in terms of authenticity.

By the beginning of the twentieth century there were just over eight thousand nuns in the country with a total of thirty five religious orders. There were 368 convents, in architectural style and design supplying a distinctive structure quite different from the Georgian or Victorian mansion or larger houses. In a comprehensive analysis of the numbers of religious (men and women) in Ireland in 1989 (using the computer methodology outlined in an earlier section of this paper), the Conference of Major Superiors has presented the researcher with figures drawn from census reports, monastic and convent archives, catholic directories and diocesan archives to present a multi-layered profile of the members of religious engaged in ministry in the catholic church in Ireland in 1989.[28] The total numbers of female religious in Ireland in 1989 was 11,415, of whom 405 were cloistered contemplatives. There were 128 religious congregations of women and twenty four monasteries of women contemplatives. The most visible change in the 1980s was the closing of thirty convents and the gradual transition of large communities to smaller groups: 141 community houses opened during the same period. The other dramatic change is the decline in vocation and the age-structure of nuns: fifty-seven per cent were over sixty years of age at the time of the *Profile's* reckoning, 1989–90.[29]

Dr Suellen Hoy, in her study, 'The Journey Out: The Recruitment and Emigration of Irish Religious Women to the United States, 1812–1913', notes that 10 per cent of the number of nuns in the US in 1915 were Irish women who had emigrated as professed nuns, novices, postulants or aspirants (there were 40,000 nuns working in the US in 1900, 175,000 in 1915).[30] Dr Hoy has placed her investigations in the context of women's experience of emigration and high on the research agenda of twentieth-century sisters in Ireland is a continuation of her work. According to J. J. Lee, the economic historian, of every 100 girls in Connaught aged between fifteen and nineteen years in 1946, 42 had left by 1951. The most the government would say in a memo from the Department of External Affairs was: 'the present high volume of emigration is due at least to causes other than economic necessity'. According to this estimate Ireland would boast the highest rate of female emigration of any European country between 1945 and 1960:

> If the comely maidens would laugh, it would be the bitter sweet laugh of liberation through emigration from a sterile society where the Bridies left behind would be glad to settle, their girlhood dreams dashed, for the Bowser Egans.[31]

Lee does not pick up on his own statistics which he quoted in an earlier essay on women and the church since the Famine, that by the 1941 census one woman out of every four hundred was entering a convent. Moreover, admissions to novitiates climbed steadily, peaked around 1960, remained stable until 1972 and then declined decisively to the present situation where 2 per cent (227) of the 11,415 nuns in Ireland are under twenty-nine years of age.[32] Clearly these statistics contain investigations of much suggestibility. Why were Irish women leaving Ireland? Is there a connection between the restrictions on entry to the United States regulated in 1917 and the swing to other parts of the world? How does the historian account for the rise in female vocations in the century which offered women undreamt of opportunities in the growing professionalisation of work? How many of those emigrant women were missionary sisters?

Though the ministerial cabinet of the Irish Free State kept referring as late as the 1930s and 1940s to the freedom of movement of Irish women to emigrate and find work as domestic servants, the reality had been that since the 1890s, there was a growing acceptance of women into university courses and of their certification in most fields of business. They also made advances into the fields of professional medicine and nursing. Dr Edmund Hogan, in his study on the Irish missionary movement,[33] has a section on 'The development of medical missions'. There he deals with the winning of the initiatives by women missionaries and the Missionary Sisters Congregations, notably the Franciscan Missionaries of Mary, the Mercy Sisters in India, the Medical Missionaries of Mary and the Holy Rosary Sisters of Killeshandra, to qualify themselves for the medical care of women and children (as surgeons, obstetricians and gynaecologists). Spelt out, this involved a struggle first with the great medical schools, and then, a prolonged lobbying of Rome, in particular of the papacy, to allow catholic sisters to study and practise medicine and to take state qualifications in midwifery. Hogan's investigations are sensitive to what Professor Margaret Thompson discerns as one of the characteristics of the 'new feminist religious history': he recognizes the actuality and need for unordained ministry, and demonstrates how laywomen and religious women worked closely together to achieve an objective. What also comes through in his study, though not overtly, is the patriarchal nature of the struggle where popes withheld dispensation and permission: not just from catholic women but also from enlightened missionary bishops. As an appendix to this study, Hogan prints in full Canon 489, which was issued in February 1936, 'Maternity training for missionary sisters'.[34] That, of course, was not the end of the story though it represents a victory for Teresa Keaveney, Mother Kevin, who in 1921 had opened a Midwifery Training School for her women in Uganda with Evelyn Connolly, a Dublin doctor, qualified in obstetrics. Keaveney herself had not succeeded in obtaining a dispensation to train in midwifery because of a Roman embargo.[35] The quest for the acquisition of professional qualifications such as those involved in surgery and obstetrics, the so-called 'forbidden skills', belongs to the area of public power, and ultimately to the area of church-state politics. The paradox of the missionary situation of the early twentieth century was that the tensions came from within the catholic structure of authority. The players were those at the top, leaders in their own domain. Three successive popes, Pius X, Benedict XV, and Pius XI, withheld dispensations (which is the normal procedure to get around a canon law). Missionary bishops of the calibre of Bishop Shanahan of Nigeria, Monsignor Wagner of Rawalpindi (who needed a hospital for women in purdah, run by women), and in the home diocese, Cardinal Bourne of Westminster, Archbishop Dougherty of Philadelphia, Cardinal Manning in Australia, all lobbied the Roman Congregation of Bishops and Regulars unsuccessfully. Fr John Blowick, founder of the Maynooth mission to China and a seasoned campaigner, organized a formidable constellation of women determined, like Teresa Keaveney, to end the embargo. Three laywomen, medical doctors all, Agnes McLaren, Margaret Lamont and Anna Dengel, came together with Teresa Keaveney, Mother Xavier Murphy, a Presentation Sister in South India, and Frances Moloney, later founder of the Columban Sisters. They were joined by two medical students, Marie Martin and Agnes Ryan. They sent Dr Agnes McLaren to speak on their behalf with the pope, Benedict XV, and other Roman officials. To no avail. Moloney went ahead and founded the Columban Sisters in 1922 'vowed to the medical care of the sick in non-christian countries and whose members would be properly qualified in medicine, surgery and midwifery'.[36] In 1924, Mary Ryan began to set up the Sisters of the Holy Rosary Killeshandra[37] and then, in 1936, Marie Martin founded the Medical Missionaries of Mary after long and careful deliberation, an institute devoted exclusively to medical and related problems.[38] From the mid-1940s a familiar sight in student medical classes and midwifery courses was a soberly-clad young woman, without adornment who took her place with her fellow students and as often as not took high grades in class results. Within fifty years of its foundation the Institute of the Medical Missionaries of Mary had some 450 members working internationally and an international hospital in Drogheda, County Louth, which has a maternity unit, and specialises in tropical diseases. The Sisters of St. Columban in their first thirty years listed nine doctors and forty two nurses among its members. In 1948 Sr Aquinas Monaghan went to Hong Kong and became a world-specialist in tuberculosis.[39]

This sketch of the politics of the women's campaign for medical training, where their resources were pitted against the highest authorities within the catholic church, is an important dimension of women's political activity in the twentieth century. It bears out a point made by Joan Wallach Scott in her article in *Past and Present*:

To ignore politics in the recovery of the female subject is to accept the reality of public/private distinctions and the separate or distinctive qualities of women's character and experience. It misses the chance not only to challenge the accuracy of binary distinctions between men and women in the past and present, but to expose the very political nature of a history written in those terms.[40]

Far less known is the history of the general nurse and her struggle for state recognition, and after that, the efforts to rescue midwifery from the irregularities of the untrained and place it on a professional footing, in line with the 1875 British parliamentary act for the training of midwives and the 1902 midwifery act of Britain which recognized the Coombe and Rotunda Hospitals as training schools.[41] Legislation passed in 1918 made it incumbent on nurses to register as midwives after training. The history of nursing dates back to the nineteenth century and Pauline Scanlon's book, *The Irish Nurse: A Study of Nurses in Ireland: History and Education, 1718–1981*,[42] and Dr Ruth Barrington's *Health, Medicine and Politics in Ireland 1900–1970* are valuable for a general background.[43] The medical profession, however, is not a homogeneous one – it is based on hierarchy and, to some extent, is also class-based. The emergence of the nursing profession, and the endeavours to train the general nurse and to set up state qualifications in midwifery, belong to the mainstream of feminist history. Here we are focusing on the nun's story which had to confront the double patriarchy of hospital administration and church control in the person of the local bishop who chaired the board of trustees. Mercy Sisters and Irish Sisters of Charity nursed side by side in the cholera epidemics of the 1830s and 1840s. When the Sisters of Mercy agreed to take over the running of the Limerick Workhouse and thereafter the other state workhouses, they received assistance and training from the 'Florence Nightingale trained nurses'. There was a perception that had to be combated by catholic women, that the quality of recruitment to the general hospital was rather low and that in the workhouses the night-attendant, who was quite often the local midwife, was not always a savoury character.[44]

The gradual assumption of administration and of senior nursing posts by trained religious sisters, gave a credibility to catholic hospitals which the Irish Free State and the government in Northern Ireland was eager to recognize. Once the Cork Mercy Hospital, founded in 1854, began to provide state training for nuns in September 1911,[45] and then much later, by arrangement with Holles Street Maternity Hospital, midwifery training, the voluntary catholic hospitals became, to some extent, victims of their own success, as church and state jockeyed for control of policy and appointments.[46]

The need for sustained analysis on the nature of twentieth-century Irish feminism has been demonstrated by Mary Cullen in her essay 'How Radical was Irish Feminism'.[47] At this point in the development of women's history in Ireland, it is difficult to chart how the female nursing and medical professions divided on lines of class and gender divisions of labour.

A study of Irish women and the professions, 1900–1936 by Clare Eager brings the debate a step further:

> Service was the watchword for Irish women who chose to work in such diverse professions as teaching, nursing and in the pursuit of the public good. With entrée into those professions assured after 1901, women's choice of career option determined the public perception of their role by a society becoming more and more conservative. One can suggest that the 'feminisation' of the professions in Ireland began in 1901 and had, by 1936, become an integral part of the state.[48]

Conclusions

There is an impression that religious life for women in twentieth-century Ireland was sterile and narcissistic and that women crowded into convents only because of economic and social conditions. As has been noted, the flow of vocations requires a different kind of analysis and the research, on which to base a viable interpretation, has only begun. We need to hear the voices of women religious, the self which is no longer annalist but the subject of the testimony. The journals of nuns exist and the voices of religious women released into familiar speech with their families and friends need to be heard. There are letters in family collections that nuns have written which are records of private feelings and thoughts, others that provide glimpses of spirituality, nuances of alternative realities to console the sorrows of bereaved relatives and friends. Dr Angela Bourke's pioneering studies of Irish women's lament poetry supplies an original methodology for a study of the spirituality of religious women. In her essay 'More in Anger than in Sorrow: Irish Women's Lament Poetry', Bourke states: 'the lament poetry considered in this essay contains messages that would have been intelligible to an inner circle of women but not necessarily to the rest of the audience'.[49] The resources of female christian spirituality in Ireland (which flourished in the teeth of Irish patriarchy) are being explored by Mary Condren, first in her book, *The Serpent and the Goddess: Women, Religion and Power in Celtic Ireland*, and in a subsequent series of essays which open up new fields of enquiry.[50] The work of Seamus Enright in examining the spirituality of Irish nuns is welcome,[51] as are the new studies of Brigid.[52] The forthcoming *Field Day Anthology* promises to capture the voices of religious women as well as the religious voices of women, in hymn, in sermon, and in diary.

On a less exalted note and as a vigorous *pis-aller* the history-writing of religious women is a shared work, possibly a collaboration, certainly one which the lay-historian is invited to venture into and research. There are situations in the lives of religious women which require analysis of an objectivity not always available to those caught up in that way of life. Caitríona Clear and Tony Fahey have both drawn attention to the anomalous position of laysisters within the nineteenth-century Irish convent. It may come as a surprise to learn that the two-tiered division within convents was only abolished in the 1960s. In the same decade apostolic religious orders of women, what used to be known as the active orders, discovered they were members of the laity.[53] By combining insights and methods drawn from a variety of disciplines, by making connections with the lives of women in faith groupings other than Roman catholicism, catholic sisters will become an integral part of Irish history and an indispensable part of the new religious history of Ireland.

from Mary O'Dowd and Sabine Wichert (eds), *Chattel, Servant or Citizen: Women's Status in Church, State and Society. Historical Studies XIX* (Belfast, The Institute of Irish Studies, The Queen's University of Belfast, 1995) pp 34–57. The essay also appeared in a special edition of *The Journal of Women's History*, Vol. 6, No. 4/Vol. 7, No. 1 (Winter/Spring 1995) and in Joan Hoff and Moureen Coulter (eds), *Irish Women's Voices: Past and Present* (Bloomington, IN, Indiana University Press, 1995), pp 49–63.

NOTES

1 Maria Luddy, Margaret Mac Curtain and Mary O'Dowd, 'An Agenda for Women's History in Ireland, 1500–1900', *Irish Historical Studies,* Vol. 28, No. 109 (May 1992), pp 1–37.

2 Linda Gordon, *US Women's History* (American Historical Association, 1991), p. 5.

3 Denis Gildea, *Mother Arsenius of Foxford* (Dublin, 1936); Bernie Joyce, *Agnes Morrogh-Bernard, 1842–1932, foundress of Foxford Woollen Mills* (Ballina, l991).

4 Rosa Mulholland, 'Skibbereen Convent of Mercy Linen Weaving', *Irish Monthly,* 18 (March 1890), pp 145–8; Mary Coleman, 'Irish Lace and Irish Crochet', in Eiléan Ní Chuilleanáin (ed.), *Irish Women: Image and Achievement* (Dublin, Arlen House, 1985).

5 Helena Concannon, *The Poor Clares in Ireland* (Dublin, M. H. Gill, 1929); 'Historic Galway convents, 1. Poor Clare', *Studies,* 38 (December 1949), pp 439–446.

6 Roland Burke, *A Valiant Dublin Woman: the Story of George's Hill, 1766–1940* (Dublin, M. H. Gill, 1940); Thomas J. Walsh, *Nano Nagle and the Presentation Sisters* (Monasterevan, Presentation Publications, 1959); Jay P. Dolan, 'New Directions in American Catholic History' in Jay P. Dolan and James P. Wind (eds), *New Dimensions in American Religious History* (Grand Rapids, Eerdmans, 1992), p. 153.

7 Angela Bolster, *The Sisters of Mercy in the Crimean War* (Cork, Mercier, 1965); *Catherine McAuley in her Own Words* (Dublin, Diocesan Office for Causes, 1978); *The Correspondence of Catherine McAuley, 1827–41* (Cork, Sisters of Mercy, 1989).

8 Sheila Lunney, 'List of twentieth-century theses on women religious orders in Ireland at post-graduate and under-graduate levels' (for the Irish Association for Research in Women's History bulletin, 1995).

9 Sheila O'Hara, *Dare to Live: Mother M. Kevin Kearney* (Dublin, Veritas, 1979); Mary Purcell, *To Africa with Love: Life of Mother Mary Martin* (Dublin, Gill and Macmillan, 1987); Colman Cooker, *Mary Charles Walker: the Nun of Calabar* (Dublin, Four Courts, 1980).

10 Lunney, *op. cit.*

11 Joseph Robbins, *From Rejection to Integration: A Century of Service of the Daughters of Charity to Persons with a Mental Handicap* (Dublin, Gill and Macmillan, 1992); Mavis Arnold, *Children of the Poor Clares, the Story of an Orphanage* (Belfast, Appletree, 1985).

12 Eileen M. Trauth and Barbara O'Connor, 'A Study of the Interaction between Information Technology and Society: An

Illustration of Combined Qualitative Research Methods' in Hans-Erik Nissen, Heinz K. Klein and Rudy Hirschein (eds), *Information Systems Research: Contemporary Approaches and Emergent traditions* (Amsterdam, Elsevier, 1991), p. 142.

13 Máire Nic Ghiolla Phádraig, 'Religion in Ireland: Preliminary Analysis', *Social Studies,* Vol. 5, No. 2 (1976), pp 113–80; 'Religious Practice and Secularisation' in Pat Clancy, Sheila Drudy, Kathleen Lynch and Liam O'Dowd (eds), *Ireland: A Sociological Profile* (Dublin, Institute of Public Administration, 1986), pp 137–54.

14 Tom Inglis, *Moral Monopoly: The Catholic Church in Modern Irish Society* (Dublin, Gill and Macmillan, 1987).

15 Tony Fahey, 'Nuns in the Catholic Church in Ireland in the Nineteenth Century', in Mary Cullen (ed.), *Girls Don't Do Honours* (Dublin, Women's Education Bureau, 1987), pp 7–30; 'Female Asceticism in the Catholic Church: A Case-Study of Nuns in Ireland in the Nineteenth Century' (Ph.D. thesis, University of Illinois at Urbana-Champaign, 1982).

16 Caitríona Clear, *Nuns in Nineteenth-Century Ireland* (Dublin, Gill and Macmillan, 1987).

17 Jacinta Prunty, *Dublin Slums 1800–1925: A Study in Urban Geography* (Dublin, Irish Academic Press, 1998).

18 Margaret S. Thompson, 'Women, Feminism, and the New Religious History: Catholic Sisters as a Case-Study' in Philip R. Vandermeer and Robert R. Swierenga (eds), *Belief and Behaviour: Essays in the New Religious History* (New Jersey, Rutgers University Press, 1991), p. 138.

19 Linda Gordon, 'What's New in Women's History' in Ineja Gunen (ed.), *A Reader in Feminist Knowledge* (London, Routledge, 1991), pp 78–9.

20 Avril Reynolds, 'From Loneliness to Loneliness: Margaret Anna Cusack, the Nun of Kenmare' (paper presented to the Society for the History of Women Conference in University College, Dublin, February 1990).

21 Margaret Mac Curtain, 'Women, Education and Learning in Early Modern Ireland', in Margaret Mac Curtain and Mary O'Dowd (eds), *Women in Early Modern Ireland* (Edinburgh, Edinburgh University Press, 1991), pp 169–70.

22 Mary L. Peckham, 'Catholic Female Congregations and Religious Change in Ireland, 1770–1870' (Ph.D. thesis, University of Wisconsin-Madison, 1993).

23 Mary L. Peckham, 'Religious Archives: A Rich Source of Social History' (paper presented to the Association of Religious Archivists of Ireland, Dublin in July 1989).

24 The Association of Religious Archivists of Ireland compiled a draft directory of Irish religious archives in 1985, under the direction of Henry O'Shea, OSB. In 1992 the association changed its name to 'Association of Church Archivists of Ireland'.

25 Angela Bolster, *Catherine McAuley: Her Educational Thought and its Influence on the Origin and Development of an Irish Training College: Two Centenary Lectures* (Dublin, Sisters of Mercy, 1980).

26 Caitríona Clear, 'The Archives of Religious Congregations: To What Purpose?' (paper presented to the Association of Religious Archivists of Ireland, Dublin in July 1989).

27 David Sheehy in conversation with author, 20 May 1993.

28 Emmet Larkin, 'The Devotional Revolution in Ireland, 1850–75', *American Historical Review,* Vol. 77, No. 3 (June 1972), pp 626, 664, 651 for nineteenth-century estimates. For late twentieth-century estimates see *Profile of Religious in Ireland, 1989/1990* (Dublin, Conference of Major Religious Superiors, 1990).

29 *Ibid.,* pp 1–97.

30 Suellen Hoy, 'The Journey Out: The Recruitment and Emigration of Irish Religious Women to the United States, 1812–1914', *Journal of Women's History,* Vol 6, No 4/Vol 7. No 1 (Winter/Spring 1995), pp 64–98.

31 J. J. Lee, *Ireland, 1912–1985: Politics and Society* (Cambridge, Cambridge University Press, 1980). p. 377.

32 J. J. Lee, 'Women and the Church Since the Famine', in Margaret Mac Curtain and Donncha Ó Corráin (eds), *Women in Irish Society: The Historical Dimension* (Dublin, Arlen House, 1978), p. 40.

33 Edmund Hogan, *The Irish Missionary Movement: A Historical Survey, 1830–1980* (Dublin, Gill and Macmillan, 1992).

34 Canon 489: Maternity Training for Missionary Sisters (Instruction, 5. Congreg. Prep. Fide, 11 February 1936), *Acta Apostolica Sedis,* 28, p. 208, quoted in full in Hogan, *op. cit,* pp 195–6 (Appendix B).

35 Hogan, *op. cit.,* pp 113–20.

36 Margaret Fairburn, 'Missionary Sisters of St. Columban', *Studies,* 36 (December, 1947), pp 451–60.

37 Mary Bridig, 'The Congregation of the Missionary Sisters of the Holy Rosary: Origin and growth', *Capuchin Annual* (Dublin, 1955), pp 254–376.

38 Mary Purcell, *op. cit.*

39 Hogan, *op. cit.,* p. 120.

40 Joan W. Scott, 'Survey Articles: Women in History: The Modern Period', *Past and Present*, No. 101 (November 1983), p. 156.

41 Jo Murphy-Lawless, 'The Silencing of Women in Childbirth, or Let's Hear it for Bartholomew and the Boys', *Women's Studies International Forum*, Vol. 11, No. 4 (1988), pp 293–8; Ian Campbell Ross (ed.), *Public Virtue, Public Love: The Early Years of the Rotunda Lying-in Hospital* (Dublin, l986).

42 Pauline Scanlon, *The Irish Nurse: A Study of Nurses in Ireland: History and Education, 1718–1981* (Leitrim, Drumlin Publications, 1991).

43 Ruth Barrington, *Health, Medicine and Politics in Ireland, 1900–1970* (Dublin, Institute of Public Administration, 1987).

44 Patricia Kelly, 'From Workhouse to Hospital: The Role of the Workhouse in Medical Relief to 1921' (M.A. thesis, University College Galway, 1972).

45 Emmanuel Browne, *Mansion of Mercy: A History of the Mercy Hospital* (Cork, Tower Books, 1988).

46 Emmanuel Browne, *A Tale of Two Hospitals* (Cork, no date).

47 Mary Cullen, 'How Radical was Irish Feminism Between 1860 and 1920?' in Patrick J. Corish (ed.), *Radicals, Rebels and Establishments* (Belfast, Appletree Press, 1985), pp 185–201.

48 Clare Eager, 'Alice Through the Looking Glass: Irish Women in the Professions, 1901–36' (paper presented to Boston College-Harvard University Irish Colloquium, 18 March 1993).

49 Angela Bourke, 'More in Anger than in Sorrow: Irish Women's Lament Poetry' in Joan Newlon Radner (ed.), *Feminist Messages: Coding in Women's Folk Culture* (Urbana, University of Illinois Press, 1993), p. 161.

50 Mary Condren, *The Serpent and the Goddess: Women, Religion and Power in Celtic Ireland* (San Francisco, Harper and Row, 1989).

51 Seamus Enright, ongoing research for Ph.D. dissertation in Maynooth College, Ireland.

52 Kim McCone, 'Brigit in the Seventh Century: A Saint with Three Lives?', *Peritia* 1 (1982), pp 107–45; Sean Connolly and Jean Michel Picard, 'Cogitosus: Life of St Brigit', *Journal of the Royal Society of Antiquaries*, No. 117 (1987), pp 11–27.

53 Austin Flannery (ed.), *Vatican Council II, the Conciliar and Post Conciliar Documents* (Dublin, Dominican Publications, 1975), p. 388.

REFLECTIONS ON WALTER OSBORNE'S
STUDY FROM NATURE

When Professor Adele Dalsimer, co-director and co-founder of the Irish Studies Program in Boston College contacted me in spring 1995 with an invitation to write an essay for the book she and Vera Kreilkamp were assembling to accompany the exhibition of Brian P. Burns' Irish paintings in Boston College's McMullen Museum of Art, my acceptance was whole-hearted. I had spent a wonderful year in the John J. Burns Library of Rare Books and Special Collections as Burns Visiting Scholar, a post which Professor Dalsimer and the Librarian, Dr Robert K. O'Neill had dreamed up for scholars of Irish Studies on a yearly basis. I am grateful to Professor Nancy Netzer, Director of the McMullen Museum, for permission to reproduce this essay originally published in America's Eye: Irish Paintings from the Collection of Brian P. Burns *(Chestnut Hill, MA, Boston College Museum of Art, 1996), and to Brian Burns for his gracious permission to reproduce this little-known painting by Walter Osborne, a delicate, gentle study of a woman gardener. I matched Osborne's reflections with my own musings on the subject of the woman gardener which could have been a painting of my own mother in her favourite garden in County Kerry. Adele Dalsimer died in February 2000. A much admired personality in Irish Studies worldwide, I dedicate this essay to the memory of Adele Dalsimer (1939–2000).*

The repose of Walter Osborne's *Study from Nature* draws the beholder into the picture to observe a seated woman in a wide-brimmed straw hat, comfortable apron and dark skirt – the garb of the woman gardener of the last hundred years. She sits on the ground gazing at her harvest of freshly-dug potatoes, having plunged the prongs of her pitchfork into the trench. Nothing in the stillness of the central figure suggests pressure.

In the right-hand corner, shafts of light and shade play over a bluish-green cabbage. Behind the foreground of what appears to be the corner of a vegetable plot, a wood-rail fence holds back from the potato patch an exuberance of natural vegetation, a branchy fruit-bearing tree, and the abundance of tall wildflowers at its base. Still further behind, a larger fence separates the scene from the more distant background. Having given his painting so general a title, Osborne invites the beholder, as well as the central figure, into a reverie withdrawn from outside distraction. Some viewers may see in the delicate range of blues and greys the dawn of an autumn day. The muted greens and whites, the shading of the dug clay, the counterpoint of amethyst shades in the woollen blouse, and the warm russet tones of the potatoes demonstrate the artist's understanding of composition. The longer the eye observes the subtle shading, the more secrets it will reveal. Is that a ladder mingling with the lower branches of the fruit-tree? How the spread branches relieve any monotony of sky the milky dawn light casts! Is that tall spire, behind the pitch-fork, an onion flower, *Allium cepa Proliferum?* Notice the tones of the wicker basket and how the light plays on the hand of the woman holding the twig.

Walter Osborne's popularity has grown steadily. A wider public came to honour his paintings during and since the exhibitions of his work at the National Gallery of Ireland and the Ulster Museum in 1983. His *Apple Gathering, Quimperlé* (1883), which hangs in the National Gallery, shows two small country girls collecting fruit. Like *Study from Nature,* it evokes the pleasures of an unsophisticated seasonal farm ritual.

'Study from Nature'
Walter Frederick Osborne, R.H.A. (1859–1903)
Oil on panel, 15 x 9¾ inches
Courtesy of the Boston College Museum of Art

As a landscape artist, Osborne preferred to paint the light and shadow of farmland, with fields, hedges and trees, and rural-looking buildings, rather than dramatic scenery.[1] He often peopled his landscapes with a lone figure, as in *Seated Boy* and *Study from Nature*. If he chose to establish an evocative autumnal mood, for example, he drew his subject-matter from life, and painted out-of-doors to capture its particular light.

Osborne belonged to the generation of Irish painters who acquainted their viewers with what was then a relatively new phenomenon in late nineteenth-century Dublin: the suburban, middle class garden. The son of an artist, Osborne grew up in Rathmines, just outside Dublin city centre on Castlewood Avenue, and he finished his life in the same house. Before the turn of the century, today's suburban Rathmines was partly in the countryside, and Castlewood Avenue houses possessed back gardens with trees, flower beds and vegetable plots. Quietly but insistently Osborne's paintings of suburban and rural life projected the aspirations of the *plein-air* circle of artists to which he belonged. This group invariably worked out-of-doors, endeavouring to infuse their subjects with the sensibility of nature as they saw it at that moment.

In *Study from Nature*, Osborne depicts a domestic landscape evoking a suburban version of rurality that accompanied major changes in economic and social life after the mid-nineteenth century. Although the painting was created in the French countryside, in the canvas Osborne celebrates the intimate garden landscape of Ireland as well as the continent. In choosing such informal scenes as subject matter, Osborne broke from the earlier convention of painting the vast geometric landscape gardens of aristocratic patrons. Placing a woman at the centre of his canvas, moreover, suggests the role Irish women have played in creating and maintaining domestic gardens throughout the centuries.

Prior to the Great Famine of the 1840s, gardens were the prerogative of the aristocracy, the ostentatious extension of the castles and great houses of Ascendancy Ireland. Ornamental shrubbery and park lands set off the houses of the nobility; herbal and flower gardens were cultivated by lesser mortals, such as Mrs. Delany, in the rectory garden at Delville,[2] and by Maria Edgeworth, the novelist, for pedagogical instruction of her father's numerous children at Edgeworthstown. But the Irish labouring classes could ill-afford the space even for a cottage garden, as the demand for potato cultivation invaded every available foot around their hovels.

Pre-Famine Ireland was a map of tessellated landscaped demesnes with forbidding boundary walls protecting their inmates from wild countryside, and wilder inhabitants who roamed it. Unless they were estate villages, towns had little aesthetic consciousness about parks or landscaping. Absorbed in surviving the tides of poverty-stricken families that fled the countryside in the decades of rising population before the 1840s, Irish towns were bleak, inhospitable refuges for the poverty stricken.[3] The appearance of urban back-gardens in post-Famine towns and cities signified a return to normality. These new garden forms represented a defensive response to the ravages of the Great Famine, and a withdrawal into an aestheticized domesticity by an expanding Victorian bourgeoisie.

In Osborne's generation, middle-class women themselves tended their flowers and vegetables, distant in both time and mentality from the elegant eighteenth-century ladies, who paced the avenues of their estates, excluded by the laws of propriety from 'working' in the gardens of their demesnes. Osborne's woman gardener is closer in spirit to a seventeenth-century settler's wife who tended the small house garden adjacent to Tully Castle in County Fermanagh. Built as a fortified tower-house in 1618 (in reality a planter's castle), its ruins today overlook the Erne river.[4] The castle was destroyed after a massacre, witnessed by the woman of the house, in the fateful 1641 Ulster Rising. Its garden, which she cultivated, was situated in the bawn, or open space, in front of the castle.[5] This Scottish planter's wife grew the flowers and herbs she loved: heartsease, love-in-a-mist, marigold, larkspur, pink campion, cornflower, and the herbs lemonbalm, marjoram, bergamo, rosemary, sweet cecily, lovage, Welsh poppy, chives, fennel and tansey. Loyal to the Scottish King James I, she planted Scottish Rose, Rose of York and Lancaster, and Jacobite Rose with older strains like the Rosa Mundi, much favoured by medieval herbalists, and Maiden's Blush.[6]

Máire Rua O'Brien's seventeenth-century garden is less gloomy. She re-designed the fortified house at Leamaneh in County Clare after her marriage to Conor O'Brien, adding a courtyard and an adjoining pleasure garden. In his 1900 ground plan of Leamaneh, T. J. Westropp, the antiquarian scholar, shows an ornamental walk, a summer house and a fishpond. Close by, a small ruined turret, called to this day 'Máire Rua's seat', overlooks the Burren countryside where alpine and arctic plants grow amid Mediterranean species. Leamaneh, with its four storeys and bartizan in its southwest wall,[7] stood sturdily on a Gaelic frontier, yet even today visitors standing in the shadow of this fortress ruin can trace the walls of a deer park, a reminder of Máire Rua's dramatic renovations to her home on the eve of the Cromwellian conquest.

With the final subduing of the rebellious Irish at the end of the seventeenth century, the victors, loyal supporters of their monarchs William and Mary, settled down to enjoy the land that was their reward. A period of ninety years ensued, uninterrupted by rebellion or invasion. The most spectacular feature of this age of property was the building boom of the new landed gentry. All over Ireland, landowners built themselves imposing residences – Palladian, Gothic-revivalist and neo-classical in style. On these spectacularly landscaped demesnes, women's personal gardening space disappeared, as professionally designed and maintained gardens took over. Care of the estate, including the demesne, was perceived to be men's work.

Like those houses of an earlier period, the classical eighteenth-century great house was designed for defense. Heavy locks, chains, and a deep moat or ditch protected entries and ground windows from unlawful entry. Beyond the trenches stretched lawns, bounded by low ditches or sunken fences, that dropped to the parks dotted with trees. Then, in a long curve as far as the eye could see, the demesne kept people out as much as they restrained animals from wandering. In her memoir of her family seat, *Bowen's Court,* Elizabeth Bowen exposes the vulnerability of the Big House and its demesne: 'the isolation is innate; it is an affair of origin'.[8]

On these isolated demesnes, in the pre-Famine years of dense population and cheap labour, scores of gardeners tended the Big House grounds. By then, the enclosed and locked 'walled garden' had become a feature of the Big House landscape. Placed close to a side-door of the mansion, such gardens permitted family and friends to enjoy the herbaceous borders, the yew and oak walks, the rock gardens and water gardens, yet remain discreetly out of sight. If space permitted, the kitchen garden, originally located some distance from the house, was incorporated within the walled garden; clipped beech hedges outlined the four quadrants of its French *potager-jardin* layout. The kitchen garden's popularity continues, and recently, Lanning Roper, the designer of Glenveagh Castle Gardens in County Donegal, has recreated its early nineteenth-century beauty in a splendid mixture of flower, fruit and vegetable.

Were it not for the testimony of an upper-middle-class clergyman's wife in her letters and diaries, and in the artistic precision of her flower collages, women as gardeners would have been overlooked in the construction of the great demesne landscapes of those centuries. Mrs. Delany's delight in her Delville garden in Glasnevin, and in the countryside around the deanery in Downpatrick, County Down, is reflected in a March 1746 letter to her sister:

> I have been planting sweets in my 'Pearly Bower' – honeysuckles, sweet briar, roses and jessamine to climb up the trees that compose it, and for the carpets, violets, primroses and cowslips![9]

For Mrs. Delany, the ability to recognize a well planned garden became a touchstone of good taste. Commenting on a friend's lack of appreciation, she wrote 'no eyes nor understanding to see that it was not a common vulgar garden'. Returning from her rambles with 'handfuls of wild plants', she would, 'search for their names and virtues in Hill – but he is not half so intelligible as old Gerard'[10] referring to her ever-present botany books. An early botanist, she identified rare specimens and classified them scientifically. Popularizing wild flowers, she rebelled against the absurdities perpetrated in the interests of formality: 'Today', she writes in her diary:

we dine at Lord Chief Justice Singleton's at Drumcondra. He has given Mr. Bristowe full dominion over house and gardens, and like a conceited connoisseur, he is doing *strange things* building an absurd room, turning fine wild evergreens out of the garden, *cutting down,* full-grown elms and planting twigs![11]

Mary Delany's gardening letters return us to the world of Walter Osborne's *Study from Nature.* He too, was a naturalist, and for years he worked in the open air, lodging in cottages and in small country inns, until winter arrived. But in the hundred years since Osborne painted *Study from Nature,* a transformation in the Irish landscape has occurred. Gone is the formally landscaped demesne of the Big House, isolated from and at odds with the world outside its walls. While its hold on the literary imagination remains hypnotic, in popular perception the Big House has been stripped of its aloofness. It has become a place to visit and to reclaim as a national heritage, an accomplishment linked to the transformation of the nation. At weekends, Irish families explore house and gardens, a testimony to the new leisure interest in gardening that has seized that very section of society for which Elizabeth Bowen expressed her class repugnance. 'The democratic smell of the Dublin bus'[12] that Bowen abhorred now mingles with the scent of old roses and lavender; the gate of the walled garden swings open to admit visitors once deemed intruders.

The suburban flower garden flourishes, its pleasures replenished from the retail garden centres that have sprung up throughout the country. The 'Tidy Towns' competition has brought trees and plants to the bare streets of Irish municipalities, and has restored elegance to neglected stone work. In their acclaimed compilation, *In an Irish Garden,* Sybil Connolly and Helen Dillon describe the gardens of 'castles, Georgian mansions, small country houses, vicarages, town houses, modern bungalows and cottages in the four corners of Ireland'.[13] The past, educating the present, has given us back the Irish garden that Osborne painted.

from Adele M. Dalsimer and Vera Kreilkamp (eds), *America's Eye: Irish Paintings from the Collection of Brian P. Burns* (Chestnut Hill, MA, Boston College Museum of Art, 1996), pp 29–32.

NOTES

1   Jeanne Sheedy, *Walter Osborne 1859–1903* (Dublin, Town House and The National Gallery of Ireland, 1991), p. 27

2   Against the wishes of her aristocratic family, Mary Granville married Dr Patrick Delany, an Irish clergyman of humble origin and modest means. Her letters and diaries, her flowered collages, and her witty personality establish her as one of the most remarkable observers of eighteenth-century Irish life. Her gardens at Delville, her painting, shell work, and needle work were, in different ways, a celebration of the flower.

3   See Anngret Simms and J. H. Andrews (eds), *Irish Country Towns, and More Irish Country Towns* (Cork, Mercier Press, 1994, 1995).

4   D. M. Waterman, 'Tully Castle', *Ulster Journal of Archaeology,* 22 (1959), pp 123–26.

5   This garden has been recently reconstructed and put in the care of the Department of the Environment for Northern Ireland.

6   The history of Tully Castle and its flowers is available from the Historic Monuments and Buildings Branch, Department of the Environment for Northern Ireland.

7   T. J. Westlopp, 'Leameneagh Castle', *Journal of the Royal Society of Antiquarians of Ireland,* 30 (1900), pp 403–07.

8   Elizabeth Bowen, *Bowen's Court* (London, Virago, 1984), p. 248.

9   Ruth Hayden (ed.), *Mrs. Delany and Her Flower Collages* (London, British Museum Press, 1980), p. 64.

10 Hayden, p. 68.

11 Hayden, p. 79.

12 Elizabeth Bowen, *Irish Stories* (Dublin, Poolbeg, 1978), p. 10.

13 Sybil Connolly and Helen Dillon, *In an Irish Garden* (London, Weidenfeld and Nicolson, 1986), p. 8.

GODLY BURDEN:
CATHOLIC SISTERHOODS IN TWENTIETH-CENTURY IRELAND

This essay was written during a period of great change for Irish sisterhoods. Castigated for their past management of orphanages and industrial schools, they were confronting the dual problems of decline in religious vocations and ageing communities of sisters. Their schools and hospitals were passing from them into increasingly state-controlled management structures. Some of their best beloved convents and institutions closed down permanently, and most humiliating of all, they had to face accusations of child abuse of children in their care and subsequent court cases. For many sisters the 1990s was a decade of heartbreak and dismay – from being actors in the building of the state in 1922 which I have examined in this essay, they became spectators of their decline. The essay was first published in Anthony Bradley and Maryann Gialanella Valiulis (eds), Gender and Sexuality in Modern Ireland *(Amerherst MA, University of Massachusetts Press, 1997).*

Into the vineyard I come in haste
Eleven sounds from its ancient tower;
So many years have gone to waste
What can I do in a single hour?

> from an Irish nun's journal, c. 1923

By 1900 there were just over eight thousand nuns and thirty-five female religious orders in Ireland. There were 368 convents. More than half of the high-walled stone buildings that became a feature of twentieth-century towns and cities were Mercy and Presentation foundations that had stemmed from the modest beginnings of Catherine McAuley's vision and Nano Nagle's aspirations to teach poor children – even before catholic emancipation had been won in 1829. The second half of the nineteenth century witnessed a dramatic growth in the number of women who entered convents – from 1,552 in the 1851 Census to 8,031 in 1901.[1] Invitations had come steadily from catholic bishops to superiors of religious orders to establish convents in their dioceses and to offer educational facilities to girls of all ages.

The terms 'sister' and 'nun' have distinct meanings in canon law but there is a wide practice of employing them interchangeably. The sisterhoods in this essay signify what canon law recognized as 'active orders' in the present century, becoming 'apostolic orders' in 1967 with the Decree on Religious Life issued by the Second Vatican Council. The problem of jurisdiction, that is, whether the religious orders were governed directly from the Vatican or by the local bishop, had been resolved by the beginning of the twentieth century in favour of the local bishop. Enclosure within the convent precincts and supervision of the convent *horarium*, as well as visitation, were potential areas of tension between bishops and the sisterhoods prior to the Second Vatican Council.

The distribution of convents in twentieth-century Ireland still lacks geographical analysis. Caitríona Clear in her study, *Nuns in Nineteenth-Century Ireland*, examined the distribution of convents after the Great Famine (1846–52) with reference to Limerick and Galway, and Dr Tony Fahey commented on the regional unevenness in the growth of congregations throughout the island, citing the 1911 Census for his statement that there were more than twice as many nuns recorded in Leinster as in Connaught: 33.8 per ten thousand women in Leinster, 17.8 per ten thousand in Connaught.[2] For Ulster there is Marie O'Connell's work, published in essay form, 'The Genesis of Convent Foundations and Their Institution in Ulster, 1840–1920'. Her appendices, where she lists, by diocese, the institutes managed and the work carried out by convents in Ulster between 1840 and 1920, are useful for their itemization of ministries. In 1840 the Poor Clare convent in Newry was the only convent in Ulster. By 1920 there were sixty-two convents: Mercy foundations numbered twenty-eight; St. Louis, five; Poor Clare, four; and Presentation, only two.[3] Research is only beginning on the subject of the sisterhoods in twentieth-century Ireland, though yearly studies of foundresses and the history of particular religious congregations exist.[4]

The centralization of the catholic church became concrete with the Dogma of Papal Infallibility in 1870 at the First Vatican Council. As well as increasing church bureaucracy, it strengthened the control of the bishop and parish priest. 'The Church', wrote Pope Pius X, 'is essentially an unequal society, comprising two categories of persons, the Pastors and the flock'. Such was the climate into which the sisterhoods settled uneasily in 1900, desperately needed as auxiliaries by bishops, possessing an ill-defined status as sisterhoods with simple vows, yet bearing the burden of enclosure and, in some orders with medieval origins, the uncertainty of not knowing whether the sisters were in simple or solemn vows. The encroachment of the bishop's jurisdiction over the movements of sisters was further augmented by the Code of Canon Law promulgated in 1917.

Vocations continued to pour into Irish convents. Suellen Hoy has analyzed the successive waves of vocations in her seminal essay, 'The Journey Out: The

Recruitment and Emigration of Irish Religious Women to the United States, 1812–1914', and she suggests that catholic emancipation and the pastoral demands in the United States made the first wave a reality after 1834. The foundations that were established in that period were generally made in the lifetime of the foundress, who exercised a fair measure of autonomy in her choice of place for the new project. Hoy situates the second wave between 1860 and 1917, when recruitment to religious orders was by way of invitation from nuns who had built the convents in regions chosen by the foundress or one of her companions. In that later recruitment, schools played a decisive role and the Sodality of the Blessed Virgin Mary (the 'Blue Ribbon', the Jesuit-inspired *Enfant de Marie*) was central to the recruiting process. Hoy demonstrates that the Sodality was not a middle-class phenomenon associated with boarding schools; it was equally effective when established in the milieu of the factory worker's club or when a domestic servant was introduced to it by the mistress of the house or by a priest confessor. Hoy further suggests that changes in immigration laws in the United States affected the flow of vocations from Ireland to convents in that country.[5]

There was no decrease in the number of entrants to Irish convents in the following decades. They continued to multiply and to find outlets for ministry throughout the world. The explanation lies partially in the missionary enterprise that marks church activity in the first half of the twentieth century. In that unprecedented growth Belgium and Ireland were at the fore. In an examination of the Irish missionary movement, Edmund Hogan describes the aftermath of the Easter Rising as a time of intense idealism in which the founding of the Maynooth Mission to China and that of the Columban Sisters to the 'Far East' took place.[6] It was a period when young people searched for outlets for a heroic life because they were disillusioned by the misplaced ardour of war. The missionary movement, as it expressed itself in Irish catholic life, provided young people with an opportunity in the decades after the civil war of 1922–23 to turn away from the troubling dilemma of legitimized physical force. It was an age when devotional catholicism peaked. The popes, Pius XI and Pius XII, vigorously advocated a style of religious observance and practice that combined expressions of piety in the context of church-based devotions. The establishment of new religious feasts – in particular the cult of Mary – and the encouragement of pilgrimages to her shrines received papal approval. Novenas such as the Miraculous Medal, the Nine First Fridays, and sodalities were assiduously promoted at parish level. The culmination of this highly charged, emotional catholicism was the promulgation in 1950 of the dogma of Mary's assumption into heaven, followed in 1954 (the year decreed by Pius XII as 'the Marian year') by an epidemic of shrine-building all over Ireland. The 1950s were the high point of female religious vocations in twentieth-century Ireland. The 1941 census revealed that one out of every four hundred women was entering a convent and admissions increased in the following decade. So great was the prestige of the sisterhoods in Ireland by the midcentury that in 1949 a lecturer from England at the annual Conference of Convent Secondary Schools in Ireland declared to the assembly:

> It is wonderful to see the power you have in education. In fact the Nuns have all the power to guide and control education policy. You have the Department of Education in the hollow of your hand.[7]

Behind the success and triumphalism of the mid-century lay the larger issue of what constituted work and/or ministry for the sisterhoods. In the previous century the convent was subsidized by dowries. The rural middle classes, daughters of substantial farmers and shopkeepers, brought to religious communities sizeable dowries; the Mercy Sisters' Account Book in Baggot Street convent in Dublin records sums between three and six hundred pounds. That sum remained constant well into the next century, and heiresses always brought large sums of money with them. By the end of the nineteenth century the dowry as asset had been augmented by the boarding school. Religious communities established fee-paying boarding schools to provide room and board for students who lived far away and whose parents sincerely desired a formative catholic environment for the education of their daughters. The decision by the government to hand over the Poor Law Union hospitals, the so-called Workhouse Hospitals, to the care of the Sisters of Mercy from the 1860s onward was decisive and significant in involving sisters in the work of the state.

The emergence of the secondary school was a major development in what constituted the ministry of the convent. The Intermediate Act (1878) was a milestone in girls' schooling, allowing girls a state qualification to enter civil service appointments and prepare for matriculation into the universities. Single sex or separate schools for boys and girls along denominational lines set the pattern for twentieth-century state schooling in Ireland. By 1922 all churches, and the Jewish community, had well-established claims on the state. A mutually beneficial relationship was hammered out between the British Ministry of Education and the Stormont government of Northern Ireland, and between the Free State and the church schools. For the Free State with its largely catholic population the gain was financial and ideological. A considerable number of day-to-day expenses were borne by religious orders. Because the system of education had inherited the single sex structure from the previous era, girls' education was largely in the hands of the nuns for the next decades. Moreover, the catholic school developed qualities the state desired in its citizens: orderliness, discipline, obedience, self-control. The involvement of the sisterhoods, and the larger church investment in education, added to the political legitimacy of the educational system as it evolved in the Dublin civil service over the next decades.

The background of this alliance between the convents and the state enables scrutiny of the policy-makers in the convents. The first university degrees were awarded in the 1890s, and, ironically, Ireland had little acceptable work for these graduates. Quite a number of them entered religious life, and the flow continued steadily and in increasing numbers until the 1940s when the rule of enclosure was relaxed to allow sisters to attend university classes and take examinations. Remarkable women, born in the 1870s, became a pioneering graduate elite – tutored in womens' colleges funded by religious orders such as the Loretos, Ursulines, and Dominicans. If they planned a career in teaching, their role models were their tutors, nuns skilled in the languages of western Europe and at home in the world of the classics. They were drawn to community life and to the positive aspects of celibacy and dedication to learning.[8] They became nuns at a later age than those who did so in the 1930s, and frequently they came bearing their masterships in arts or in science. They knew they were a pioneering generation as the new century precipitated them into the franchise debate and the subsequent agitation for the vote.

A substantial number joined religious orders after the Civil War and claimed membership in Cumann na mBan while at university. Catherine Dixon cycled across Dublin during curfew and delivered Eamon de Valera's American passport to him in the tense aftermath of Easter Week 1916. She subsequently joined the Dominican nuns in Sion Hill convent in Blackrock outside Dublin. Marie Martin, the foundress of the Medical Missionaries of Mary had served as a Volunteer Aid Detachment nurse in World War I. How did that idealistic and high-spirited generation deal with the growing authoritarianism of the political and church climate in the 1930s, '40s, and '50s? Did they assume leadership at a sensitive time? What solutions did they offer to problems like the growing inequalities in the society they ministered to?

One situation in convent life that was not addressed until the mid-century was the status of the lay sister. Lay sisters are present in records from the abbeys and monasteries of the middle ages when it was customary for wealthy women who entered the cloister to bring their serving women with them, or, if they were very young, their nurses. There is no evidence that there was such a division in the small groups of Irish nuns who came together in dwelling houses during the eighteenth century when convents and catholic schools were forbidden to function by state law. With the resurgence of religious life for women in nineteenth-century Ireland the lay sisters became a visible structure within the convent. They entered without dowry, coming from small farming families or artisan backgrounds. They were responsible for support tasks in the convent: cooking, laundering, working in the farm, cleaning the school and dormitories. They led a hidden life. They possessed no vote in community affairs and they did not elect to the leadership of the community; nor were they eligible for election as superior.

Yet the lay sisters were not perceived as domestic servants in an age when Dublin had fifty servants for every thousand women. They had a freedom to converse with men on the farm, to supervise the entrance door as portresses, and to attend the sick. The ideology of the time held that the home and work done therein were suitable for girls or women, so domestic service appealed to parents as a safe occupation for daughters despite the isolation of the work and poor marriage prospects.[9] Convent life with its rhythm, its security, and its sense of space was a desirable option for girls without dowry. What is perplexing is that the two-tiered system remained in existence in Ireland long after it was abolished in the new world of America and Australia. The anomaly of the Irish twentieth-century lay sister contributed to the stratification of Irish society for many decades. Hierarchy within the convent reflected public life in twentieth-century Ireland.

From the mid-nineteenth century, protestant missionaries had taken the lead in sending thousands of missionaries to Asia: doctors, catechists, leaders of mission stations in far-off places like outer Mongolia or deepest Africa. Early in 1912 the Maryknoll Missionary Sisters were founded in the United States by an Irish-American woman, Mollie Rogers. A decade later the Columban Missionary Sisterhood was founded by Frances Moloney, a widow. In 1924 Mary Ryan founded the Holy Rosary Sisters of Killeshandra for mission in Africa. In 1902, previous to these endeavours, Teresa Keaney had gone to equatorial Africa, and gradually it became clear to her that the resources of catholic church missions in issues of disease and health care were inadequate. Thereafter, she crusaded tirelessly for hospital training, including midwifery certification. Finally she established her own sisterhood, the Franciscan Missionaries to Africa, and opened a midwifery training school in Uganda.[10] The quest for the acquisition of professional qualification in surgery and obstetrics, Rome's 'forbidden skills', is the subject of a section of Hogan's study of the Irish missionary experience in the twentieth century. At the heart of the struggle lay the embargo, enshrined in the 1917 Code of Canon Law, forbidding Sisters to take studies in midwifery, obstetrics, and all branches of medicine, including surgery and gynæcology. The struggle to win recognition from the great medical schools was complicated by the necessity to lobby the papacy, and the Roman curia. Pope Benedict XV remained impervious and the capitulation to a clamant demand on the part of missionary bishops and heads of religious orders occurred in 1936 when Pius XI issued Canon 489: Maternity Training for Missionary Sisters.

The Medical Missionaries of Mary, founded by Marie Martin in 1936, were, possibly, the most innovative of the Irish missionary orders of women in twentieth-century Ireland. Her institute was devoted to health care and her Sisters studied all branches of medicine and qualified as surgeons. Their example was quickly followed by other missionary groups. An examination of the politics of the religious women's campaign for medical training reveals the adventurous dimension of the religious calling in decades that were perceived as dehumanizing to sisters working in Irish orphanages and boarding schools. These were the same decades in which Austin Clarke chided nuns for choosing a 'tidy bed,/Full board and launderette', thereby robbing themselves of spontaneity. And somewhat later Edna O'Brien arrested a moment of icy institutional coldness in her description of her convent boarding school.[11]

There were two areas in the daily lives of sisters where the burden of religion sat heavily on their shoulders. The first was the Code of Canon Law as it applied to women religious. By 1900 apostolic activity as a legitimate exercise of a convent's mission had been acknowledged both by Rome and by local bishops. There was recognition that travel, dress, and the strict laws of enclosure needed modernization. The 1917 Code of Canon Law set, for decades to come, the limits of autonomy for women religious: weekly confession, daily Eucharist, set hours for prayer including meditation. Laws of fast and abstinence were strictly enforced in convents during Lent and Advent and each Friday of the year. The practice of religious life became a process of fulfilling a series of obligations. Catholicism, until the Second Vatican Council, was a religion of authority concealed by the beauty of the liturgical revolution, which revitalized Gregorian chant and brought ritual into the lives of ordinary church-goers. It was an age of pageantry and ritual; the liturgical plainchant of the choir office became an art form in convent culture and drew an appreciative audience to the solemn liturgies of Holy Week, Easter, and Christmas. It took its toll on the health of the sisters already overburdened in classroom and hospital ward. The shock of recognition and the identification with the central character in *The Nun's Story* (played by actress Audrey Hepburn) was a prelude to acknowledging a reality that would later cause women who had spent a number of years in religious life to leave the convent.[12]

The image of the nun in mid-century Ireland (and elsewhere) was that of a docile and submissive figure clad in a black or white or blue sweep of garment with a medieval headdress who rarely raised her voice or eyes. Yet these same women were major players in church-state relations below the official level of the catholic hierarchy. Owners and matrons of the main hospital system in the country, they were entrusted by the state with the state's industrial schools and orphanages and with the reponsibility of implementing the state's fragile and largely underdeveloped welfare policy.[13] Though set in wartime France, Eiléan Ní Chuilleanáin's elegy for her aunt Anna encapsulates the contradictions and perplexities of the nun's role in that period.

> When young in the Franciscan house at Calais
> She complained to the dentist, I *have a pain in our teeth*
>
> ... Stripping the hospital, loading the sick on lorries,
> While Reverend Mother walked the wards and nourished them
> With jugs of wine to hold their strength.[14]

One canon of the 1917 Code is frequently overlooked: catholics were forbidden to attend schools open to non-catholics. That stricture was brought to bear in the negotiations between the catholic hierarchy and the Free State Department of Education in 1924, formally recognizing catholic schools as state schools. Salary scales were implemented, capitation and building grants were agreed upon. Examining convent accounts,[15] it is evident that, initially, the relief was great: the burden of teaching extracurricular subjects, such as music, singing, voice projection – for necessary revenue – was lifted. Then, in 1929, came Pope Pius XI's encyclical, *The Christian Education of Youth,* which put a seal of approval on the ministry for educating the young at school and college level. Thus, far from discouraging sisters from acquiring professional qualifications, Pius XI urged the heads of religious orders to qualify sisters for the schools and colleges he advocated. It should have been the beginning of the modernization of the Irish sister. She now attended university or hospital as a student (wherever possible one with a catholic ethos). If unable to study by day because of other work, she studied by night and during weekends. Summer schools were not offered in the Ireland of that period. It was in truth an age of 'eternal verities'. The sisterhoods represented an eternity on earth: clothes, ways of thinking, rules were changeless. The imposition of cloister and the frequent canonical and episcopal strictures on its enforcement placed women religious in Ireland in a culturally rigid role. Impossible burdens of work and unrealistic asceticisms dried up human affectivity in the increasingly younger aspirant to religious life who moved from the institutionalized boarding school into the structured novitiate.

In 1950 Pope Pius XII, concerned with evidence that the level of professional excellence among many of the sisters was far below that of their lay counterparts, summoned an international congress of superior generals to Rome and exhorted them to educate their subjects on a par with their lay colleagues. Inspired by his mandate, the 1950s was a decade of summer schools in theology, scriptural studies, and the updating of subjects taught at school level. Sisters began to take higher degrees and lectureships at third level. On the eve of the Second Vatican Council, the sisterhoods had organized themselves into confederations and were talking among themselves, comparing experiences and inviting sisters from other religious orders to address them. The isolation was breaking down. One of the lightning conductors was the development of the theology and spirituality of religious life. The Pontifical Institute of Regina Mundi was set up in Rome by directive of Pius XII in 1954 to offer three-year religious courses for women, both lay and religious, and those who enrolled returned to positions of responsibility within novitiates.[16]

They brought back a new concept of the mission of religious orders, one that placed emphasis on vowed poverty as a way of witnessing and serving the needy in society. Celibacy was valued in its ability to give greater freedom of time and energies to those in need. Obedience was interpreted as listening to the Gospel values and to the overall mission of the Church. Thus it can be argued that the renewal of religious life anticipated the mandates of Vatican II. The change that seemed so gradual in the first sixty years of the twentieth century was unthreatening to Rome and to convent structures. Popes had encouraged it. In the earlier part of the century the Irish state and the Stormont government in Northern Ireland had facilitated church-state relationships in granting recognition to the apostolic ministries of teaching and social welfare, as well as bestowing positions of responsibility on sisters, without examining their professional qualifications. The Vatican had, in turn, granted dispensations for the professionalization of the sisters that seemed harmless enough, such as permission to travel singly, to discard the religious garb if studying medicine, to absent oneself from the common table and even common prayer. Too late it was perceived that removal of the Canon concerning cloister was a structural change of such magnitude that it would affect all elements of religious life in the convent in twentieth-century Ireland.

There were other factors certainly; change was in the air in the early sixties, but the demands of professional work standards and the obligations of conventual living set in a nineteenth-century mould were to prove incompatible. In Ursula Le Guin's *Earthsea Trilogy*, the second adventure – *The Tombs of Atuan* – tells the story of the priestess, Tenar.[17] She is given a choice: either to stay and be afraid of the dark and make her peace with those she serves in the Temple or to leave the Tombs of Atuan and begin another story and another life. By stopping on the threshold of the post–Vatican Two era there is a completion to the narrative. What happened next belongs to a new Ireland and a questioning catholicism.

from Anthony Bradley and Maryann Gialanella Valiulis (eds), *Gender and Sexuality in Modern Ireland* (Amerherst MA, University of Massachusetts Press, 1997), pp 245–256.

NOTES

1   Tony Fahey, 'Nuns in the Catholic Church in Ireland in the Nineteenth Century', in Mary Cullen (ed.), *Girls Don't Do Honours: Irish Women* in *Education* in *the Nineteenth and Twentieth Centuries* (Dublin, Women's Education Bureau, 1987), p. 7. Data for years 1851 and 1901, 'Tables of Occupation', Census of Population of Ireland.

2   For an analysis of nineteenth-century distribution of convents, Caitríona Clear, *Nuns in Nineteenth-Century Ireland* (Dublin, Gill and Macmillan, 1987), pp 36–68; Tony Fahey, 'Female Asceticism in the Catholic Church: A Case Study of Nuns in Nineteenth-Century Ireland' (Ph.D. thesis, University of Illinois, 1981), pp 66–74.

3   Marie O'Connell, 'The Genesis of Convent Foundations and Their Institutions in Ulster, 1840–1920', in Janice Holmes and Diane Urquhart (eds), *Coming into the Light: The Work, Politics and Religion of Women in Ulster 1840–1940* (Belfast, Institute of Irish Studies, 1994), pp 179–201.

4   Margaret Mac Curtain, 'Late in the Field: Catholic Sisters in Twentieth-Century Ireland and the New Religious History', in Mary O'Dowd and Sabine Wichert (eds), *Chattel, Servant or Citizen: Women's Status in Church, State and Society* (Belfast, Institute of Irish Studies, 1995), pp 34–44.

5   Suellen Hoy, 'The Journey Out: The Recruitment and Emigration of Irish Religious Women to the United States, 1812–1914', *Journal of*

Women's History, Vol. 6, No. 4, Vol. 7, No.1 (Winter/Spring 1995), pp 64–98.

6   Edmund Hogan, *The Irish Missionary Movement: A Historical Survey, 1830–1980* (Dublin, Gill and Macmillan, 1992), pp 95–97.

7   Report of Conference of Secondary Schools in Ireland 1949 (Archives Education Secretariat, Conference of Religious of Ireland, Milltown Park, Dublin).

8   Research in progress by author. See Margaret Mac Curtain, 'Women of Eccles Street', *The Lanthorn* (Dublin, Dominican Publications, 1982), pp 54–60.

9   Suellen Hoy and Margaret Mac Curtain, *From Dublin to New Orleans: The Journey of Nora and Alice* (Dublin, Attic Press, 1994), pp 30–31.

10 Hogan, *op. cit.,* pp 114–16.

11 Austin Clarke, 'Living on Sin', *Collected Poems* (Dublin, Dolmen Press, 1974), p. 271; Edna O'Brien, *The Country Girls* (London, Penguin Books, 1960).

12 The exodus from Irish convents of sisters who had spent a substantial part of their lives in religious vows became noticeable in the 1970s and continued as a significant trend for well over a decade.

13 Sheila Lunney, 'Institutional Solutions to a Social Problem: Childcare in Ireland 1869–1950', (M.A. thesis, University College Dublin, 1995).

14 Eiléan Ní Chuilleanáin, 'J'ai mal a nos dents', *The Magdalene Sermon* (Dublin, Gallery Press, 1989), p. 29.

15 The Conference of Religious of Ireland was founded in 1961 as the Conference of Major Superiors. For some years it was a loosely knit group meeting periodically. From the beginning, one of its main tasks was to bring the managerial and ownership structures of the complex school systems of the catholic religious orders under its jurisdiction.

16 Patricia Wittberg, *The Rise and Decline of Catholic Religious Orders* (Albany, State University of New York Press, 1994), p. 211.

17 Ursula K. Le Guin, *The Tombs of Atuan* (London, Victor Gollancz, 1972).

WOMEN AND THE RELIGIOUS REFORMATION IN EARLY MODERN IRELAND

For sheer spread of writings by Irish women and for texts centred on women in Ireland, The Field Day Anthology of Irish Writing, IV–V *(Cork, Cork University Press, 2002) was the outstanding Irish publication of a decade. Eight women editors and a number of contributing editors participated in a decade-long multi-disciplinary enterprise. The two volumes are organized into eight large sections: 'Medieval to Modern, 600– 1900'; Religion, Science, Theology and Ethics, 1500–2000'; 'Sexuality, 1600–2001'; 'Oral Traditions: Women in Irish Society, 1200–2000'; 'Politics, 1500–2000'; 'Women's Writing, 1700–1960', and 'Contemporary Writing, 1960–2001', in all over 3000 pages. From its tentative beginnings in 1992 to the completed hard and paperback editions in 2002 the project was a stunning combination of collaborative scholarship and co-operation with a courageous university press. The following essay is the introduction to the section on texts associated with women and the religious reformation in the 16th and 17th centuries.*

The religious Reformation, which Irish society experienced from the mid-1530s onwards, changed the denominational composition of the small population of the country significantly. At first sight it seemed an act of state, imposed upon a section of the island to which the Tudor king of England laid claim in the 1530s. In similar fashion, European crowned heads were favouring alternative modes of religious Reformation in their realms in this, the age of Martin Luther, John Calvin and the Council of Trent. The establishment of the Church of Ireland, following the Anglican model, was, in the main, the work of the Tudor monarchs Henry VIII, his son, Edward VI, and his daughter, Elizabeth I. By the middle of the seventeenth century, the Reformation had claimed different constituencies on the island. The government elites gave their allegiance to the established church, the Church of Ireland. The majority of the inhabitants, then estimated variously at under a million, declared for a renewed Roman Catholicism, rejuvenated by the decrees of the Council of Trent and mediated to Ireland through a European-educated clergy and hierarchy. Yet a third group who had come to Ireland during these formative centuries of the early modern period were settlers, different from the medieval Viking, Norman, or later English adventurers, who had formed the core of English administration in Dublin and its surrounding area, the Pale. As colonizers, the settlers of early modern Ireland had the support of the monarchy. Mainly interested in land investment, their general religious configuration was protestant. Within that classification were contained lines of religious demarcation. Elizabethan settlers, with a few noteworthy exceptions, belonged to the Church of Ireland. Scottish settlers came in significant numbers to designated areas of Ulster in the Jacobean period. Presbyterians, with the characteristics of the Lowland Scot, their religious identity was rooted in the Calvinism of John Knox.

How did the position and status of women change throughout the Reformation centuries? Did reformed christianity address itself to the religious needs of women? Is it possible to trace the links that connect pre-Reformation expressions of religion which emerged in the refounding of catholic religious life for women in eighteenth-century Ireland? In the prevailing vision of Ireland's past, a fissure of discontinuity separates the long and shared cultural perceptions of early and medieval Irish society from the genuinely historical changes that characterize the transitional nature of early modern Ireland.

All historians are seduced by the persuasiveness of a master narrative which neatly divides the medieval world from the modern by a chronology which situates all the significant changes in the contemporary world of a hypothetical but real period designated as 'early modern'. It was 'then' that western civilization encountered humanism. It was 'then' that reformed christianity shattered the unity of christendom. The discovery of the New World occurred during that period and, with it, the rise of capitalism, nation states and national monarchies. For Ireland there was the added experience of incorporation into the British Empire, with the Tudor expansion accompanying a colonial experiment of settlement from the neighbouring countries of England, Scotland and Wales. In subscribing to a master narrative, historians section off the medieval world, isolating it so that its society and culture belong to a past extraneous to what follows. Historians of early modern Ireland succumb to the attraction of a great transition, but uncertainty prevails over the beginning and ending of the traditional periodization. Does the historian include the era of the Penal Code in the first half of the eighteenth century? Or was a new canon established in 1976, by giving the magisterial volume three of *A New History of Ireland* an end date with the final victory of the Williamite forces and the consolidation of the land settlement in favour of settlers?

There is consensus about the starting point for early modern Ireland. It is the Fall of the House of Kildare, with the liquidation of its leading members in the 1530s. Attempts to shift the emphasis back have not altered the master narrative. It is convenient for historians to establish a canonicity around the centuries that designate early modern Ireland. It privileges scholarship and offers compartmentalized sanctuary for medievalists as well as for early modern historians. In this arrangement, the distinction between the condition of medieval women and of early modern women carries with it pejorative assumptions. Women's lives worsened in the early modern period. Women lost ground in sixteenth-century Ireland and women's status and choices were drastically curtailed in the following century. Thus the notion of a major transition for women between the medieval and early modern centuries persists as integral to the master narrative instead of challenging it.

The historiography of early modern Ireland retains the configuration of an emerging political map. The traditional issues of historical investigation, such as the visible political developments, military events, and the impact of religious changes which received a major reinforcement of research in the 1960s with the study of the ruling elites, have remained the *longue durée* of sixteenth- and seventeenth-century Ireland. Intersections between racial, ethnic, gendered and class identities attracted little research and the methods of the new 'social' history developed in the 1970s, such as quantitative analysis (borrowed from economics), the interpretation of symbols, such as the role of the poet or *file* (from anthropology), and the study of gender, using the tools of gender analysis, are conspicuous by their absence. The important theoretical models that have been built around women as gendered historical change-objects have not been addressed by mainstream historians of early modern Ireland. Certainly the perception of a categorical, dramatic change in women's lives between 1534 and 1691, wherever it is tested, holds up to scrutiny, but the uncritical assumption of a negative transition for women is a forceful and compelling paradigm in the developing field of Irish women's history. Like the model of a medieval and early modern divide, this secondary model of (liberated) medieval, (oppressed) early modern women fits into the master narrative because the areas tested are women, law and property, extrapolating too rapidly from that experience of diminishment of women's rights to an over-generalized picture of, and extinguishing of, women's presence in early modern Ireland.

Did the experience of women in the Reformation century go from bad to worse? How did women regard their religious experience in a reformed christianity?

The most powerful and, in many respects, most independent women in the late medieval church in Ireland remain hidden from historical scrutiny. There are no mystical writings from the period, either before or after the Black Death, such as the English anchoress Julian of Norwich produced. There is no Catherine of Siena, doctor of the church and patroness of Italy, to recall the Irish church to its sense of mission, no Bridget of Sweden, who is credited with the vision of Ireland where she saw souls fall into hell like leaves in wintry weather. In point of fact there are no Irish women saints in this long period of medieval Ireland, when Rome gradually assumed. control of who should be 'raised to the altars of the church'.

Of the major monasteries that were dissolved in the first distribution, 1536–7, during the reign of Henry VIII, two out of the seventeen monasteries dissolved by Crown Commissioners were nunneries: Graine, County Kilkenny, and Hogges Lane in Dublin. In the second distribution, 1539–46, a number of other nunneries are listed, of which Kilculliheen abbey and its abbess are the most frequently cited as evidence of moral decay. Citations from the document 'An Instrument Concerning Elicie Butler', translated in full for the first time in *Field Day*, have presented a picture of unmitigated decadence on the eve of the Reformation. The text in its entirety tells a different story. It is clear from the final section of the document that Elicie Butler and the abbey properties of Kilculliheen were victims of the rival jurisdictional claims of two neighbouring bishops. Deposed the following year, Elicie Butler retained a privileged position in her abbey and was awarded a pension at the dissolution of Kilculliheen.

Alison White was the spirited abbess of Grace Dieu, the most renowned Augustinian monastery and girls' school within Ireland when one of the commissioners for the dissolution, Patrick Barnewall, evicted her and her community, and adapted the buildings for his family mansion. Visitation records of Grace Dieu exist from the previous century and give a picture of a well-run establishment, where the 'divine offices are duly celebrated'. Studies of these sixteenth-century women, who administered large properties and had jurisdiction over many subjects, have yet to come. The aged Countess of Ormond, who died in 1542, was representative of a generation of propertied women of the ruling class and both she and Margaret Ball afford a glimpse of how women of their class carried out their religious duties. In the following century, Honor Fitzmaurice, Lady Kerry, conveys poignantly the sense of being obedient to a higher authority when law and order had broken down.

With the religious changes in sixteenth-century Ireland, the nunneries and their lively occupants disappear and information begins to flow about the reformed women. Their lives were difficult, particularly for the wives of the first reform bishops. Bishop John Bale of Ossory split his diocese asunder when he married. Archbishop Loftus of Armagh dismayed his subjects by marrying a local woman, and her sister married his successor. Nine of the first generation of reform bishops married: a new role for women had been created, the clergyman's wife. The protestant idealization of motherhood, propelled by Luther's theology of the family, in turn influenced the Council of Trent's regulations on marriage. The history of marriage in this century suggests evidence of an improved status for women. Loss of property was continuous throughout the period but the miseries of clandestine marriages, abandonment and the injustices that beset the ordinary woman in the late middle ages, which we find in the filings of the Armagh registers, in the Gormanston records and in Archbishop May's registers, do not surface in the Irish Chancery Court after 1570. By that time extensive legislation relating to marriage had been enacted both in the civil and ecclesiastical courts. The Council of Trent restored marriage as a sacrament. The Book of Common Prayer introduced a splendid marriage liturgy, and the dispensations from the impediments of consanguinity and affinity were allowed for annulment purposes in Rome. Gone was the earlier reckless wife-swapping atmosphere of the 1530s; instead the Elizabethan church settlement made divorce difficult.

The paradigm of a diminishment in women's status in the post-Reformation era does not hold, despite an intensification and reinforcement of a patriarchal model of authority. In the following century the incidence of women writing about their religious experience, together with the feminization of domestic religion within the home, testify to the spiritual vigour that women discovered in their chosen religious affiliations. The diary of Mary Rich, née Boyle, deserves serious scholarly attention. Through its pages the reader is introduced to the intimacy of the Puritan female mind and discovers a clear exposition of the Puritan doctrine of daughterly obedience. By then, women of Quaker affiliation had entered Irish society. Their non-aristocratic background, their ability to take their own space in their assemblies, preaching, discussing, even interrupting sermons, testify to the spiritual freedom of Nonconformist women. Rediscovering the religious voices of women in the age of Reformation challenges the master narrative. Religious history is developing significant inter-connections and parallels with other branches of the new 'social' history. The readiness to acknowledge the importance of unordained ministry and to examine the changing constructs of hagiography is a sign of that change. Possibly the most courageous leap forward that the new feminist religious history has made in the field of historical practice is its preparedness to adopt the techniques of qualitative analysis, to look at frameworks derived from feminist theology and biblical research, and to uncover the implications of the ongoing patriarchal control of organized religion for society in general and for the lives of men and women.

from Angela Bourke, Siobhán Kilfeather, Maria Luddy, Margaret Mac Curtain, Geraldine Meaney, Máirín Ní Dhonnchadha, Mary O'Dowd, Clair Wills (eds), *The Field Day Anthology of Irish Writing: IV–V: Irish Women's Writing and Traditions* (Cork, Cork University Press, 2002).

WRITING GRIEF INTO MEMORY
WOMEN, LANGUAGE AND NARRATIVE

This essay grew out of a paper I delivered at the annual conference of the International Association for the Study of Irish Literatures held in the University of Limerick in 1998. Its delivery and the task of preparing the paper for publication afforded me an opportunity to examine literary texts in a setting which drew on history and literature. Hitherto I had appropriated such themes as the classical lament for a dead chieftain for historical purposes and I had perceived the role of the Poet (An File) in sixteenth-century Irish as that of an influential political figure in the Irish world. Influenced by my work as an editor of The Field Day Anthology of Irish Writing *for the writing of the IASIL paper I selected women writers and the overall theme of grief, and I surveyed women's writings on grief in two languages, Irish and English from the late eighteenth century to the present day.*

What delighted me was the richness and variety of lament poetry in Irish which women have published in the second half of the twentieth century and the manner in which they picked up in the written form of the language the thread of grief expressed in the great oral repertoire of the eighteenth and nineteenth centuries. The full significance and complexity of women's poetry is an exciting field for literary criticism; my interest in this essay was to look at the historical space women's poetry occupied and how significant that space was to the communities they addressed.

Originally I had intended to concentrate on the memoir written in English and to offer reasons why the memoir was a satisfying vehicle for writing about grief at the end of the twentieth century. As IASIL invites research and discussion in Irish as well as in English, I took full advantage of my brief and reached back into the memories of Peig Sayers, and marvelled afresh at the culture of the Blasket island writers.

This final essay I dedicate to the students who attended my history option in UCD 'Learning in Elizabethan and Jacobean Ireland' over several years. Drawn from a number of cognate disciplines their insights enriched the course and made all participants reflect on 'otherness' and diversity. The essay was first published in Patricia A. Lynch, Joachim Fischer and Brian Coates (eds), Back to the Present, Forward to the Past *(Amsterdam, Rodopi, 2006).*

Memory, the ability to recall past events and remember the names and deeds of past generations, was regarded at the end of the twentieth century as the most precious power of the intellect which humans possess. Together with language, it is the characteristic that provides humans with a history of their own. It underlines all learning, the core feature of which is retention, and even though there may be learning without remembering, the activity of the memory covers recognition and recall.

Mnemosyne, the Greek goddess of memory, was the mother of the Muses; thus, the Greeks distinguished between two different states of existence, mortality and immortality. The generic word for goddess is oppositional to muse, and underscores the structural parallel between the human agent created by the mating of the goddess with a mortal man whose offspring becomes the narrator while the Muses, divine and remote, create the narrative. Without the human voice of the mediating narrator, poet, bard, singer, the narrative with its dangerous detachment from the suffering world seduces the listener into forgetfulness and oblivion. The Greeks believed the Muses had a heart without the capacity for grief; their concern was the formal dirge. In contrast, the bard, while having access to their distant world, belonged in the suffering of human experience.[1]

The study of memory was first developed by the German psychologist, Hermann Ebbinghaus, in 1885. Since then theories about memory have characterized the twentieth century and as Minerva, goddess of wisdom and memory in Roman civilization, carried the owl as the symbol of her power, the twentieth-century goddess of memory has been worshipped under the image of the computer. Memory and loss of memory haunt humanity at the end of the century. Memory has always been the consolation of growing old, and being remembered is a ritual enacted by and within the community when someone departs from this world. Particularly painful is that loss of memory associated with Alzheimer's disease, paralysing for a philosopher and novelist as eminent as Iris Murdoch.[2]

What I propose to examine in this article is how women's voices use memory to create a narrative around mourning and grief. Rewriting the literary landscape in order to reconfigure the canon was one of the aims of the editors of *The Field Day Anthology* which was published in three volumes in 1991, and evoked a storm of protest for its failure to give women writers their place within the recasting of the canon. The decision to add a fourth volume devoted exclusively to women's writings met with a lukewarm reception, but the project got underway in the autumn of 1992 with an editorial board of seven women editors and Seamus Deane, the general editor of *Field Day*.[3] Working with commissioned editors in sub-sections of the main areas, the project made slow progress throughout the 1990s. As general editor for women's religious writings over the last five hundred years in Ireland, I worked with section editors to select from printed works and published documents in the sphere of religious and spiritual writings, the thoughts and sentiments of women in sermon, letter, diary, hymn, poem and religious controversy. Though not strictly religious, expressions of women's grief appeared frequently in poetry and autobiography, and this article gives me the opportunity to comment on the ways women wrote grief into Irish literature.

It is rare for a historian to be given the opportunity of working on the texts I here examine and to think about narratives within their historical context and outside the framework of academic history. Perhaps my understanding of the role of the *file*, the poet in sixteenth-century Irish life, allowed me to feel comfortable about investigating the theme of lament poetry composed by women poets in the Irish language. Did the status and immense authority of the *file* admit women into their ranks? Were the bardic poets impervious to the genius of creativity in their daughters and how did those daughters overcome obstacles of gender and training? Máirín Nic Eoin's ideological critique of Irish literature and the literary output of women, *B'ait Leo Bean: Gnéithe den Idé-Eolaíocht Inscne i dTraidisiún Liteartha na Gaeilge*,[4] ranges over more than a thousand years of the Irish literary tradition, and argues compellingly that some of the best known poems of the Old Irish period were written by women. Exclusion of women poets followed the general European trend in the middle ages, and in Ireland the bardic schools did not admit women. When the bardic tradition declined women poets regained their voices. Their remarkable contribution to lament-poetry was a feature of their re-emergence.

Although there is ample literary evidence concerning the expressions of women's grief during the Elizabethan conquest of Ireland in the sixteenth century and the self-imposed exile of its nobles in the episode known as 'The Flight of the Earls' in 1607, when the chieftains of the North sailed away from Ulster and left that province defenceless, my starting point is the middle of the next century. The most remarkable poem of the eighteenth century written in Irish was a lament attributed to a woman, Eibhlín Dubh Ní Chonaill. According to Seán Ó Tuama in his edition of the poem in Irish, *Caoineadh Airt Uí Laoghaire* (in English, 'The Lament for Art O'Leary'), it was composed for public recitation. Ó Tuama identified a number of elements characteristic of the lament genre: the address to the dead person, the use of formulaic language, the plea to rise up from the dead, the orchestration of praise, the sympathetic mourning of nature for the dead one, and the curse laid on those responsible for the slaying of the hero.[5]

Composed in five different movements, it is an absorbing drama concerning a quarrel between two neighbours, Morris, a protestant law-enforcer and Art Ó Laoghaire, a catholic landowner and a former colonel of the Austrian imperial army in good standing with the Empress Maria Theresa. The context of the quarrel was a series of Irish laws with a religious bias, known as the Penal Code, which the victorious protestant minority imposed on catholics and nonconformists, depriving them of civil rights in the years following the English Revolution Settlement 1689–1714. Designed to protect the privileges of a small propertied minority, the penal laws affected every aspect of life for the disenfranchised. In this incident Art Ó Laoghaire's magnificent brown mare was at the heart of the dispute between the two men. By invoking a statute of the Irish Parliament, popularly described as a penal law, a protestant of the established church was entitled to buy a horse from its catholic owner for as little as £5. The purpose of the law was to render powerless the dwindling catholic gentry who had obstinately held on to profession of the catholic religion as a mark of their identity over two centuries. At an estimated £5 a horse was valued as the trappings of a military man, so it was a calculated insult to offer Art Ó Laoghaire, remnant of the catholic nobility, reputable soldier of the Austrian army, such a contemptible sum of money. Art Ó Laoghaire repudiated the offer and openly threatened to be revenged on Morris. On the night of 4 May 1773, Art Ó Laoghaire was murdered and his brown mare arrived home, splashed with blood, tense with alarm and fear, reins loose and trailing, to Art Ó Laoghaire's widow, Eibhlín Dubh Ní Chonaill. The first sequence of the poem is Eibhlín's address to her dead husband which includes her response to the appalling news:[6]

> Mo chara thú go daingean!
> Is níor chreideas riamh dod mharbh
> Gur tháinigh chugham do chapall
> Is a srianta léi go talamh,
> Is fuil do chroí ar a leacain
> Siar go t'iallait ghreanta
> Mar a mbitheá id shuí 's id sheasamh.
> Thugas léim go tairsigh,
> An dara léim go geata,
> An tríú léim ar do chapall.
>
> My friend you were forever!
> I knew nothing of your murder
> Till your horse came to the stable
> With the reins beneath her trailing
> And your heart's blood on her shoulders
> Staining the tooled saddle
> Where you used to sit and stand,
> My first leap reached the threshold,

My second reached the gateway,
My third leap reached the saddle.

The heart of the poem is the centrality of Eibhlín's grief and how personally it is expressed:

Do bhuaileas go luath mo bhasa
Is do bhaineas as na reathaibh
Chomh maith is bhí sé agam,
Go bhfuaireas romham tú marbh
Cois toirín ísil aitinn,
Gan Pápa gan easpag
Gan cléireach gan sagart
Do léifeadh ort an tsailm
Ach seanbhean chríonna chaite
Do leath ort binn dá fallaing –
Do chuid fola leat 'na sraithibh;
Is níor fhanas le hí ghlanadh
Ach í ól suas lem bhasaibh

I struck my hands together
And I made the bay horse gallop
As fast as I was able,
Till I found you dead before me
 Beside a little furze-bush
Without Pope or bishop
Without priest or cleric
To read the death-psalms for you,
But a spent old woman only
Who spread her cloak to shroud you –
Your heart's blood still flowing;
I did not stay to wipe it
But I filled my hands and drank it.

One of the best commentaries on the 'Lament for Art O'Leary' is Eiléan Ní Chuilleanáin's, who, discussing these stanzas, writes:

This striking passage as well as conveying passion and grief shows us a woman whose image of herself emphasizes action and movement. By contrast with the lone mourner who might be death personified, the *seanbhean chríonna chaite* whom she finds attending Art's body, she is all decisive vigour. It is her self-portrait that gives the poem its central life, though the *Caoineadh* contains several descriptions of her husband.[7]

Ní Chuilleanáin understands how the poem reflects the social nature of keening, the ritualized public form of giving voice to grief where one mourner takes up and responds to the previous speaker. Yet the principal narrator, Eibhlín, is the active voice who articulates the grief of the community and speaks with the responsibility of avenging the honour of her murdered husband. This blazing anger, the proclamation of personal action are, according to Ní Chuilleanáin, the levers which transform 'The Lament for Art O'Leary' from the *caoineadh* (the English keening), as a vehicle for communal mourning, into 'an assertion of personal freedom' which Ní Chuilleanáin connects to the atavistic grief for a dying Gaelic aristocracy:

> Tá fhios ag Íosa Críost
> Ná beidh caidhp ar bhathas mo chinn,
> Ná léine chnis lem thaoibh,
> Ná bróg ar thrácht mo bhoinn:
> Ná trioscán ar fuaid mo thí,
> Ná srian leis an láir ndoinn,
> Ná caithfidh mé le dlí,

> Jesus Christ knows
> I'll have no cap on my head,
> Nor a shift on my back,
> Nor shoes on my feet,
> Nor goods in my house,
> Nor the brown mare's harness
> That I won't spend on lawyers;

The 'Lament for Art O'Leary' passed into numerous oral versions at the end of the eighteenth century and in its written form the following century was attributed to

Eibhlín Dubh Ní Chonaill. Máire Mhac an tSaoi[8] disputes Eibhlín's authorship rather dismissively ('Poor Nelly – she has been demoted; she is no longer a poet, only a poem') but as Ní Chuilleanáin points out, the poem builds upon a framework in which Eibhlín and her lover/husband are alternatively active and passive. Though 'The Lament' gives us a vivid sense of what Art Ó Laoghaire was like, it is Eibhlín's own self-realization that gives the lament its vigour. It is incontestable that the professional keening women were present at Art Ó Laoghaire's obsequies. One in particular, Norry Singleton, recited the *Caoineadh* thirty years later for a transcriber, thus beginning its cycle again as one of the most impressive literary achievements of modern Irish writing.

Memory and recall are central to women's elegiac poems. Voice is what gives it body. Angela Bourke assigns the keening woman her primary role in the performance of the lament and her active agency in the composition of the lament-form in Irish literature. Lament poetry, she suggests, is verbal art, and the women who gave voice to the *Caoineadh* were skilled in the dramatic arts. Developing her thesis further Bourke writes:

> Her [the keening woman's] willingness to experience disturbing emotions to the full provided a catharsis for everyone who witnessed her performance. She used her appearance, her voice, and her poetry to work on the emotions of her audience. The cry of the keener has been described as 'blood-curdling', 'horrible' and 'hideous'; yet young girls used to practice to get the right effect.[9]

Whereas Ní Chuilleanain, and Mhac an tSaoi read the lament poems as literary texts for interpretation, Bourke connects the lament poet with oral performance and with acquired skills of transforming the private grief of the mourner into the public expression of experiencing loss. Bourke interrogates the poem to find the story behind the occasion for creating the lament and addressing the deity. She looks for the clues that allow the woman narrator to reveal secrets that normally were locked away in the community or household memory. Because the narrator, who may have composed the lament, was wild in manner and conveyed to her audience a reckless behaviour akin to madness, according to Bourke the extravagant expressions of grief were choreographed for a purpose:

> The 'madness' of the lament poet at a wake or funeral would clearly have the effect of protecting her from the consequences of her outspoken behaviour. The inner circle of mourners – women who had lamented their own dead and the younger women who listened to learn – must have recognized that there was method in that madness however … The assumed madness of mourning could be used to cloak statements about sexual and personal identity. By baring their breasts and loosening their hair, by referring to sexual pleasure, or the absence of it, in their relations with their husbands, and by frequently referring to pregnancy and childbirth, lament poets asserted their identity as women in a way that contrasts sharply with the accepted norms of modesty and reticence in Irish society.

In crossing over to the nineteenth century, when lament poetry was a popular genre, it also became part of the oral tradition. Bourke cites a lament poem composed by the mother of a young farmer killed in a fall from his horse in 1860, still popular in Irish-speaking gatherings eighty years later in the 1940s. Whereas Eibhlín Dubh Ní Chonaill spoke for a class, the dwindling Gaelic aristocracy of the eighteenth century, in the following century the keening women, whether makers or vehicles for grief, daringly expressed anger, protest and mockery for a rural community of small farmers and fisherfolk. The 'keeners' relayed coded messages to an appreciative audience who read reality out of their crazy outrageous behaviour and their sometimes covert satire.

Before moving to the twentieth-century narratives of grief written for the printed page, the writings of Peig Sayers, the Blasket Island storyteller, permit the reader of the published texts of her memoirs to experience second-hand the anguish of a seafaring community subsisting on a small mountainous island off the coast of the Dingle peninsula in County Kerry. Peig Sayers' memories were published when she was in her mid-sixties in three books, *Peig: A Scéal Féin*, edited by Máire Ní Chinnéide (Dublin, Talbot Press, 1936) and translated several times, most notably by Bryan MacMahon in 1973, *Scéalta ón mBlascaod* (Dublin, Talbot Press, 1938) and *Machtnamh Seana-Mhná* (1939), translated by Séamus Ennis as *An Old Woman's Reflections* with an Introduction by W. R. Rodgers (London, Oxford University Press, 1962).

The Great Blasket Island is known and celebrated throughout the world as the home of three Irish writers, Tomás Ó Criomhthain, Peig Sayers and Muiris Ó Súileabháin, whose mastery of the art of storytelling first in the Irish language for their own island community and then for a larger audience was communicated through the published translations of their stories dictated to the scholars who came to visit them, Robin Flower from Oxford, Kenneth Jackson from Edinburgh and George Thompson from Manchester. Into the traditional art of oral storytelling, with its repertoire of legends and fantastic exploits of the other-world, these celebrated islanders incorporated the real-life episodes of the close-knit families who were their audience. Seal-hunting, storms at sea in curraghs (frail coracles), drownings, all the hazards of sea and cliff are woven into their narratives. Peig Sayers in particular gives a unique picture of a way of life, recognizably modern yet caught in a time-warp, that lasted until the island was abandoned in 1952. Her selective and impressionistic memoirs are crucial for an understanding of what it was to be a woman from the mainland, married to a Blasket fisherman, to bear children, to lose children in childhood and in adult life, to part with a beloved daughter who emigrated.

Peig Sayers married into the Great Blasket in 1893 at nineteen years of age. Her father and brother made a match for her with Pádraig Ó Guithín, an island man whom she met for the first time ten days before she married him. She came from a family of Irish-speaking storytellers in Dunquin, and she inherited a store of folk traditions, classical stories, prayers, wisdom aphorisms, calendar observances. She could recite the Fenian cycle and the exploits of Fionn Mac Cumhaill in their entirety, imparted to her by her father. Robin Flower, the Oxford scholar who came regularly to the Great Blasket when she became a renowned storyteller, called her:

> a natural orator, with so keen a sense of the turn of a phrase and the lilting rhythm appropriate to Irish that her words could be written down as they leave her lips, and they would have the effect of literature.[10]

Her talents as a storyteller were diverse. She entertained an adult audience nightly with her tales and anecdotes, and she enthralled her listeners with her salty, humorous style of narrative. But she was also elegiac and lyrical. Seán Ó Dálaigh, the folklore collector recalls:

> I never heard anything so moving in my life as Peig Sayers reciting a lament of the Virgin Mary for her Son, her face and voice getting more and more sorrowful. I came out of the house, and I didn't know where I was.[11]

Peig Sayers had lost her husband and four children by mid-life. An extract from her third book, *Machtnamh Seana-Mhná (An Old Woman's Reflections)* sounds and reads like a lament:

> My spell on this little bench is nearly finished. It's sad and low and lonely I am to be parting with it. Long as the day is, night comes, and, alas, the night is coming for me, too. I am parting with you, beautiful little place, sun of my life. Other people will have your pleasure in future, but I'll be far away from you in a kingdom I don't know ... I thought there was nothing in the things of this life but poverty – this place full today and empty tomorrow – hadn't I got it to be seen, clearly. The people I knew in my youth, it was often they had the stone in the gauntlet for each other. They were strong, courageous, strong-worded, but they all fell, they were cleared out of the world ... There are people and they think that this island is a lonely, airy place. That is true for them, but the peace of the Lord is in it. I am living in it for more than forty years, and I didn't see two of the neighbours fighting in it yet. It was like honey for my poor tormented heart to rise up on the shoulder of the mountain footing the turf or gathering the sods on each other. Very often I'd throw myself back in the green heather, resting. It wasn't for bone-laziness I'd do it, but for the beauty of the hills, and the rumble of the waves that would be grieving down from me, in dark caves where the seals of the sea lived – those and the blue sky without a cloud travelling it, over me ...[12]

The extract, in its printed form less than three pages, contains over twenty references to sorrow, grief, hardship, heart-torment. The original Irish version expresses eloquently the asceticism of a life pared down to the simplicity of empty spaces, living on the edge of the Atlantic with long winters and great crashing seas. Like the Caribbean poet, Derek Walcott, Peig Sayers thought constantly about the island life, those who lived and died there, and those who went away. She too 'gave voice to one people's grief' and like the narrator in Walcott's 'The Schooner Flight', she loved and blessed her island.[13] Freed from the tyranny of being a school textbook, her account of life on the Great Blasket in the first half of the twentieth century is now read for its undeluded, nuanced transparency.

With the departure of the last family from the Great Blasket Island in 1952, it seemed as if the voices that passed on the oral tradition of storytelling, and of the spoken lament to the next generation were stilled. Joan McBreen records 'the silence which surrounded the voices of women in poetry throughout the decades after 1930', puzzling in its complexity but, perhaps, a necessary wintering time for women poets to create the new forms demanded by publishers and readers alike.[14] How and where the professional Irish woman poet acquired her skills is outside the scope of this inquiry. What is germane is the fidelity of the woman poets to the legacy of the lament form as an entitlement from their foremothers. 'What foremothers?' Nuala Ní Dhomhnaill asked in a *Poetry Ireland Review* article but she knew the answer, as Máire Mhac an tSaoi, poet and critic, observes in her Introduction to Ní Dhomhnaill's *Rogha Dánta/Selected Poems*. 'Her command of the medium she has chosen is absolute; the literary tradition to which she adheres is unique'.[15]

Máire Mhac an tSaoi (1922–) mapped the landscape for the women poets who followed her in the Irish language and who published their poems in journals and in collections of their own poetry. As a child she spent her summers in Dunquin in the Kerry Gaeltacht where her uncle, the scholarly Monsignor Pádraig de Brún, had a house. She took a degree in Celtic Studies and Modern Languages and an MA in Classical Modern stimulating perspectives on the Irish housewife. The irreverent approach of Margaret O'Callaghan in her sub-section, 'Women and Politics in Independent Ireland, 1921–1968', in Bourke *et al* (eds) *The Field Day Anthology of Irish Writing, V* (Cork, Cork University Press, 2002) and Diarmaid Ferriter, *Mothers, Maidens and Myths: A History of the ICA* (Dublin, The Irish Countrywomen's Association, 1995) is refreshing and insightful. Maryann Gialanella Valiulis has focussed attention on gender and citizenship in the Irish Free State with her frequently-cited 'Defining Their Role in the New State: Irishwomen's Protest Against the Juries Act of 1927', in *Canadian Journal of Irish Studies*, Vol. 18, No. 1 (July 1992); 'Engendering Citizenship: Women's Relationship to the State in Ireland and the United States in the Post-Suffrage Period' in Valiulis and O'Dowd (eds) *op cit*; 'Power, Gender and Identity in the Irish Free State' in *Journal of Women's History*, Vol. 6, No. 1/Vol. 7, No. I (1995); 'Neither Feminist nor Flapper: The Ecclesiastical Construction of the Ideal Irish Woman' in Mary O'Dowd and Sabine Wichert (eds), *Chattel, Servant or Citizen: Historical Studies 19* (Belfast, Institute of Irish Studies, 1993). Rosemary Cullen Owens' work on Irish suffragism, the subject of a path-breaking MA thesis in 1976 culminated in her important study, *A Social History of Women in Ireland 1870–1970* (Dublin, Gill and Macmillan, 2005). Hilda Tweedy, *A Link in the Chain: The Story of the Irish Housewives' Association 1942–1992* (Dublin, Attic Press, 1992) is a case of history making history, it is now a collector's item.

Moving back into the nineteenth century the work of Maria Luddy dominates the post-Famine period: *Women and Philanthropy in Nineteenth-Century Ireland*, (Cambridge, Cambridge University Press 1995); *Women in Ireland 1800–1918: A Documentary History* (Cork, Cork University Press 1995). Her section, 'Philanthropy in

Nineteenth-Century Ireland' in Bourke *et al* (eds) *The Field Day Anthology of Irish Writing* contains her specialised studies of prostitution, women's work and charitable organizations. David Fitzpatrick has offered tantalising glimpses of the Irish woman as emigrant in his valuable essays, however the Irish-American historians' strong contribution captures the attention, such as Janet Nolan's *Ourselves Alone: Women's Emigration from Ireland 1885–1920* (Lexington, KY, University of Kentucky Press, 1989), and *Servants of the Poor: Teachers and Mobility in Ireland and Irish-America* (South Bend, IN, University of Notre Dame Press, 2004). Maureen Murphy's meticulous editing of Asenath Nicholson's two classic accounts of the Irish Famine, *Ireland's Welcome to the Stranger* (Dublin, The Lilliput Press, 2002) and *Annals of the Famine* (*Ibid*, 1998) are a prelude to her work, 'the life and times of Asenath Nicholson'. Her research of the Irish servant in the United States is ongoing. Annie O'Donnell's letters to James Phelan, *Your Fondest Annie* (Dublin, University College Dublin Press, 2005) expand our understanding of the Irish servant girl which Hasia Diner introduced in her book, *Erin's Daughters In America: Irish Immigrant Women in the 19th Century* (Baltimore, Johns Hopkins University Press, 1983).

The surprise emergence of professional studies on catholic nuns and sisterhoods owes much to the organized efficiency and hospitality of convent and religious orders' archivists in Ireland, Britain, Rome and the United States. Despite the embargoes placed on archival material because of legal cases arising out of accusations of child abuse in religious-run institutions, Suellen Hoy found good-will and helpfulness in her searches for her collection, *Good Hearts: Catholic Sisters in Chicago's Past* (Urbana and Chicago, University of Illinois Press, 2006); 'The Journey Out: The Recruitment and Emigration of Irish Religious Women to the United States, 1812–1914', is a must-read for emigration studies. Caitríona Clear, *Nuns in Nineteenth-Century Ireland* (Dublin, Gill and Macmillan, 1987) set a standard for subsequent studies. The willingness of religious women to use their archives in graduate studies has yielded high returns such as Máire M. Kealy's doctoral dissertation, *Dominican Education in Ireland 1820–1930* (Dublin and Portland, OR: Irish Academic Press, 2007). Jacinta Prunty, *Margaret Aylward 1810–1889* (Dublin, Four Courts Press, 1999) needs to be read in conjunction with Mary Peckham Magray, *The Transforming Power of the Nuns: Women, Religion and Cultural Change in Ireland, 1750–1900* (New York and Oxford, Oxford University Press, 1998).

Phil Kilroy, while engaged in writing her fine biography of the founder of the Society of the Sacred Heart, *Madeleine Sophie Barat: A Life* (Cork, Cork University Press, 2000), wrote two essays on the subject of religious archives, 'The Use of Continental Sources of Women's Religious Congregations and the Writing of Religious Biography: Madeleine Sophie Barat, 1779–1865' in Valiulis and O'Dowd (*op cit*, 1997) and 'The writing of religious women's history: Madeleine Sophie Barat (1779–1865)' in Rosemary Raughter (ed.), *Religious Women and Their History: Breaking the Silence* (Dublin, Irish Academic Press, 2005). In 2006 Dr Caroline Bowden and Dr Carmen Mangion developed and update a website, 'The History of Women Religious of Britain and Ireland' which is read worldwide. For details contact c.mangion@history.bbk.ac.uk.

The eighteenth century for women in Ireland was a world of letter-writing, keeping of journals and diaries and of capturing in words the process of self-identity. Rosemary Raughter's section in Volume 4 of *The Field*

Day Anthology of Irish Writing: Irish Women's Writings and Traditions (Cork, Cork University Press 2002) titled 'Eighteenth-Century Catholic and Protestant Women' introduces the reader to the private world of women's thoughts and impressions which Raughter carries over to her sub-section, 'Philanthropic Institutions of Eighteenth-Century Ireland' in Volume 5, *op cit.* Kevin O'Neill's long study of Mary Leadbeater's two volume writings including her journals and the *Annals of Ballitore* is a drop by drop experience, 'Mary Shackleton Leadbeater: Peaceful Rebel' in Dáire Keogh and Nicholas Furlong (eds), *The Women of 1798* (Dublin, Four Courts Press, 1988) gives us another distillation of his anticipated study of the Quaker village of Ballitore. Is it too much to hope that Phil Kilroy will re-visit her Quaker and reformation women at a future date, having given us a sample in her sub-section. 'Memoirs and Testimonies: Nonconformist Women in Seventeenth-Century Ireland', in Volume 4 of the *Field Day Anthology*, (*loc. cit.*)?

Mary O'Dowd, *A History of Women in Ireland 1500–1800* (Harlow and New York, Pearson Longman, 2005) displays a superlative familiarity with primary sources. She quotes other scholars of the early modern period on reading sources 'against the grain, of asking where women are absent as well as present in the document'. Reading her extensive bibliography supplies the key to her meticulous scholarship. The publication of primary sources has a long and respectable pedigree in medieval Irish studies. In the period I am surveying (mainly the 1990s), Professor Donnchadh Ó Corráin as founder and editor of *Peritia (1981–) Journal of the Medieval Academy of Ireland* and founder of CELT: Corpus of Electronic Text has explored the status of women in the Law Tracts, principally the Cáin Lánamna, the law tract on marriage, and has edited and authored the sub-section, 'Early

1973

'Education: A Church-State Problem in Twentieth-Century Ireland', *The Furrow,* Vol. XXIV, No. 1, pp 3–12.

1974

'Pre-Famine Peasantry in Ireland: Definition and Theme', *Irish University Review,* Vol. IV, pp 188–198.

Review of Brendan Bradshaw, *The Dissolution of the Religious Orders in Ireland Under Henry VIII* (London, Cambridge University Press, 1974), *The Tablet,* Vol. CCXXVIII, No. 7011, p. 1106.

Review of Hugh Fenning, *The Undoing of the Friars of Ireland: A Study of the Novitiate Question in the Eighteenth Century* (Louvain, Publications Universitaires de Louvain, 1972), *The Tablet,* Vol. CCXXVIII, No. 6975, p. 227.

'Women – Irish Style', *Doctrine and Life*, Vol. XXIV, No. 4, pp 182–197.

1975

'The Fall of the House of Desmond', *Journal of the Kerry Archaeological and Historical Society,* No. 8, pp 28–44.

Review of Shevawn Lynam, *Humanity Dick* (London, Hamilton, 1975), *The Tablet,* Vol. CCXXIX, No. 7054, pp 866–867.

Review of M. Perceval-Maxwell, *The Scottish Migration to Ulster in the Reign of James I* (London, Routledge and Kegan Paul, 1973), *History: The Journal of the Historical Association,* Vol. LX, pp 453–454.

1978

Margaret Mac Curtain and Donncha Ó Corráin (eds), *Women in Irish Society: The Historical Dimension* (Dublin, Arlen House: The Women's Press), 125pp.

'Preface', *Women in Irish Society,* pp vii–viii.

'Women, the Vote and Revolution', *Women in Irish Society,* pp 46–57.

1979

'Preface', Irene ffrench Eagar, *Margaret Anna Cusack: One Woman's Campaign for Women's Rights* (Dublin, Arlen House: The Women's Press), pp vii–xii.

'Rural Society in Post-Cromwellian Ireland', in Art Cosgrove and Donal McCartney (eds), *Studies in Irish History: Presented to R. Dudley Edwards* (Dublin, University College Dublin), pp 118–136.

Mark Tierney agus Máiréad Nic Curtáin a scríobh; Tomás F. Mac Anna agus Seán Mac Pháidín a d'aistrigh, *Éire sa Nua-Aois* (Baile Átha Cliath, Oifig an tSoláthair, 248pp).

1980

Review of Nicholas Canny, *The Elizabethan Conquest of Ireland: A Pattern Established, 1565–1576* (Hassocks, Harvester Press, 1976), *History: The Journal of the Historical Association*, Vol. LXV, pp 302–303.

Review of T. W. Moody, F. X. Martin and F. J. Byrne (eds), *A New History of Ireland, Vol. III: Early Modern Ireland 1534–1691* (Oxford, Clarendon Press, 1976), *History: The Journal of the Historical Association*, Vol. LXV, pp 301–302.

'Towards an Appraisal of the Religious Image of Women', *The Crane Bag*, Vol. IV, No. I, pp 26–30.

1981

'The Roots of Irish Nationalism', in Robert O'Driscoll (ed.), *The Celtic Consciousness* (Toronto, McClelland and Stewart, 1981), pp 371–382. (Republished in 1982 in Irish, US and UK editions; Mountrath, Dolmen Press; New York, Braziller; Edinburgh, Canongate).

1982

'Women of Eccles Street', in E. Kane (ed.), *The Lanthorn: Year Book of the Dominican College, Eccles Street, Dublin. Centenary Year* (Dublin, Dominican College).

Review of Cyril Falls, *Elizabeth's Irish Wars* (London, Constable, 1996), *Irish Times, Weekend*, 23 March, p. 7.

Review of Maria Luddy, *Women in Ireland, 1800–1918: A Documentary History* (Cork, Cork University Press, 1995), *The Irish Reporter*, No. 22, p. 80.

Review of Anne Thurston, *Because of Her Testimony: The Word in Female Experience* (Dublin, Gill and Macmillan, 1995), *The Furrow*, Vol. XLVII, pp 121–122.

1997

'Godly Burden: Catholic Sisterhoods in Twentieth-Century Ireland', in Anthony Bradley and Maryann Gialanella Valiulis (eds), *Gender and Sexuality in Modern Ireland* (Amherst, MA, University of Massachusetts Press), pp 245–256.

1999

'Foreword', Robert Tweedy, *The Story of the Court Laundry* (Dublin, Wolfhound Press), pp 9–10.

2000

'Foreword', Marie O'Neill, *Grace Gifford Plunkett and Irish Freedom: Tragic Bride of 1916* (Dublin, Portland, OR, Irish Academic Press), pp ix–xi.

2001

'Godly Burden', in Alan Hayes and Diane Urquhart (eds), *The Irish Women's History Reader* (London and New York, Routledge), pp 146–151.

'Hogan and Tudor Ireland', in Donnchadh Ó Corráin (ed.), *James Hogan: Revolutionary, Historian and Political Scientist* (Dublin, Four Courts Press), pp 80–88.

2002

General Editor of Section 'Religion, Science, Theology and Ethics, 1500-2000', *The Field Day Anthology of Irish Writing* (Cork, Cork University Press), pp 464–753.

2004

'Tending the Wells of Memory – Sharing Sources of Hope', in Geraldine Smyth (ed.), *Distance Becomes Communion: Dominican Journeys in Mission and Hope* (Dublin, Dominican Publications), pp 38–53.

'Late Medieval Nunneries of the Irish Pale', in Howard B. Clarke, Jacinta Prunty, Mark Hennessy (eds), *Surveying Ireland's Past: Multidisciplinary Essays in Honour of Anngret Simms* (Dublin, Geography Publications), pp 129–143.

'Foreword', Alan Hayes and Diane Urquhart (eds), *Irish Women's History* (Dublin and Portland, OR, Irish Academic Press), p ix.

2005

'Foreword', Annie Ryan, *Witnesses: Inside the Easter Rising* (Dublin, Liberties Press), pp 23–28.

'Foreword', Elgy Gillespie (ed.), *Vintage Nell: The McCafferty Reader* (Dublin, Lilliput Press), pp 9–14.

2006

'Writing Grief into Memory Women, Language and Narrative', in Patricia A. Lynch, Joachim Fisher and Brian Coates (eds), *Back to the Present, Forward to the Past. Irish Writing and History Since 1798: Volume 1* (Amsterdam, New York, Rodopi), pp 255–277.

'Foreword', Yvonne McKenna, *Made Holy: Irish Women Religious at Home and Abroad* (Dublin, Portland, OR, Irish Academic Press).

'Famine Silences', in Maureen Murphy, Alan Singer, Charles F Baker (eds), *Potatoes Rot: Famine Plagues Ireland* (Peterborough, NH, Cobblestone Pub).

2008

Ariadne's Thread: Writing Women into Irish History (Galway, Arlen House), 400pp.

Reader's Notes

Reader's Notes

Reader's Notes

Reader's Notes

English, Dr Ada 96
Ennis, Séamus 343, 347–8, 352, 363
Enright, Seamus 292, 297
Erasmus, Desiderius 226–7
Eucharistic Congress 30
European Economic Community 46, 81, 167, 276
Eustace, Sir Christopher 149
Eustace, Jenet, 148–149, 233
Eustace, Rose 149
Eustace, Sir Walter, 148
Evans, Prof R. J. 256, 364

Fahey, Tony 273, 281, 293, 295, 310, 323
Falkland, Lord 242
Falkland, Lady 234, 251
Farrell, Alderman 87
Farrer, Austin 102
Feminist History Forum 26
Fenton, Catherine 243
Ferriter, Diarmaid 43, 56, 369
Field Day Anthology 18, 24, 34–5, 226, 325, 332, 333, 335, 354, 362, 369, 372–3
Finlay, Fr S.J. 73,
Fischer, Joachim 334, 362
Fitzeustace, Roland 148
Fitzgerald, Alice 147, 149
Fitzgerald, Lord Edward 129
Fitzgerald, Emily Duchess of Leinster 129
Fitzgerald, Garret 38
Fitzgerald, Joan Butler 123
Fitzgerald, Maud 147
Fitzgerald, Sir Maurice 149
Fitzgerald, Richard 147
Fitzgerald, Silken Thomas 146, 149, 229

Fitzmaurice, Honor, Lady Kerry 330
Fitzpatrick, David 268–9, 273, 370
Flower, Robin 123, 207, 269, 343–4, 363
Fogarty, Richard 178
Foley, Maribel 38
Fondo Santa Sede 15
Forristal, Desmond 27
Franciscan Missionaries for Africa 203, 279, 287, 318
Furlong, Nicholas 372

Gabbet, Joe 198
Galway, Mary 86
Gavan Duffy, Louise 74, 92, 99, 206
Gearóid Óg, Earl of Kildare 147
Gill, Colette 198
Gillespie, Raymond 33, 250, 252
Ginnell, Mrs 97
Gonne, Maud 93, 219
Gordon, Linda 278, 282, 294–5
Gordon, Mary 358
Gore-Booth, Eva 93,
Gormlaith 121
Grace Dieu 37, 233, 330
Grattan, Henry 130
Gregory, Lady Augusta 35, 84, 93, 99, 355–6, 359, 361, 364
Gregory, Robert 355
Griffith, Arthur 93
Gunnel, William 227, 249

Hackett, Rosie 97, 217

Hapsburg, Empress Maria Theresa 337

Harrison, Miss 87

Haslam, Anna 83–4, 93, 98, 131

Haslam, Thomas 83–4, 98

Hayden, Mary 13, 60, 70–1, 75, 79–80, 84–5, 88, 98, 216, 366

Healy, Isabel 163

Healy, Tim, MP 87

Hearn, Mona 218, 223

Hearne, Dana 220

Heck, Barbara 36

Hederman, Mark Patrick 101

Heffernan, Bishop 200–2

Helferty, Seamus 284

Hepburn, Audrey 319

Hillmann, James 169

Hobson, Bulmer 93

Hochburgher, Mother Albertus 71

Hoff, Joan 56, 277, 293

Hogan, Dr Edmund 287, 296, 312, 296, 324

Hogan, James 13, 48

Holland, Ailsa 284

Holland, Mary 163–4, 173

Holy Ghost Order (CSSP) 203

Holy Rosary Sisters of Killeshandra 203, 287, 289, 317

Howlin, Fr John 230, 250

Hoy, Suellen 29, 286, 296, 311, 323–4, 370

Hughes, Kathleen 102

Hughes, Sam 198

Hufton, Olwyn 367

Hussey, Joan 147

Humanae Vitae 45

Hyde, Douglas 74

Inchiquin, Lord 151

Inghinidhe na hÉireann 88, 93

Inglis, Tom 281

Iníon Dubh 122

International Association for the Study of Irish Literatures (IASIL) 34, 39, 333

International Committee for Historical Science 49

International Federation for Research in Women's History 49

Irish Anti-Apartheid Society 27

Irish Association for Research in Women's History 48–49, 294

Irish Citizen, The 86, 91, 98–99

Irish Citizen Army, 94

Irish Countrywomen's Association 44, 56, 369

Irish Feminist Information 161

Irish Historical Studies 18, 54, 56, 58, 294, 365

Irish Housewives' Association 46–47, 56, 369

Irish Republican Army 14

Irish Sisters of Loreto 31, 72, 76–7, 129, 132, 186, 202, 279, 315

Irish Times, The 15, 32, 58

Irish Women's Suffrage Federation 86

Maintenon, Madame de 73, 234

Markievicz, Constance 89, 91–97, 99, 134, 211, 219–20

Markola, Pirjo 52–3, 57

Marlborough, Duke of 262

Martin, F. X. 20, 23, 99, 250–1, 253

Martin, Mother Marie 30, 203, 279, 289, 294, 316, 318

Marx, Karl 258

Meaney, Geraldine 332

Medical Missionaries of Mary 203, 279, 287, 289, 316, 318

Meek, Christine 373

Merici, Angela 232, 238

Merriman, P.J. 71

Merriman, Brian 136

Meyer, Kuno 102, 107

McAuley, Catherine 129, 279, 294, 296, 310

McBreen, Joan 346, 353, 363–4

McCafferty, Nell 26, 163–4, 173

McCarthy, Mary 217

McCoole, Sinéad 367

McKenna, Siobhán 16

McKenna, Sr M. Bonaventure 16

McKiernan, Prof Eoin 115

McKillen, Beth 21

McLaren, Agnes 288–9

McMorrough, Dermot 213

McQuaid, John Charles Archbishop 16, 188

McQuarrie, John 181

Mac Cana, Proinsias 117

Mac Cionnaith, Prof Eoin 16

Mac Cumhaill, Fionn 344

Mac Curtain, Mrs 299

Mac Curtain, Seán 14

Mac Curtain, Tomás 14

MacCarthy, B. G. 34

Mac Donagh, Thomas 91, 95–6

Mac Mahon, Bryan 174, 209, 343

MacNeill, Eoin 13, 118, 137

MacNeill, Máire 18

Mac Réamoinn, Seán 167

Mac Swiney, Mary 96

Magee Presbyterian Theological College 62

Magray, Mary Peckham 275, 371

Mallin, Cmdt Michael 94

Mangan, James Clarence 352

Mangion, Carmen 371

Maude, Caitlín 35, 352–3, 363–4

Mhac an tSaoi, Máire 35, 341, 346–9, 352, 363

Mill, James 131

Mill, John Stuart 83, 131

Millet, Jean-Francois 258

Milton, John 242, 246, 254

Minotaur 55

Missionary Sisters of the Holy Rosary 203, 296

Mnemosyne 334

Molloy, James Lyman 260–1, 272

Moloney, Frances 289, 317

Molony, Helena 90, 93, 97

Monaghan, Sr Aquinas 289

Moody, Theo 56, 255

More, Margaret 227

More, Thomas 142, 226–7, 249–50

Morris 337–8

O'Connell, Daniel 130–1, 138, 215
O'Connell, Marie 311, 323
O'Connor, Anne V. 179, 209, 273
O'Connor, Frank 116, 124, 128, 136
Ó Corráin, Donncha 19, 98, 118, 120, 137, 296, 372
Ó Criomhthain, Tomás 182, 343
Ó Dálaigh, Seán 344
O'Daly, Dominic 14–5, 240, 253
O'Day, Alan 50
O'Doherty, Lady Rosa 123, 234
O'Donnell, Annie 370
O'Donnell, Red Hugh 122
O'Donohue, John 24
O'Dowd, Mary 27, 54, 56, 58, 137, 223, 225–6, 249, 277, 293–5, 323, 332, 365, 368–9, 372
Ó hEoghusa, Eochaidh 352
O'Faolain, Nuala 358–9, 364
O'Farrell, Nurse Elizabeth 213
O'Farrelly, Agnes 74, 85, 91
Ó Faoláin, Seán 28, 106, 112, 172
Ó Guithín, Pádraig 344
Ó hÓgáin, Dáithí 165, 173
Ó hÓgartaigh, Margaret 373
Ó Laoghaire, Art 337–8, 341
Ó Laoghaire, S.J., Diarmuid 180
Ó Laoghaire, Peadar 121
O'Loughlin, Thomas 19
O'Malley, Gráinne 122, 213, 233, 251

O'Neill, Earl Hugh 123, 234
O'Neill, Eoghan Roe 123
O'Neill, Kevin 372
O'Neill, Dr Robert 299
O'Rahilly, Egan 127
Ó Rathaille, Aodhgán 270, 273
Ó Súileabháin, Muiris 182, 343
O'Sullivan, Donal Cam 233
O'Sullivan, Lady Ellen 233
O'Sullivan, Niamh 367
Ó Tuama, Seán 123, 273, 337, 362
Ó Tuathaigh, Gearóid 125, 138
Omolo, John 204, 210
Ormond, Thomas, Earl of 233
Osborne, Walter 23, 299–304, 307–8
Owens, Rosemary Cullen 98, 369

Pankhursts 83, 87, 98
Parnell, Anna 83, 98, 211, 213, 220
Parnell, Charles Stewart 61, 83, 213, 215
Parnell, Fanny 83, 211, 213
Párliament na mBan 247–8, 254
Pearse, P. H. 74, 90, 93, 98, 110–1
Pearse, Mrs 96
Perrot, Michelle 52, 57
Phelan, James 370
Plummer, Charles 104
Plunkett, Sir Horace 85
Pope Benedict XV 288–9, 318
Pope Gregory XIII 233, 251